12.50

THE MYTH OF INVARIANCE

Ernest G. McClain

THE MYTH OF INVARIANCE

The Origin of the Gods, Mathematics and Music From the Ṛg Veda to Plato

Introduction by Siegmund Levarie

Edited by Patrick A. Heelan

Nicolas-Hays, Inc.
York Beach, Maine

First published in 1976 by
Nicolas-Hays, Inc.
P.O. Box 612
York Beach, ME 03910

This paperback edition, 1984

Distributed exclusively by
Samuel Weiser, Inc.
York, Beach, ME 03910

ISBN 0-89254-012-5

Library of Congress Cataloging in Publication Data

McClain, Ernest G
The myth of invariance.

Includes index.
1. Music—Philosophy and aesthetics. 2. Music and mythology. 3. Music—Theory—To 400. I. Title.
ML3800.M15 780'.1 76-28411

Printed in the United States by
Mitchell-Shear, Inc.
Ann Arbor, MI

This Child is Augusta's

Let us with tuneful skill proclaim these
generations of the Gods,
That one may see them when these hymns
are chanted in a future age.

Ṛgveda 10.72.1

"It was clear to me for a long time that
the origins of science had their deep roots
in a particular myth, that of *invariance*."

Giorgio de Santillana
Preface to *HAMLET'S MILL*

CONTENTS

CHARTS AND TABLES

CHARTS AND TABLES

INTRODUCTION

Ernest McClain's book constitutes an intellectual breakthrough of utmost significance. It offers a persuasive explanation of crucial passages in texts of world literature—the *Ṛg Veda*, the Egyptian Book of the Dead, the Bible, Plato—that have defied critics of the separate concerned disciplines. All these passages deal with numbers. What sounds like mathematical nonsense or literary gibberish has been given life and meaning by McClain's incisive thoughts. The recurrence, moreover, of identical and similar numbers in Babylon, Egypt, Greece, and Palestine confirms ever growing speculations on the historical continuity and direction of a basic spiritual tradition.

Dr. McClain's method is simple enough: he recognizes music as the one force capable of projecting a philosophic synthesis. For this approach he is not likely to earn the immediate approval and support of theologians, philosophers, philologists, mathematicians, and others who have become too specialized to view the whole rather than the detail. Nor is he likely to find on his side musicians who consider their art primarily a branch of amusement and musicologists who are instinctively afraid of numbers.

Yet his approach, neglected for centuries, is anything but new. He learned it by taking Plato literally. Plato insists on the superior role of music in the education of the whole man. In *Phaedrus* he writes: "The soul which has seen most of truth shall come to birth as a philosopher, or beauty lover, or fervent musician" (248d). In the *Republic* he writes: "Education in music is most sovereign, because more than anything else rhythm and harmony find their way to the inmost soul" (3.401d). These statements have generally been interpreted sentimentally. Dr. McClain, by taking Plato's directions literally, found the open-sesame.

To give one of many examples: when Plato states that the tyrant is 729 times as bad as the good man, the philologist "simplifies the text" (as Francis Cornford has done in his famous English translation), and the mathematician calls it a "literary license." The trained musician, however, knows that every tone is both a number and a quality, neither one explaining the other one-sidedly, but each corresponding to the other exactly. Thus the ratio 1:2 does not explain the experience of the musical octave any more than the sound of this interval would explain the quantity involved; but the two facets of tone mutually illuminate each other. Now the number 729 chosen by Plato (*Republic* 587e) corresponds to the musical quality of the tritone (3^6 = six fifths above the fundamental), the worst possible dissonance in the musical systems known to Plato and, for that matter, in all Western tonal systems for two thousand years after him. What Plato evaluated by the number 729 was the relation between the good man and the tyrant as that of the greatest possible tension within a civilized system.

One sympathizes with the puzzlement of nonmusicians facing such numbers. To appreciate the analogy involved, one must realize (as Plato took for granted) that in antiquity musical symbolism was understood directly by all educated and many less educated people. When in the course of history the role of music as a spiritual force was increasingly sacrificed to that of individual expression or entertainment, the interpretation of once very clear texts suffered. McClain's great accomplishment lies in his recognition of music as the spiritual model par excellence throughout antiquity and in his courageous and self-critical application of this insight to other fields. He has provided philologists, philosophers, theologians, historians, mathematicians, and musicians with a sound basis for further explorations in their own fields.

As a musician, I should like to comment on one particular musical feature of the book. McClain's emphasis on tuning systems is not an arbitrary device but, on the contrary, fundamental to all musical process and thought. One normally accepts a tonal system as given without remembering the discerning and painstaking ingenuity that has always preceded the establishment of any such system. The physical world contains an infinity of tones from which the musician must necessarily select a finite number. The built-in difficulty (of which the inevitability is easily proven by mathematics) derives from the internal incompatibility of any selection. To "get along" with each other—in technical terms, to fit within the octave—the tones of every conceivable system must submit to a compromise. The kind of compromise determines the tuning, that is, the definition of the tones used within a system. Just tuning, meantone temperament, equal temperament, and others are different compromise solutions without which disorder would disrupt functioning. A similar internal incompatibility characterizes the movements of the heavenly bodies in relation to a fixed observer. No wonder that astronomy and music served Plato and others as, respectively, heavenly and artistic models for the conception of a well-functioning political state. Thus McClain's reconstruction of various tuning systems, far from being an isolated concern, deals with a central issue of life and human endeavor.

Siegmund Levarie
Professor of Music at
Brooklyn College of the
City University of New York

ACKNOWLEDGMENTS

My book was conceived as a musical companion for *FOUR-DIMENSIONAL MAN*: *The Philosophical Methodology of the Ṛg Veda* by Antonio T. de Nicolás. In his first edition of that work de Nicolás showed how a profoundly mathematical logic pervades the sacred hymns of our ancient Hindu "mother" culture, a culture in which *sound* has remained the primary vehicle of truth. From his general schema I have developed those details familiar mainly to musicians through their experience with tuning theory. De Nicolás has freely shared his insights into ancient and modern Indian cultures, making available both his personal library and his unpublished manuscripts, so that what is offered here is essentially a progress report on a continuing dialogue between a philosopher and a musician. The work has grown beyond its intended scope—reaching now into Sumerian, Babylonian, Egyptian and Hebraic mythology—largely on account of the extraordinary fecundity of de Nicolás' ideas and his untiring personal support.

The musical ideas exploited here are those of two colleagues, Siegmund Levarie and Ernst Levy, who have been generous with advice and assistance throughout the several years of my "Pythagorean" studies. The fundamental mathematical ideas are those of Robert Brumbaugh, who was particularly helpful during my work on Plato's mathematical allegories. I owe immense debts to many other friends and correspondents: Malcolm Brown, Edwin Davis, Fred Fisher, Christopher George, David McClain, Jean Le Mée, Wendell Mordy, John Rouse, Marius Schneider, Harvey Wheeler and Francis Wormuth. Richard Sacksteder, my mathematical advisor, wrote an important summary for Chapter 12. Patrick Heelan not only inspired the logical framework of *FOUR-DIMENSIONAL MAN* but has provided thoughtful editorial guidance for its companion. The entire manuscript has had the benefit of advice from de Nicolás, Heelan, Levarie, Levy and Sacksteder, but I must emphasize that I have never been able to do justice to all the insights of my technical advisors and have allowed imagination to roam beyond the bounds of cautious scholarship, and so must accept alone the responsibility for having erred.

ACKNOWLEDGMENTS

It is a pleasure to be able to thank Patrick Milburn, associate editor of *MAIN CURRENTS IN MODERN THOUGHT*, for perceiving the relevance of my Plato studies to de Nicolás' work on the *Ṛg Veda*, for bringing us together, and for providing an inexhaustible fund of relevant ideas and source materials.

Translations from the *Ṛg Veda* are from *A PHILOSOPHY IN SONG POEMS* by J. B. Chethimattam and Antonio T. de Nicolás and from *THE HYMNS OF THE ṚG VEDA* by Ralph T. H. Griffith. The philological commentary is mainly from *FOUR-DIMENSIONAL MAN*, supplemented by Griffith's notes, which draw heavily on earlier generations of Sanskrit commentary. Alain Daniélou's *HINDU POLYTHEISM* proved invaluable for insight into Hindu geometric symbolism.

Beyond these debts there are incalculable debts to others, not least to the nameless singers who have kept the 10,800 verses of the *Ṛg Veda* a living tradition for four or more millenia.

Motilal Banarsidass, Indological Publishers & Booksellers of Delhi, India, has graciously allowed the quotation of considerable material from the New Revised Edition of *THE HYMNS OF THE ṚG VEDA* by Ralph T.H. Griffith. The author and publisher also gratefully acknowledge permission to reproduce the following copyrighted illustrations:

Egyptian mathematical notation and the Eye of Horus, from *MATHEMATICS IN THE TIME OF THE PHARAOHS* by Richard J. Gillings: The MIT Press, Cambridge.

Babylonian Cuneiform Tablet YBC 7289 and its interpretation, from *MATHEMATICAL CUNEIFORM TEXTS* by Otto Neugebauer and A. Sachs; American Oriental Society, New Haven.

Triangular "group" motif, from *A HISTORY OF MATHEMATICS* by Carl Boyer; John Wiley & Sons, Inc., New York.

Ptolemy's tonal zodiac, from "Ptolemaios Und Porphyrios Uber Die Music" by Ingemar Düring; The Publications' Committee, Gothenburg University and Professor Düring.

Three diagrams (charts 7, 44, and 45) from "Musical Marriages in Plato's Republic," (figures 8, 12, and 16); Journal of Music Theory, Vol. 18.2, Fall 1974.

Harrappan seal writing and the potters' marks of the Quetta Valley, from *THE ROOTS OF ANCIENT INDIA*, 2nd, Ed. and an hexagonal drawing from Çatal Hüyük, from *THE THRESHOLD OF CIVILIZATION*; Walter A. Fairservis, Jr.

Painted pottery types, from *EARLIEST CIVILIZATIONS OF THE NEAR EAST* by James Mellaart, and a schematic Vinca figurine from

ACKNOWLEDGMENTS

THE GODS AND GODDESSES OF OLD EUROPE by Marija Gimbutas; Thames & Hudson Ltd., London.

Charts 10 and 19, from "The Scroll and the Cross," by the author; The Catgut Acoustical Society Newsletter, May 1, 1975.

Cartoon: "No! No! I said build an ark!"; *SATURDAY REVIEW* and Orlando Busino.

Cartoon: "Pretty good, but I'll bet you can't hit him again."; *THE NEW YORKER* and Charles Barsotti

The author owes a special debt to the staff of Nicolas Hays, Ltd. for its courtesy and resourcefulness.

GLOSSARY OF TERMS

Arithmetic mean—an intermediate value between two extremes; there is always a *larger ratio* between the *smaller numbers*. (For example, 3 is the arithmetic mean between 2 and 4, but the ratio 2:3 is a musical fifth while the ratio 3:4 is a musical fourth.)

$$\text{formula: } M^a = \frac{A + B}{2}$$

Calendrical scales—a term introduced here to include Didymus' Diatonic scale and Ptolemy's Diatonic Syntonon together with their reciprocal scales and pentatonic subsets, that is, all scales which can be defined by integers $2^p3^q5^r \leq 720$, "the days and nights" of a schematic year.

Cent—the modern unit of interval measure, the hundredth part of an equal-tempered semitone, with the ratio

$$\sqrt[1200]{2}.$$

Circle of Fifths—the arrangement of the tones of equal-temperament by fifths either rising (F C G D, etc.) or falling (B E A D, etc.). When fifths are defined as the ratio of two integers, 2:3, however, as in this study, they produce a tone *spiral* rather than a tone *circle*.

Comma—a small disagreement between two different definitions of a tone; the two most important ones are the syntonic comma and the Pythagorean comma, subliminal in some circumstances but not in others, hence a continually nagging problem.

Diaschisma—the comma of ratio 2025:2048, worth about 20 *cents*, which arises in Just tuning (for instance, after four perfect fifths C-G-D-A-E plus two pure thirds E-G♯ and G♯-B♯ when B♯ is compared with the starting C).

Diesis—The interval of 125:128 (roughly 41 *cents*, or 1/5th of a tone) which arises between two tones in Just intonation which need to be enharmonically equivalent, for practicality, as for instance A♭ and G♯.

Ditone—a major third defined as two successive wholetones of 8:9, having the ratio $(9/8)^2 = 81:64$, slightly larger than the thirds of equal-temperament.

Ditonic comma—see Pythagorean comma.

Epimoric ratio—see Superparticular ratio.

Equal temperament—the division of the octave into twelve equal parts or semitones, each of which has the ratio

$$\sqrt[12]{2} \sim 1.059461^{+}.$$

Geometric mean—that intermediate value which divides an interval *proportionally* (into two intervals with the *same* ratio), as for instance 2 is the geometric mean between 1 and 4 and 3 is the geometric mean between 1 and 9. In equal-temperament the semitone is geometric mean within the wholetone, the wholetone within the major third, the major third within the augmented fifth, etc., but in ancient tunings it was present in the scale only under exceptional circumstances.

$$\text{formula: } M^g = \sqrt{A \times B}$$

Harmonic mean—the "sub-contrary" of the arithmetic mean, with the larger interval between the larger numbers. For instance, 9 is the arithmetic mean in the octave double 6:12 (dividing it into a fifth of ratio 2:3 and a fourth of 3:4) while 8 is harmonic mean with the fifth of 2:3 at 8:12 and the fourth of 3:4 at 6:8.

$$\text{formula: } M^h = \frac{2AB}{A + B.}$$

Index—any integer considered arbitrarily as the limit of available integers, generally functioning here as an expansion of 1 = geometric mean in the field of rational number to whatever limit allows fractions to be cleared in some model octave, hence, metaphorically, a "mask of god" (= unity).

Just tuning—a system based on the octave 1:2, the fifth 2:3 (or the complementary fourth 3:4) *and* the pure major third of 4:5.

Monochord—a string stretched over a resonator in such a way that one bridge can be moved without altering the tension, i.e., so that intervals can be defined as measures of string length. The same name is applied to instruments with several strings similarly arranged.

Pythagorean comma—the ratio 524288:531441, worth about 24 *cents*, which arises between the reference pitch and the twelfth tone tuned by pure fifths of 2:3 or fourths of 3:4 (numerically, between 3^{12} and the nearest power of 2).

Pythagorean tuning—a system based on the octave 1:2 and the fifth 2:3 (or complementary fourth 3:4).

Schisma—the difference between the syntonic and ditonic commas, with the ratio 32805:32768, approximately 2 *cents*.

Superparticular ratio—strictly speaking a ratio in which the antecedent exceeds the consequent by 1, as 2:1, 3:2 etc., equivalent to the Greek *epimoric* ("a part added"). (For ease in reading, the smaller number is given first here.)

Syntonic comma—the interval between a pure major third of 4:5 and a Pythagorean ditonic third of 64:81, that is 80:81, roughly 22 *cents*. It is the fundamental problem in Just tuning, rendering it wholly impracticable where modulation is involved.

Temperament—any system of tuning which slightly modifies the normative roles of superparticular ratios. (See Equal temperament.)

CHART 1

Foundations of Mathematical Harmonics

Equivalent representations of the basic Hindu-Greek scale (Ptolemy's Diatonic Syntonon).

Idealized Aulos

Monochord

Generation from ratios of the first six integers

(similar tetrachords)

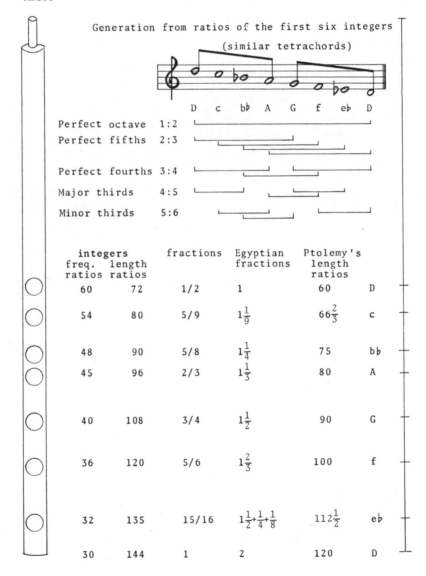

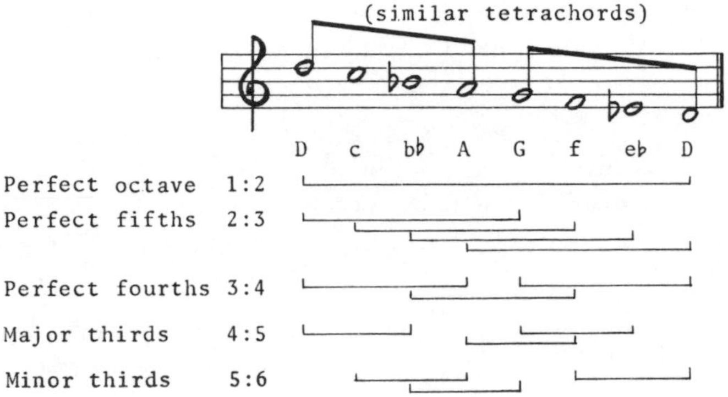

integers: freq. ratios	integers: length ratios	fractions	Egyptian fractions	Ptolemy's length ratios	
60	72	1/2	1	60	D
54	80	5/9	$1\frac{1}{9}$	$66\frac{2}{3}$	c
48	90	5/8	$1\frac{1}{4}$	75	b♭
45	96	2/3	$1\frac{1}{3}$	80	A
40	108	3/4	$1\frac{1}{2}$	90	G
36	120	5/6	$1\frac{2}{3}$	100	f
32	135	15/16	$1\frac{1}{2}+\frac{1}{4}+\frac{1}{8}$	$112\frac{1}{2}$	e♭
30	144	1	2	120	D

1

INTRODUCTION

THE PROBLEM

The song-poems of the *Ṛg Veda*, India's oldest sacred book, abound in mysterious arithmetical and geometrical details. Its hymns link Sun and Moon and all creation to incestuous couplings within a pantheon of deities in which sons create their own mothers and all are counted. The universe emerges as a victory of gods over demonic forces which can be defeated but never eradicated, and both the frays and the forces are counted. The spoils of war are counted along with the singers and their syllables and tones, the ribs of the cosmic horse, the sticks of the sacrificial fire, rivers, tribes, holy chalices, footsteps, twin sons, mountains, cattle, dogs, sheep, storm gods, the seats and wheel-spokes of celestial chariots, and castles, priests, and sacred stones. The poets seem concerned with the exact number of everything they encounter and alive to location in space, but why they cared is seldom clear. Their own riddles are addressed directly to other singers (R.V. 10.28). And their own faith is invested in the power of song!

The gods of the *Ṛg Veda* are dependent on an elaborate cult of sacrifice, vigilantly maintained by Brāhman priests, in which the chanting of hymns plays the central role. It is the singers who "with their mind, formed horses harnessed by a word" for the chariot of the gods (1.20.2). "The choirs established Indra king forever" (7.31.12). The priests themselves are "car-borne, through song" (the refrain in hymns 4.16, 17, and 19 through 24). "Heaven's fair light" is "made apparent" by the hymns of seven singers whose songs "cleft e'en the mountain open," bringing rains so copious that cattle "walk knee-deep" in water (4.16.6 and 1.37.10). Agni, savior and god of fire, is himself "the holy Singer who precedes the sages, . . . waxen mighty by laudations," and the secret he alone can impart is a certain "lofty hymn" (3.5.1–2 and 4.5.3).

Few poems have suffered more in translation. Not even in Sanskrit is the intention of the poets clear, and translators who treat every verse with reverence are quick with apologies. Not only are many shades of meaning lost, but sometimes no sensible meaning can be understood from the plethora available. In *Four-Dimensional Man* Antonio T. de Nicolás observes that although Indian thought originates in the *Ṛg Veda*, somehow the *Ṛg Veda* "remained peripheral to the subsequent development of Indian thought," so that today, ironically, it is largely a "text out of context."[1]

THE CHALLENGE

"What the *Ṛg Veda* does not have, no other external source can supply," de Nicolás declared as he embarked on the effort to retrieve its meaning by "internal comparison and reconstruction."[2] What he found by that method was a "lattice logic" consisting of four "languages":

1) the language of Non-Existence (*Asat*),
2) the language of Existence (*Sat*),
3) the language of Images and Sacrifice (*Yajña*), and
4) the language of Embodied (*Ṛta*) Vision (*Dhīḥ*).

These four languages are the expressions of a sensorium which organizes itself primarily on a model of sound. "Sound," de Nicolás writes, "is the greatest clue we have to interiority, our own and that of others."

> It would be the greatest understatement to say that the Rgvedic methodology draws its main clue to interiorizing all perception, the whole sensorium, from sound. Ṛgvedic man was enveloped by sound. He was surrounded by sound, excited by sound, made aware of presences by sound, looked for centers of experience in the experience of sound, found the model of complete, absolute instantaneity and communication in sound. He structured the sensorium in such an interiorist way as to become, in one instant moment, the total presence and power of absolute and efficient communion. The *Ṛg Veda*'s song-poems were not only oral creations but also chanted creations. While the other sensory media provided discontinuity, sound alone, in spite of its evanescence, gave Ṛgvedic man the instance of eternal presence and unity he so well used to further develop the world of *ṛta*, the well-formed instant.[3]

Now in the Pythagorean cosmology of ancient Greece the "well-formed instant" in the sound continuum was defined by number. That tradition bequeathed us a fund of arithmology and related mythology in Plato's mathematical allegories.[4,5,6] De Nicolás' discovery of a logical structure within the *Ṛg Veda*, his summary of the arithmetical elements in its creation hymns, and his emphasis on the role of sound constitute a major challenge to musicians: Were the Indian poets, like Plato, speaking a mathematical metaphor derived from a musical model? Can the poets' numbers, like all of Plato's, be analyzed according to the principles of Greek tuning theory? Is it possible, as the distinguished authors of *Hamlet's Mill* have claimed, that Plato really is our "living Rosetta Stone" to the more obscure science of earlier cultures?[7]

De Nicolás has charted a new course in the Western effort to rediscover its Eastern roots, a new adventure for the imagination. I aim to follow his clues as far as number can guide a musician.

A MUSICAL HYPOTHESIS

This study will develop the hypothesis that the "lattice logic" which de Nicolás perceives in the *Ṛg Veda* was grounded on a proto-science of number and tone. The numbers Ṛgvedic man cared about define alternate tunings for the musical scale. The hymns describe the numbers poetically, distinguish "sets" by classes of gods and demons, and portray tonal and arithmetical relations with graphic sexual and spatial metaphor. Vedic concerns were with those *invariances* which became the focus of attention in Greek tuning theory. Because the poets limited themselves to *integers*, or natural numbers, and consistently used the *smallest integers possible* in every tonal context, they made it possible for us to rediscover their constructions by the methods of Pythagorean mathematical harmonics.

The four Ṛgvedic "languages" de Nicolás defines have their counterparts in the foundation of all theories of music. His "language of Non-Existence" (*Asat*) is exemplified by the pitch continuum within each musical interval as well as by the whole undifferentiated gamut—chaos—from low to high. His "language of Existence" (*Sat*) is exemplified by every tone, by every distinction of pitch, thus ultimately by every number which defines an interval, a scale, a tuning system, or the associated metric schemes of the poets, which are quite elaborate in the *Ṛg Veda*. The "language of Images and Sacrifice" (*Yajña*) is exemplified by the multitude of alternate tone-sets and the conflict of alternate values which always results in some accuracy being "sacrificed" to keep the system within manageable limits. The "language of Embodied (*Ṛta*) Vision (*Dhīḥ*)" is required to protect the validity of alternate tuning systems and alternate metric schemes by refusing to grant dominion to any one of them. We are dealing with a *primitive* science of music and number, and a *mature* philosophy.

As our study unfolds it will raise serious questions about the early development of mathematical thinking, about debts which the calendar and scale may owe to each other, and about the possible origins of both the mathematics of music and its related mythology. They are among the many questions we cannot answer satisfactorily as long as a vast amount of archaeological material lies in disarray, unexamined or still undecipherable, much of it untranslated, and as long as a considerable amount of the surviving literature of classical times still remains inaccessible for want of a key. Historians of science have barely begun to cope with certain kinds of material available to them, and we must await their judgment on many issues. A musical analysis of Ṛgvedic imagery will provide, we believe, a new tool for the study of the origins of science, of our calendar, of musical theory, and of the roots of our civilization.

The great moral of Greek Pythagoreanism as it applies to music was drawn by Aristotle and his pupil Aristoxenus when they cut the umbilical cord which tied tone to number. The ear rules the universe of tone, they declared, at a time when Plato and the Pythagoreans had mastered the insights number provided acoustical theory. By that radical act they preserved for music the flexibility of definition—a certain elasticity in intervals—which the evolving science of mathematics could no longer tolerate. Only musicians, henceforth, could speak of "wholetones" and "semitones" rather loosely, defining them with great precision at one moment and then ignoring discrepancies the next. Our modern musical terminology is a jungle to the uninitiated. Indian musicians are rigorously "Aristoxenian" in declining to use Pythagorean ratios in their tuning theory. They learned, early in history, that numerical definitions of intervals lead to great "strife"—a Ṛgvedic lesson—and they have preserved the *moral* of the Ṛgvedic musical poets, not their materials. Thus it is the very great respect which Indians display for their past which makes it impossible to ground our "protopythagorean" analysis in their present habits. That is a truly delicious irony. We have the double burden of first explaining why Ṛgvedic numbers are musical, and then showing how the Ṛgvedic lesson was preserved by abandoning "tone-numbers" altogether.

We are crediting Vedic poets with understanding "tuning theory" as well as any people in history. We assume they knew something about string-length ratios on their primitive harps and that they developed further insight by purely arithmetical methods. What we are investigating, then, is actually a realm of number theory in which music sets the problems, since musical patterns elevate certain numbers to a prominence pure number theory would not accord them. Musical values introduce a hierarchy into the number field: as we shall show in Chapter 3, *even* numbers which *define* the octave matrix are "female," *odd* numbers which *fill* that matrix with "tone-children" are "male," and the *smaller* numbers define intervals of *greater* importance. That part of the continuum of *real* number which lies beyond *rational* number belongs to Non-being (*Asat*) and the Dragon (Vṛtra). Though to a mathematician all numbers may be holy, to a musician some are "divine," others "human," and certain ones "bestial," depending on the context.

The specific mathematical methods required for analyzing "Pythagorean" allegories were suggested twenty years ago by Robert Brumbaugh in *Plato's Mathematical Imagination*: a) the musical octave, ratio 1:2, functions as a matrix for number theory, b) whatever the context, relations are defined by the *smallest integers* possible, and c) the logic is essentially geometrical and is best studied via appropriate diagrams alluded to in the texts but not otherwise transmitted.[8] The full implications of Brumbaugh's suggestions have never been explored in respect to Plato, and their far-reaching implications are quite unknown to scholars in many related fields.

A century ago Albert von Thimus called attention to many arithmetical and graphical structures in the tonal imagery of the ancient world, particularly to the Greek chi *X*, Plato's symbol for the "World-Soul," the Hindu "Drum of Śiva," understandable as the intersection of powers of 2 with powers of 3, or of sequences of octaves and fifths.[9] Thimus called attention to the role of 720 in defining the Just scale, essential to the musical cosmology of all ancient civilizations. Thimus, with his priceless clues to Plato and the past, has been unduly neglected.

The most important idea we need to understand Ṛgvedic thinking is the notion of *reciprocity*. The tonal implications of the Pythagorean affection for *opposites* have been the subject of essays and lectures by Ernst Levy for forty years. Inspired in part by Thimus, Levy has recovered the Pythagorean musical imagination. Levy's treatises on harmony, in which he applies Pythagorean methods and metaphor to modern harmonic analysis, unfortunately have never been published. They would provide an ideal background for scholars wishing to understand the past in terms of the present, and vice versa. The *Ṛg Veda*'s poets, we believe, were suffused with the poetic feeling for number and tone as explained by Levy and his colleague Siegmund Levarie in *Tone: A Study in Musical Acoustics*.[10]

Relevant also to our study of the *Ṛg Veda* is a wealth of ancient commentary which has not yet been re-evaluated from the historical perspectives which are now emerging. Sanskrit scholars have never enjoyed the luxury of knowing how much Vedic mathematics and Vedic imagery may have contributed to Greek science and mythology. Going back in time, we shall glean from the Greeks much that is useful in explaining the pre-conceptual science of the *Ṛg Veda*. The key elements, common to both, were number and tone. Number theory will be pursued rigorously by the methods of Nicomachus, and musical theory will be developed from the models of Archytas and Ptolemy. Musical allegory will be interpreted according to clues derived from Philolaus, Plato, Crantor, Plutarch, and Proclus.

To the Pythagoreans 10 was "divine." It was the sum of the "dimensions" of experience:

```
1 = point           o
2 = line          o   o
3 = plane       o   o   o
4 = solid     o   o   o   o
```

A triangular array of ten pebbles formed the "holy tetractys." Ṛgvedic poets likewise never tire of celebrating the significance of ten. The ten fingers, so helpful in computation, are ten "sisters," ten "daughters" of Tvaṣṭṛ, maker of the gods. Ten "sister maids of slender form" press the Soma juice ceremoniously imbibed by the priests and thereby "animate the devotions," and ten months is the gestation period for a god. Ten is also the appropriate number of gifts for a god (chariots, horses, treasure chests, and lumps of gold), and ten is the number of piles of wood for the fire in which Agni is born as well as the number of his secret "dwelling places." *Puruṣa* ("the soul and original source of the universe") not only fills the universe but within man occupies "a space ten fingers wide" (the region of the heart, and locus of the soul).[11] The same "sisters ten" who drive the god's "car-horse" to the "resting places," "pouring out the rain together," also "blow the skin musician-like" (a possible allusion to a bagpipe?).[12] Ten-ness dominates the arithmetic of the *Ṛg Veda* in ways never suspected until the appropriate triangular yantras (algebraic arrays of integers) are developed for each cosmic cycle according to the examples of Plato and the rules of Nicomachus.

The logic of India is profoundly geometric. Its maṇḍalas and yantras present the observer with static forms which could only be achieved by dynamic processes. Our problem here is to learn to see those forms as Socrates yearned to see his own ideal forms, "in motion."[13]

PROCEDURE

Since the Ṛgvedic poets never give a systematic account of their cosmology, I have had to invent one based on a succession of tone-maṇḍalas and algebraic yantras on which the Ṛgvedic text is a commentary. This will carry the reader step by step from the simplest numerical constructions toward the largest and most complicated. I shall present a systematic account of tuning theory and related number theory in the form of charts which only experts in acoustical theory should expect to understand at a glance. All the relevant technical information necessary to check the charts, however, is given in detail and it can be studied at leisure. I employ modern musical and mathematical notation freely for the power and clarity they provide, but I also use along with them pebble patterns in the ancient style and sectioned circles, probably once drawn in the sand, two "notations" available to the ancient world even before the invention of writing.

I shall quote the *Ṛg Veda* extensively to support the analysis being offered.[14] The analysis, however, has two parts: 1) a mathematical part on musical harmonics, easily verified since number theory leaves little room for opinion, and 2) an imaginative interpretation of the mathematical and musical metaphor. The latter is a personal reconstruction, the plausibility of which the reader must judge, for there is no way of proving that a poet meant what we think he may have meant. My lesson in mathematical acoustics is clearly implied, I believe, by the wealth of implications in the hymns, by the contexts the poets created for particular sets of numbers. In considering plausibility, however, we must remember that there is also a substantial body of arithmetical material which cannot be explained by my methods. My work, then, is essentially a first effort at bringing musical order out of mathematical chaos.

Chapters 2 through 7 will carry Ṛgvedic mathematical analysis as far as possible. Chapter 8 will explore systematically the arithmetic of the calendar and the scale, making audible and visible their many arithmetic and geometric coincidences. Chapters 9 through 11 will draw upon Ṛgvedic insights to analyze the musical mythology in the *Book of Revelation*, its Sumerian and Babylonian prototypes, and their related Greek and Egyptian mythologies. Chapter 12 will aim at cautious conclusions, befitting a work still in progress.

Throughout my study I shall focus on *invariances*, that is, on *patterns* which remain the *same* in different *contexts*. This theme of invariance was expressly formulated by Marius Schneider:

> In view of the inconstancy of the world of form, primitive man questions the reality of static (spatial) phenomena and believes that transient (temporal) dynamic rhythms are a better guide to the substance of things.[15]

Schneider affirms that "sound represents the original substance of the world" for the historian of culture, and points out that the Indian tradition emphasizes the "luminous nature of sound" in the similarity between *svar* (light) and *svara* (sound).[16] My mathematical presentation can be regarded as a very specialized development of Schneider's general view of the role of music in the spiritual history of man.

FOOTNOTES

1. Antonio T. de Nicolás, *Four-Dimensional Man: The Philosophical Methodology of the Ṛg Veda* (Bangalore: Dharmaram College Studies No. 6, 1971), p. 8.
2. *Ibid.*
3. *Ibid.*, p. 134.
4. Ernest G. McClain, "Plato's Musical Cosmology" (*Main Currents in Modern Thought*, vol. 30, no. 1, September/October 1973, pp. 34–42).
5. ———, "Musical Marriages in Plato's Republic," (*Journal of Music Theory*, vol. 18.2, Fall 1974, pp. 242–272).
6. ———, "A New Look at Plato's *Timaeus*," (*Music and Man*, vol. 1, no. 4, 1975), pp. 341–360.
7. Giorgio de Santillana and Hertha von Dechend, *Hamlet's Mill*, (Boston: Gambit, 1969), p. 311.
8. Robert S. Brumbaugh, *Plato's Mathematical Imagination*, (Bloomington: Indiana University Press, 1954; New York: Kraus Reprint Corporation, 1968), pp. 3, 74, 221–229, and 295. Many of Brumbaugh's drawings can be read directly as graphs of "tone-numbers," and he provides the most accessible summary of the geometric-arithmetic symbolism of ancient commentary on Plato.
9. Albert von Thimus, *Die harmonikale Symbolik des Altherthums*, (Köln, M. DuMont-Schauberg, 1868 and 1876).
10. Siegmund Levarie and Ernst Levy, *Tone: A Study in Musical Acoustics*, (Kent: Kent State University Press, 1968), Chapters 2 and 14.
11. Ralph T. H. Griffith, *The Hymns of the Ṛgveda* (Delhi: Motilal Banarsidass, 1973, New Revised Edition) p. 602. (First edition, Delhi: 1889.)
12. *Ibid.*, p. 472, footnote on R.V. 9.1.8.
13. Plato, *Timaeus*, 19b.
14. In *Avatāra: The Humanization of Philosophy Through the Bhagavad Gītā*, (New York: Nicolas Hays, Ltd., 1976), de Nicolás suggests how many of the diagrams presented here are also relevant to the *Bhagavad Gītā*. (See Chapter 6.)
15. Marius Schneider, "Primitive Music," *The New Oxford History of Music*, vol. 1, (London: Oxford University Press, 1957) p. 43.
16. *Ibid.*, pp. 45–49. Schneider's essay anticipates many of the themes in my book. Especially significant is his appreciation of the male-female sexual imagery involved with the instruments and their playing, "bisexuality" proving to have an interesting arithmetical meaning. Schneider also emphasizes the "friction" necessary to sound a tone, and points to the sound-box as "a kind of sacrificial cavern" (pp. 46–51), ideas which will prove important in later chapters. I deeply regret that the *magnum opus* which he now has in progress, summarizing his life's work in musicology and ethnomusicology, is not yet available, for it is obvious that Schneider and I are concerned with the same topics, although from quite opposite perspectives which must eventually be coalesced.

2

TONE-MAṆḌALA AND SUN'S CHARIOT

THE SINGLE-WHEELED CHARIOT OF THE SUN

The central geometrical image in the *Ṛg Veda* is the maṇḍala of the "single-wheeled chariot of the Sun," harmonizing moon months with solar years and the signs of the zodiac.

> Formed with twelve spokes, by length of
> time, unweakened, rolls round the
> heaven this wheel of during order.
>
> Twelve are the fellies, and the wheel is single.
>
> *(R.V. 1.164.11 and 48)*

If time were perfectly cyclic and celestial motion limited to perfect circles and invariant velocities, if the twelve constellations of the zodiac were evenly spaced and twelve moon months were exactly equal to one solar year, then the tone-circle symbolizing our modern Western equal-tempered scale could serve as a geometrical emblem—visual and acoustical—for the *temporal* periodicities of the universe. Each "felly" would be the interval of a *semitone*, and the twelve "spokes" which locate the tones could be thought of as the "rays" of twelve Vedic sun-gods (*Ādityas*).

Ṛgvedic cosmogony does not *begin* with this vision, however, but *ends* with it.

> The Gods are later than this world's production.
> Who knows then whence it first came into being?
>
> *(R. V. 10.129.6)*

CHART 2

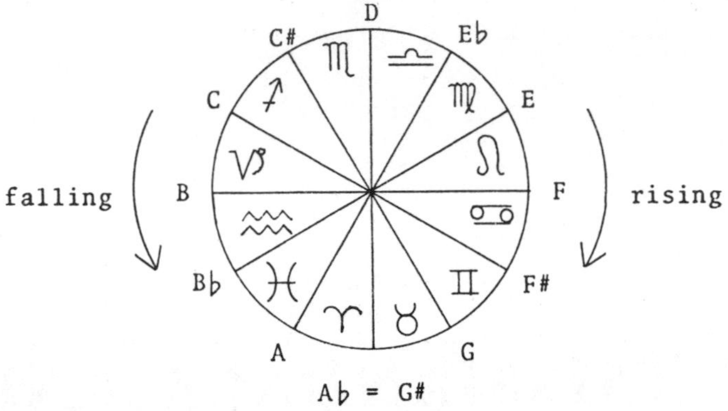

Maṇḍala of The Single-Wheeled Chariot of the Sun

This hypothetical "tonal zodiac" shows how a twelve-spoked maṇḍala harmonizes music and astronomy at an abstract geometrical level. In ancient times neither the constellations nor the intervals of the chromatic scale divided the cycle equally.

♉ Taurus (Bull)	♏ Scorpio (Scorpion)
♊ Gemini (Twins)	♐ Sagittarius (Archer)
♋ Cancer (Crab)	♑ Capricorn (Goat)
♌ Leo (Lion)	♒ Aquarius (Water bearer)
♍ Virgo (Virgin)	♓ Pisces (Fish)
♎ Libra (Balance)	♈ Aries (Ram)

That question frames our entire study with its challenge to explain how the extremely complicated Vedic world "came into being."

The chariot of the gods is actually a "wheel-less car . . . fashioned mentally" (10.135.3). The Celestial Race itself "was made by singers with their lips," and the same singers "with their mind formed horses harnessed by a word" to drive the chariot, "a light car moving every way" (1.20.1–3). Of the car itself, in what I assume to be an allusion to rotation and counter-rotation in the tone-circle, we hear that it "works on either side," the car-pole to which the horses are harnessed thus "turning every way" (10.102.1 and 10.135.3). We are told explicitly that the car "was not made for horses or for reins": a hymn is addressed to

> Ye Sapient Ones who made the lightly-rolling car
> out of your mind, by thought,
> the car that never errs.
>
> *(4.36.1–2)*

We are studying what the poets described as "a spirit-fashioned car," or a "word-yoked car" (10.85.12 and 1.7.2). Throughout the *Ṛg Veda* allusions to music and to the power of the musician are explicit and ubiquitous, and so is insistence that the imagery be read as allegory.

A tone-maṇḍala whose spokes are evenly distributed can correlate only with equal-temperament. The Greeks achieved the geometric ability to tune an equal-tempered monochord scale when Archytas, Plato's Pythagorean friend, solved the problem of doubling the volume of the god's cubical altar at Delphi, the allegorical form of the problem of establishing the third root of 2. Now the cube root of 2 establishes an equal-tempered major third within the monochord octave:

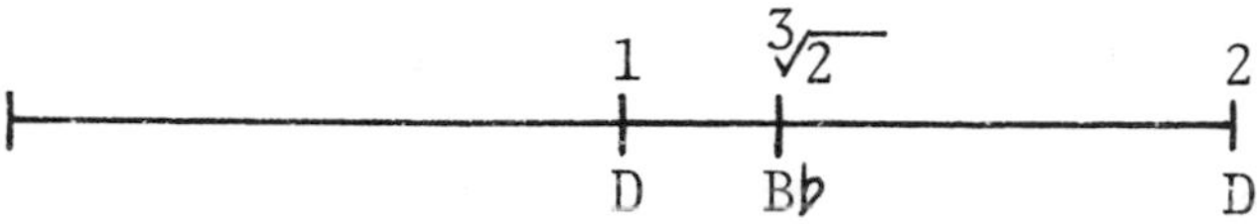

From that beginning, the equal-tempered wholetone is the geometric mean *within* the major third, and the equal-tempered semitone is the geometric mean within the wholetone. Iterations of this procedure will produce all twelve tones in equal-temperament. The necessity of tempering the *pure* intervals, defined by the ratios of *integers*, is one of the great themes of Plato's *Republic*. In his allegorical form, "citizens" modelled on the tones of the scale must not demand "exactly what they are owed," but must keep in mind "what is best for the city."[1] Tempering is implicit in Aristoxenus' arguments.[2] Neither the early forms of the scale nor the zodiac were based on exactly equal divisions of their cyclic maṇḍalas. Ptolemy normalized the zodiac in the form we know it today c. 150 A.D., giving it the musical labels shown in Chapter 8, with "temperament" implicit.[3] We are concerned here with what happened earlier.

The vernal sun rose in Taurus (the Bull) between 4000 B.C. and 2000 B.C., when the mathematical system postulated in this study was apparently first developed and the earliest poems conceived, but it shifted to Aries (the Ram) before the *Ṛg Veda* was completed.[4] Indra, leader of the gods, is the "Bull of Heaven" in many poems and the "Ram" in others. As leader of the Maruts (storm-gods), he is "the Thunderer," the "Mighty

Steer'' who bellows "upon the height above earth's breadth" (7.49.1, 9.106.1, and 10.28.2). As the Ram, "Stone-hurler," he "hastens with his troop," and "finds the light of heaven" (8.2.40, 1.10.2, and 1.52.1).

In the modern Western world we are inclined to think of tones as "points" in the continuum of pitch, an idea quite inappropriate in either ancient Greek or modern Hindu tuning theory. The Greeks named the tones with the strings of the lyre, considering certain tones to be fixed and the others variable over a certain range. Hindu theory allows pitch to vary from as little as a quarter-tone (the smallest perceptible difference) to as much as three quarter-tones. It is this *range of variability* which justifies the associations of tones with constellations, as in Ptolemy's own "tonal zodiac."[5]

Today equal-temperament conceives the octave cycle, defined by the ratio 1:2, to be subdivided into 1200 *cents* (equal logarithmic units) so that each semitone is worth 100 *cents*, or $\sqrt[12]{2}$, and all larger intervals are an integral number of semitones. For the ancient world, however, limited to *rational numbers*, this simplicity was beyond reach of their arithmetic. The maṇḍala in Chart 2, then, has only the value of an abstract ideal against which to measure the practicable, and the actual. In Chart 3 I have tried to show how Plato's "Atlantis" tuning—arithmetically the most economical available—approximates "the Sun's Chariot."

THE HINDU-GREEK SCALE: A CYCLIC SPACE OF "THIRTY REGIONS"

The smallest integers which can define a diatonic scale with two similar tetrachords—a fundamental concept in both Hindu and Greek tunings—occupy a "space" of thirty units in the "octave-double" 30:60 shown in Chart 3. The numbers 30, 32, 36, 40, 45, 48, 50, 54, and 60 exhaust the tonal implications of integers $2^p3^q5^r \leqq 60$, as will be shown in Chapter 10, but they constitute only one of very many alternate definitions of the scale, as shown in Chart 1. The oldest explicit reference to this tuning is Ptolemy's.[6] I claim that this tuning is implicit in the musical cosmology of several earlier cultures for all of the complicated reasons to be gradually unfolded here. Furthermore, these numbers function as ratios both of wavelength and frequency, and I claim that this tonal reciprocity was fully understood in the ancient world in a slightly different guise: integers functioned as both *multiples* and *submultiples*, specifically of monochord string-length, but in general of any quantified matter studied under the aspect of ratio theory. In Chart 3 the Hindu-Greek scale rises via the same sequence of ratios that its reciprocal scale (our modern major scale) falls. This tuning, which Ptolemy labelled *Diatonic Syntonon*, and one other in which the major

CHART 3

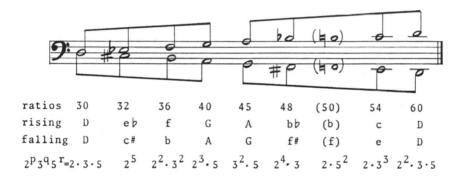

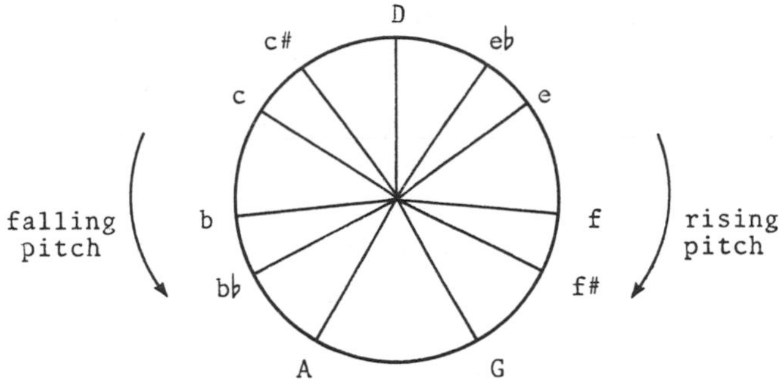

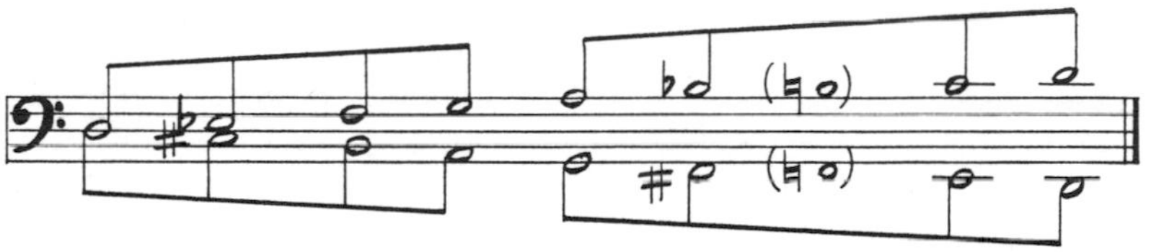

ratios	30	32	36	40	45	48	(50)	54	60
rising	D	e♭	f	G	A	b♭	(b)	c	D
falling	D	c#	b	A	G	f#	(f)	e	D
$2^p3^q5^r$=	$2\cdot3\cdot5$	2^5	$2^2\cdot3^2$	$2^3\cdot5$	$3^2\cdot5$	$2^4\cdot3$	$2\cdot5^2$	$2\cdot3^3$	$2^2\cdot3\cdot5$

The Hindu-Greek Diatonic Scale and Its Reciprocal

The smallest integers which can define the rising Hindu-Greek diatonic scale or its falling reciprocal scale lie within the octave double 1:2 = 30:60. Three tones, A, D, and G in the notation used here, are common to both scales so that there are only eleven total "cuts" in the tone-maṇḍala. There are wholetones of both 8:9 and 9:10 and oversized "semitones" of 15:16, hence the divisions of the maṇḍala are distinctly unequal. The numbers 50 and 36, representing f and b, are redundant in the maṇḍala. Capital and small letters distinguish two classes of tones, the first "fixed," the second "movable."

and minor wholetones of 8:9 and 9:10 are reversed within the tetrachords and which he labels *Didymus' Diatonic*, contain pure octaves, fifths, and thirds, and are called "Just tunings" today. To both Greek and Hindu the scale is essentially a falling form, but with many modal variants and tuning permutations of little interest to mathematics. What the mathematician strives for is "aesthetic economy," meaning simplest or most powerful formulas. In Chapter 11 we shall note the elegant economy in Plato's formula for this tuning; meanwhile we must grow comfortable with the variety of ways in which it can be achieved, and become aware of its flaws.

Ancient cosmology required just enough number theory and just enough musical theory to harmonize the heavens with the scale and the calendar. "The Moon is that which shapes the years" (R.V. 10.85.5) by dividing the Sun cycle into approximately twelve sub-cycles, and so it is likewise the Moon that arouses interest in dividing the octave cycle into twelve parts even though musicians need a maximum of only seven at a time. The reciprocal scales of Chart 3 define eleven tones of the octave, but they are by no means equally spaced. There are two sizes of "wholetones" (8:9 at 32:36, 40:45, and 48:54, and 9:10 at 36:40 and 54:60), and the "semitones" of 15:16 (at 30:32 and 45:48) are considerably oversized. The proper location of the missing twelfth tone, A♭ or G#, is the subject of a considerable part of the mythology being analyzed later.

That the Ṛgvedic poets knew this tuning is an inference from the way they stressed the role of 30 and 60 in defining cycles, and the roles of 7 and 11, the number of tone-values in diatonic and chromatic sets, and from their insistence on linking these numbers to tone. The Vedic year consisted of twelve months of thirty days each, with an occasional intercalary month also of "thirty members," and the Vedic day contained thirty hours of sixty minutes.[7] The months seemed to have been grouped in pairs of "double months," periods of sixty days, giving the year "six seasons."[8] The Sun was conceived metaphorically as the "Bird" whose "morning song, representing prayer, is supreme through all the divisions of the world."[9] Those divisions number thirty:

> Song is bestowed upon the Bird; it rules
> supreme through thirty realms
> throughout the days at break of morn.
>
> *(10.189.3)*

Uṣas, Dawn, mother of light and daughter of the Sun, resplendent in her own shining chariot, can daily "traverse thirty regions, and dart across the spirit in a moment" (1.123.8). In the metaphor of the cosmic "cow" we hear that "stretching her head and speaking loudly with her tongue, she hath gone downward thirty steps" (6.59.6). A cycle of thirty units harmonizes the month with the diatonic scale at the *arithmetic* level; later we shall see how the reciprocal scales harmonize the chromatic scale with the 360-day year. Modern astronomers scorn the notion that their predecessors ever invented such inconvenient calendar units as the 30-day month and 360-day year, since observations would quickly have shown them to be false.[10] Musicians, on the other hand, need units of these sizes for a systematic exploration of the octave.

15

THE HINDU-GREEK SCALE: A CYCLIC SPACE OF "THIRTY REGIONS"

The seven-day week was established for Hindus and Hebrews long before it was introduced into Egypt and Greece. In the poems the seven tones of the diatonic scale—the scale which elevates 30 and 60 from mere metric convenience to the status of *a necessary base*—become "seven holy singers" guarding the "beloved firmly-settled station" of the Sun (3.7.7 and 4.16.3). We shall probably never know whether there is an allusion to the basic *tetrachord* (four strings) in the reference to the four who "bear him up and give him rest and quiet," or the four "swift-footed" red and purple steeds which Vāyu, wind, yokes to his chariot (5.47.4 and 1.134.3). The seven together, however, are a "team of Seven" (Vālakhilya 7.5), "seven Bay Steeds" for the Sun's chariot (1.50.8), seven rays shining through "Earth and Heaven" (1.55.8–9), "seven-priests, the brother-hood, filling the stations of the One" (9.10.7). Later we shall see that these seven tone-numbers are "seven male children" generated by the *odd* numbers 3 and 5 within the womb of Uṣas, symbolized by the female number 2 which defines the octave matrix as an arithmetical "double." Here we see these seven yoked in two different ways "to the one-wheeled chariot . . . bearing seven names" (1.164.1–2). We shall avoid the temptation to pursue a reference to "the mighty ones, the seven times seven" Maruts (storm gods) as an allusion to seven possible modal permutations of the scale because we know nothing about any Vedic modal theory. The total set of eleven tones in Chart 3, however, does command attention.

Notice that the eleven tones in Chart 3 are grouped in symmetric pairs about the reference tone, D. In Plato's "Atlantis" myth these eleven elements represent "Poseidon and his five pairs of twin sons."[11] In the *Ṛg Veda*, Uṣas in her role as universal "bride" is offered the following wedding prayer:

> Vouchsafe to her ten sons, and make
> her husband the eleventh man.
>
> *(10.85.45)*

A Upaniṣad describes man's body as "a city with eleven doors."[12] According to Daniélou, the number of the Rudras—"the working class of heaven"—is usually given as eleven.[13] The notion that where ten men gather to pray God is also present lives on in the Hebrew requirement of ten to form a *minyan*, the quorum necessary for public worship. In the *Ṛg Veda*, "the Viśvadevas (sun-gods), as a separate troop or class of Gods, are ten in number"; they are especially worshipped at funeral obsequies.[14] The Ṛgvedic curse on a man who defames one is: "May he lose all his ten sons together" (7.104.15). There are ten "yoked to the far-stretching car-pole of the sun's chariot" (1.164.14).

Sexual imagery was applied to sets of tones and numbers. It is clear, then, that we need a theory which relates tones and tonal relationships to "fathers," "sons," and "mothers." The next chapter will reconstruct the eleven tones of Chart 3 by a systematic "generation" from one given reference tone.

FOOTNOTES

1. Socrates debunks the notion that justice means giving "to each what is owed" commencing at *Republic* 331e, and insists that justice must be modeled on the musical scale where "moderation" reigns, and all can "sing the same chant together" (*Republic* 432*a*).
2. *The Harmonics of Aristoxenus*, Henry S. Macran ed. and translator (Oxford: Clarendon Press, 1902). Aristoxenus' discussion is in Book II, pp. 55–58, and Macran's commentary is on pp. 285–286. By allowing "perfect" intervals "an inappreciable locus" of variation, Aristoxenus gains the equivalent of an argument in equal-temperament, but his argument rejects any mathematical definition of the intervals.
3. Ptolemy's own "tonal zodiac" can be found in Book III of his *Elements of Harmony*. (See "Ptolemaios und Porphyrios über die music" by Ingemar Düring, *Goeteborgs Hoegskolas aarsskrift*, 1934:1, pp. 122–128.)
4. The "precession of the equinoxes" through a cycle of about 25,000 years means that the vernal sun moves from one constellation to the next about every 2000 years. For a gracious discussion of astronomical complexities and a study of ancient records see *The Dawn of Astronomy* by J. Norman Lockyer (Cambridge: The M.I.T. Press, 1964, first edition by Cassell and Company, 1894).
5. See 3 above. Ptolemy allots the *two* octaves of the Greek "Perfect System" to his circle, hence one octave occupies only a semicircle; a wholetone, ratio 8:9, is thus worth 30 degrees, and a whole "sign." His ratios are "arc" measurements, not string-length ratios, and thus correspond with our equal-temperament, rather than with earlier Pythagorean tunings. If I followed his example and represented the whole octave within a semicircle, then my spacing between "spokes" would be reduced by half, and we should end up with double the number of Ṛgvedic spokes in each instance. I follow what I believe to be Plato's habits. Ptolemy's mathematics and astronomy belonged to a new age. (See Chapter 8.)
6. Ptolemy preserved many tunings devised by his predecessors and invented several new ones which, so far as we know, had little influence on musicians. They are most accessible in Chapter 2 of *Tuning and Temperament: A Historical Survey*, by J. Murray Barbour (East Lansing: Michigan State College Press, 1953). This particular tuning he labelled *Diatonic Syntonon.* (See Barbour, page 20, Table 20, where tone-names are one step higher, E D C B A G F E, but ratios are the same.)
7. Sukumar Ranjan Das, "Scope and Development of Indian Astronomy," *Osiris* II, 1936, pp. 197–219.
8. See Griffith's footnotes on pp. 13, 110, 194, and 195 of *The Hymns of the Ṛgveda* (Delhi: Motilal Banarsidass, 1973, New Revised Edition).

17
FOOTNOTES

9. *Ibid.*, p. 651.

10. See Lockyer, *op. cit.*, Chapter 24. "Had ignorance led to the establishment of a year of 360 days, yet experience would have led to its rejection in a few years." (He is quoting Ideler, on p. 245.) He adds: "If observations of the sun at solstice or equinox had been alone made use of, the true length of the year would have been determined in a few years" (p. 246).

11. *Critias* 114.

12. Alain Daniélou, *Hindu Polytheism*, (New York: Pantheon Books, 1964), p. 43.

13. *Ibid.*, p. 103.

14. Griffith, *op. cit.*, p. 17.

3

MUSICAL GENERATION

"GOD" AND "MOTHER"

A vibrating string of any reference length can be halved to sound the octave higher or doubled to sound the octave lower. Since all tones recur cyclically at the octave—as the "Same" tone in one sense, but a "Different" tone in another—any octave can serve as the model for all possible octaves, at least for the general purposes of tuning theory. The cyclic structure of the octave is the *invariant* common to all systems of tuning. The tone-circle functions as a cyclic matrix within which derivative tones come to birth, as shown in Chart 4.

The Greeks spoke of "three genera"—diatonic, chromatic, and enharmonic—so that the apt metaphor of musical "generation" has always been part of the Western tradition. In tuning instruments like the piano and organ we start with a given reference pitch and generate the tones of the scale one at a time according to an established schema of rules. Unless one has the experience of actually tuning an instrument, behaving as "midwife" to successive tones, the metaphor of generation may have little meaning. Plato's genetic theory, however, with its sexual metaphor, was a theory of tuning. This metaphorical sense which numbers acquire in a tonal context is what we need for the *Ṛg Veda*.

The number 2 is "female" in the sense that it creates the matrix, the octave, in which all other tones are born. By itself, however, it can only create "cycles of barrenness," in Socrates' metaphor, for multiplication and

CHART 4

harmonic progression

1:2

1:2

reciprocal harmonic progression

$D = 1 = n^o = 2^n$

division   multiplication

1.75   1.25

1.5

$A\flat = G\# = \sqrt{2}$

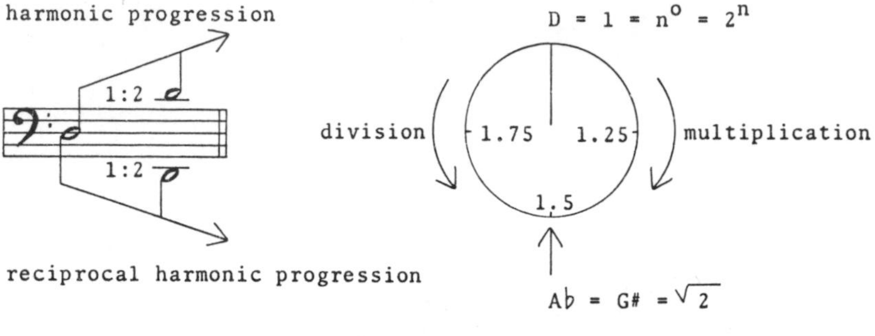

The Tonal Matrix: "God" and "Mother"

When the Divine Unity ("1") splits itself, it creates the model octave "double" of ratio 1:2 within which all possible tones have one octave incarnation, *i.e.*, as one "cut" in the circle. Thus "2" becomes the female number, defining the cyclic spaces within which all other numbers are interpreted according to a logarithmic scale on base 2. Multiplication and division by 2 never changes the locus of a "cut" in the tone-maṇḍala.

logarithmic scale (base 2)

| 0 | .1 | .2 | .3 | .4 | .5 | .6 | .7 | .8 | .9 | 1 |

| D | c | | b♭ | A | | G | f | | e♭ | D |
| 1 | $\frac{10}{9}$ | | $\frac{5}{4}$ | $\frac{4}{3}$ | | $\frac{3}{2}$ | $\frac{15}{9}$ | | $\frac{15}{8}$ | 2 |

$\sqrt{2} = G\# = A\flat$

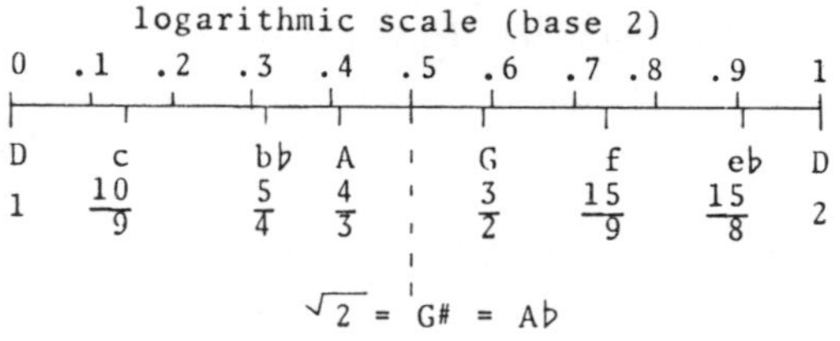

division by 2 can never *introduce* new tones into our tone-maṇḍala.[1] In musical arithmetic, the powers of 2 ($2^{\pm n}$) generate cyclic identities; that is, they leave the musical relationship of the octave cycle invariant. Other numbers show their tonal implications by reduction to a logarithmic scale of base 2, and the omission of the characteristic or whole-number portion of the logarithm. Although we are accustomed to thinking of logarithms as a modern invention, any ancient culture which mathematized the scale actually possessed in the tone-cycle diagram a kind of circular logarithmic scale of base 2.[2] Today we subdivide that matrix into 1,200 equal logarithmic units called *cents*, so that the semitones of equal-temperament are exactly 100 cents each. It proves convenient to study the ancient cosmological tunings as approximations to equal-temperament, using the language of cents to discuss small variations in pitch. Conversion tables are given in Appendix I. Most of the puzzling changes in numerosity which arise in this study involve the fact that multiplication by $2^{\pm n}$ is an identity operation for the tone-maṇḍala, the transformation in number representation or "appearances" having been brought about solely to eliminate fractional forms.

It is a theme of much ancient mythology that the Divine Unity is a hermaphrodite, producing a daughter, "2," by a process of division without benefit of a mother. God is "1," but he cannot procreate except via his daughter, "2," the female principle and mother of all. Numerical and musical relationships provide the metaphor: ratio theory *is* "music" for the ancients.[3] The incest theme pervades the *Ṛg Veda*. When the tone-maṇḍala is filled with children it is the womb of Uṣas, daughter of the Sun; when it is an "undifferentiated continuum," as in Chart 3, it belongs to the dragon, Vṛtra, and to *Asat* (Non-Existence).

For de Nicolás the starting point of the *Ṛg Veda*'s intentional life is the *Asat*, the non-existent, "the whole undifferentiated primordial chaos" ruled by the dragon Vṛtra.[4] *Asat* is "a place of silence," "self-destruction," "disappearance," "the lap of *Nirṛti*" (in-activity). It is a place for those "incapable of following the norm, the *Ṛta*."[5] In their verbal roots both *Asat* and Vṛtra (*As-* and *Vṛ-*) stand for "an activity of covering—or not letting exist that which longs to exist."[6] Plato defines "mother" as "matrix," "Receptacle of what has come to be visible and otherwise sensible."[7] De Nicolás describes the *Asat* similarly as "Space" or "field-condition" out of which all differentiation in human experience emerges for the poets. "It is a necessary field of sound emergence and of all communication."[8] "Vṛtra is also called *dharuna*, the original receptacle—foundation—of the waters."[9]

In Chart 3 the undifferentiated circle belongs to the dragon, the ratio 1:2 belongs to mother, and every point in the circle which we can define by an integer belongs to God. The model for all Existence (*Sat*)—hence of everything which can be named or numbered—is Indra:

> His form is to be seen everywhere
> for of every form He is the Model.
>
> *(6.47.18)*

The continuum of the circle (Vṛtra) embraces all possible differentiations (Indra). The conflict between Indra and Vṛtra can never end; it is the conflict between the field of *rational* numbers and the continuum of *real* numbers. Integers which introduce new "cuts" in the tone-maṇḍala demonstrate "Indra power" over Vṛtra; Vṛtra is "cut to pieces" in every battle with the Gods, but his death would be their own. "Without the *Asat* or its equivalent Vṛtra, the Dragon, there would be no Indra, nor even the gods for he is their container."[10]

The etymology of Vṛtra, however, contains an even more interesting notion: the root *vṛt-* means "twirl, to turn around."[11] Our tone-maṇḍalas must be thought of "in motion," *multiplying* numbers to whatever size is required to avoid fractions. Vedic gods are produced, de Nicolás notes, by "turning, twirling, churning" of the original "waters."[12] Every revolution is a multiplication by 2, and it will require dozens of such revolutions—to integers of fifteen digits—for our lesson in Vedic arithmetic. The "churning of the sea" is a mythical motif Giorgio de Santillana and Hertha von Dechend pursue around the world in *Hamlet's Mill*; many forms of that myth have strong Vedic overtones. The dragon, Vṛtra, seems never to have lost some of the qualities de Nicolás assigns him: "It is the ground of perception: *Vṛtra in potentia* is Indra and the rest. Indra, the Sun, etc., *actu* are Vṛtra."[13]

Indra slays Śuṣṇa, like Vṛtra one of the "demons of drought," by "circumambulating" him in a particular direction:

> Thou slewest, turning to the right, Śuṣṇa
> for every living man.
>
> *(10.22.14)*

I shall interpret rotation to the right (clockwise) in the tone-circle as meaning *multiplication*, for it is by multiplication that we achieve larger integer sets and give Indra more victories over the undifferentiated continuum. Since whatever exists for us to divide already belongs to Indra, a poet can sing,

> From thy body thou has generated
> at the same time the Mother and the Father.
>
> *(10.54.3)*

If the tone-maṇḍala represents the world, then the "world-halves" are separated by a diameter which locates, tonally, the equal-tempered A♭ = G♯ directly opposite our reference tone D. This has the arithmetical value of the square root of 2, an "irrational" number which is the focus of much of our following discussion. Since no integer can substitute for it, Vedic imagery must wrestle with it:

> Between the wide-spread world-halves is
> the birthplace: the Father laid the
> Daughter's germ within it.
>
> *(1.164.33)*

We need a "spoke" at that locus, but not until Chart 13 will we discover a Ṛgvedic way of locating one there.

How "the sonless gained a grandson from his daughter" we can discover by studying the odd "male" numbers in Chart 5 (3.31.1–2).

CHART 5

The Harmonic Series and Its Reciprocal

∧ = higher than notated
∨ = lower than notated

each degree = 1200/360
= 10/3 cents

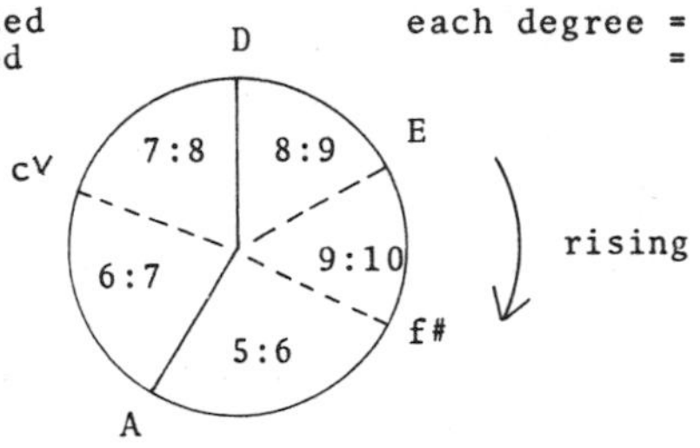

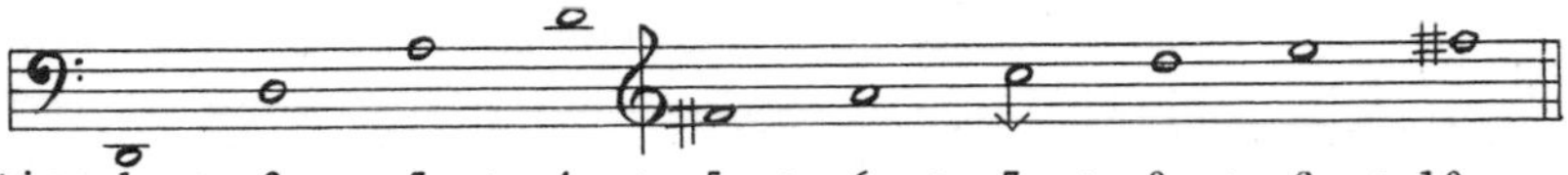

ratios	1 :	2 :	3 :	4 :	5 :	6 :	7 :	8 :	9 :	10
tones	D	D	A	D	f#	A	c∨	D	E	f#
cents		1200	702	498	386	316	267	231	204	182
equal temperament notation		1200	700	500	400	300	-	-	200	200

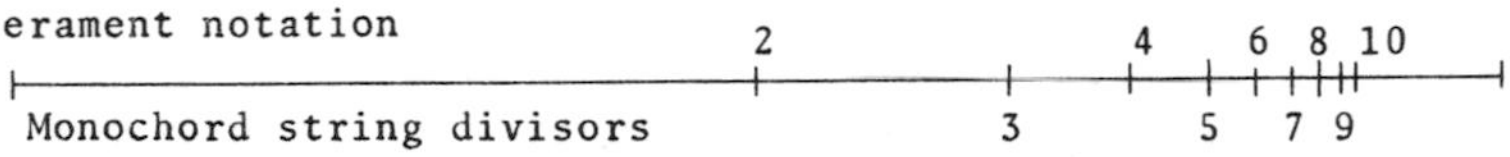

a) The Harmonic Series

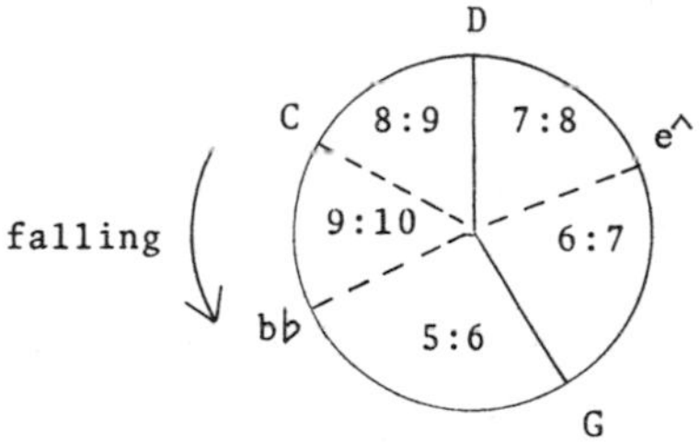

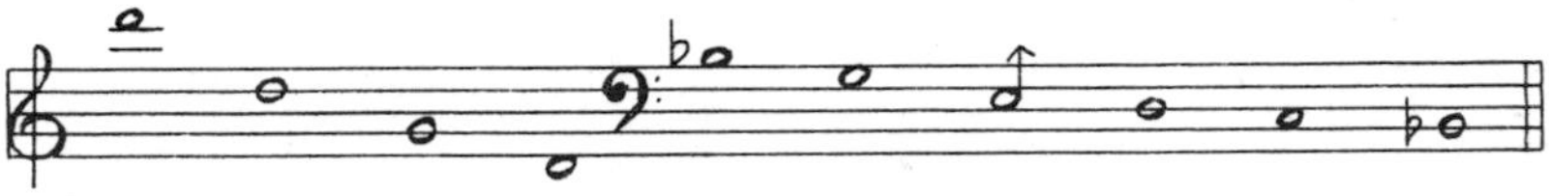

ratios	1 :	2 :	3 :	4 :	5 :	6 :	7 :	8 :	9 :	10
tones	D	D	G	D	b♭	G	e^	D	C	b♭

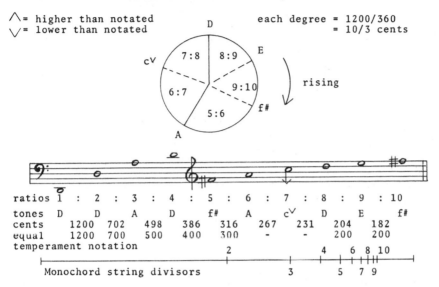

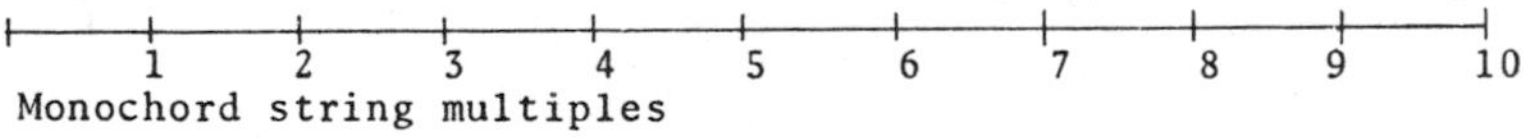

b) The Reciprocal Harmonic Series

See Appendix I for tables of ratios, cents and degrees, and for conversion formulas.

FATHERS AND SONS

Within the female "womb" or matrix of the octave cycles generated by 2^n, the odd numbers introduce new tones and thereby justify the notion that they are "male," the female being supposed to play a passive role genetically.[14] In Chart 5a the tonal functions of the first ten integers can be read directly from their locus in the harmonic series: any pair of numbers defines a ratio according to their respective ordinal positions in the series, functioning as divisors of string length and multiples of frequency.

In Chart 5b the first ten integers are shown as an arithmetic series representing multiples of string length; from a tonal perspective we get a "reciprocal harmonic series." Later we shall examine *reciprocity* as one of the most rigorous ideas in the *Ṛg Veda.* Throughout this study we must never fail to examine the opposite, reciprocal functions of the numbers in both arithmetic and harmonic series, that is, as both multiples and submultiples of some basic unit.

The male odd numbers take precedence over their female octave "doubles" not only because they lie closer to god = 1, but presumably because they permit the divine unity to be subdivided rigorously according to the principle of unity: if we limit generative ratios, as Greek musical theory did traditionally, to those between two consecutive integers (*i.e.*, differing by unity, ratios called *superparticular* in Latin and *epimoric* in Greek) then each odd number (oddness itself being due to an element of unity) functions as the arithmetic mean for an earlier superparticular ratio, and subdivides it according to the same principle. We can schematize this subdivision as follows:

1					2
2			3		4
4		5	6	7	8
8	9	10			

Thus 3 (or $\frac{3}{2} \times 2$) functions as an arithmetic mean between 1 and 2, 5 between 2 and 3, 7 between 3 and 4, 9 between 4 and 5, etc. We are not attributing any harmonic theory or any theory of "means" to Ṛgvedic poets. We are simply noticing that if *division* is always of the simplest kind, by the arithmetic mean, the division of successive ratios will require larger but still successive integers. Every division, however, creates a larger tonal interval between the smaller pair of numbers. We assume Ṛgvedic man noticed this, and that he made reciprocity an integral element in his thinking. What we now call the "harmonic" series was actually called the "sub-contrary" series until the time of Archytas; that means that what we today call the "reciprocal harmonic series" was once taken as the norm, that is, as an arithmetic series of string-length ratios. The explanation is so much more complicated than the fact: any ratio can be sung in either direction.

Every odd number has a unique "angular value" in the tone-maṇḍala. Since Hindu cosmic cycles are numbers divisible by 2, 3, and 5, we can examine their potential musical implications by plotting the location of all products of the prime numbers 2, 3, and 5 in relevant tone-maṇḍalas, as in Chart 3, where reciprocal meanings were plotted for all numbers $2^p3^q5^r \leqq 60$ (p, q, and r being integers including zero). The "divine male number 3" will generate cuts or "spokes" which lie within about half a degree of the idealized twelve spokes of equal-temperament. (The ratio 2:3 is worth about 702 cents, and the complementary ratio 3:4 is worth about 498.) The "human number 5" will generate "poorer" spokes: the ratio of the major third, 4:5, is worth about 386 cents, and its complementary minor third of ratio 5:6 is worth about 316.[15]

What about the prime number 7? In ancient times the ratio 7:5 was a valued simplification of the square root of 2. Notice that in the maṇḍalas of Chart 5 the ratio 7:5 defines a pair of tones which nearly lie on a diameter. This approximation is not good enough for the *Ṛg Veda*'s poets. We shall encounter 7 not as a "tone-value," but as the most important limiting number in several sets, particularly in its role as exponent.

Plato defined "father" as "the model in whose likeness that which becomes is born."[16] The only fathers we need from here on are "3" and "5," which appear to have meant in the *Ṛg Veda* exactly what they meant long afterward in the *Republic*. In a sense, 3 "fathers" 9 (*i.e.*, as 3^2), and 3 and 5 together "fathered" all eleven tones in Chart 3.

In the tonal functions of odd numbers we see represented within the ancient religions we are considering a strong male bias. The female principle was deified, but it was exclusively the male element on which the world developed and differentiated itself.

The patterns in Chart 5 can be rotated to the right or left to plot all possible tones generated by these intervals. Every set of tones, however, will have a unique "numerosity," depending on a particular point of view within a particular context. In Chart 6 we see what happens when the reciprocal meanings of "3" are plotted in the same circle.

INDRA AND THE AŚVIN PAIR

Three tones provide the framework on which Western musical theory developed from its earliest Greek foundations up through the nineteenth century. They are shown in Chart 6 both in cyclic, maṇḍala form and in linear scale order as defined by the "musical proportion" 6:8::9:12 which

CHART 6

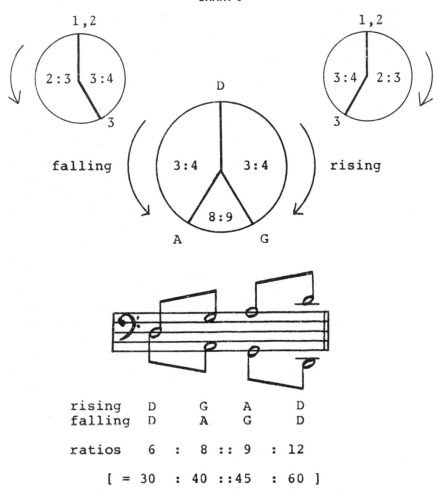

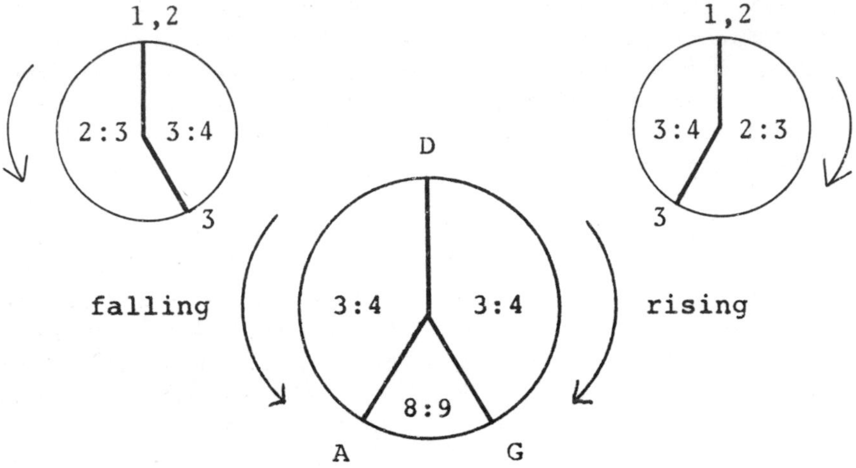

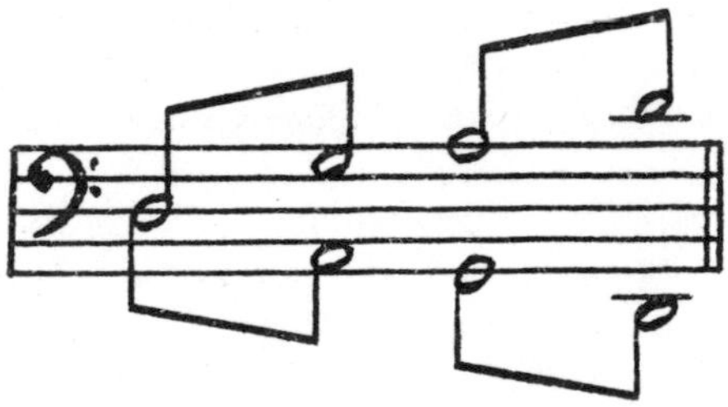

rising	D		G		A		D
falling	D		A		G		D
ratios	6	:	8	::	9	:	12
	[= 30	:	40	::	45	:	60]

The Musical Proportion 6:8::9:12

These three tones play interchangeable roles as arithmetic, harmonic, and geometric means, and define the limits of two tetrachords. In Vedic metaphor they are apparently symbolized by "Indra and the Aśvin Pair." In modern musical theory these tones are tonic, dominant, and subdominant. In the maṇḍala we see D as the geometric mean *between* the arithmetic and harmonic means, a totally different perspective than that provided by the staff notation or by the proportion 6:8::9:12

Pythagoras reputedly brought home from Babylon.[17] In ratio theory the number 9 is the "arithmetic mean" within the octave module (6:12 = 1:2) and 8 is the "sub-contrary" or "harmonic" mean. "Numerosity" is simply a result of the decision to display all results as a sequence of integers, or whole numbers. The arithmetic mean subdivides the octave into a perfect fifth of ratio 2:3 (= 6:9) and a complementary perfect fourth of ratio 3:4 (= 9:12), that is, with a *larger* ratio between the *smaller* numbers. The "harmonic mean" reverses the order of intervals in a "sub-contrary" direction (6:8 = 3:4 and 8:12 = 2:3) to establish the perfect inverse symmetry which characterized not only Plato's arithmetic but a vast amount of art in many ancient cultures. The Greeks conceived these two "means" as being the fixed limits of their *tetrachords* (see Chart 3) within each of which the two interior strings were "movable" in pitch. Western musicians think of these tones as "dominant" and "subdominant" in the harmonic vocabulary of recent centuries. In our tone-maṇḍala, with D as reference tone, G and A are simply the "opposite" meanings of 3, as 3^1 and 3^{-1}.

In Ṛgvedic imagery the arithmetic and harmonic means—so I believe—are "the Aśvin pair," twin children of the gods who function as the "two Bay Steeds" of Indra's chariot. They are among the most mysterious characters in the poems, present at all of Indra's exploits, yet their identity is never made clear. We meet them most often as "twin heralds of the Dawn," or as "physicians," "miracle workers," and "first teachers of agriculture."[18] Their musical identity can be gleaned from Hymn 1.34 which addresses the Aśvins with the cyclic notion of "threeness" over thirty times in a mere dozen verses.

1) Ye who observe this day be with us even thrice . . .

2) Three are the fellies [rim segments] in your
honey-bearing car . . .
Three are the pillars set upon it for support . . .

3) Thrice in the self-same day, ye Gods who banish
want, sprinkle ye thrice today our sacrifice
with meath;
And thrice vouchsafe us store of food . . .

4) Thrice come ye to our home, thrice to the righteous
folk, thrice triply aid the man who
well deserves your help. . . .

5) The Sun's daughter hath mounted your three-wheeled car. . . .

9) Where are the three wheels of your triple
chariot, where are the three seats
thereto firmly fastened?

To that last question the tone-maṇḍala in Chart 6 provides a highly suggestive answer.

What cannot be made clear all at once is that all of the material in the tone-field will function as arithmetic and harmonic means in allied number sets. The scales in Chart 3 and the more complicated material to be presented later can be generated solely by taking successive cuts in derivative modules according to this pattern of arithmetic and harmonic means. "Indra-power"—meaning ratio theory in the broadest sense known to Nicomachus, called by him simply "music"—needs no other tools. It does not even require a theory of means. If cuts are made in the most obvious way—in the middle of a string or interval ratio—and if the derivative intervals are studied under the aspect of *perfect inverse symmetry*, then the Aśvins would appear as twins carrying "Indra" to every part of the continuum of sound which mathematics can differentiate, and to whatever limits anyone cares to investigate the limitless field of rational numbers.

It is the poets' idea—not mine—that the Aśvins are linked to "the Seven Mother Streams" (1.34.8), and these life-giving streams or rivers to "the seven tones" and "seven holy singers" (3.7.1 and 7) shown first in Chart 3. Every "mother" tone or number can give birth to the harmonic and reciprocal harmonic series of Chart 5. It was very appropriate that the Aśvins became the "Twin Horse-headed Gods of Agriculture" in later Hindu methology.[19]

Two further refinements are worth noting: 1) the "third wheel of their chariot, standing by itself in front, is especially ornamental."[20] And the car itself is a tonal creation:

> That circumambient Car, worthy of sacrifice,
> we call with our pure hymns at
> earliest flush of dawn.
>
> *(R.V. 10.41.1)*

These three tones (with D doubled at the octave) frame the tetrachords of Chart 3, and they remain fixed elements in every construction which follows. In the "marriage" allegory of the *Republic* and in his legislation concerning "wedding feasts" in *Laws*, Plato has shown us how "Pythagorean marriages" between the ratio of the perfect fourth, 3:4, and the "human" number 5 can fill these frames with tone children.[21]

INDRA AS DANCER AND LORD OF THE FIVE TRIBES

The tetrachord frames in Chart 6 can be filled with "movable sounds" generated by the prime number 5 according to exactly four patterns, shown in Chart 7. Notice the following structural considerations: a) every pattern

CHART 7

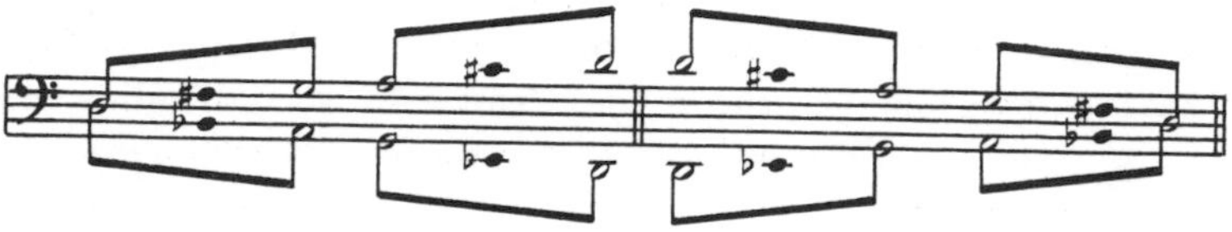

	24	30	32	36	45	48	30	32	40	45	48	60
Tonal Inverses	D	f# bb	G A	A G	c# eb	D	D	c# eb	A G	G A	f# bb	D
	6	:	8 ::	9	:	12	6	:	8 ::	9	:	12

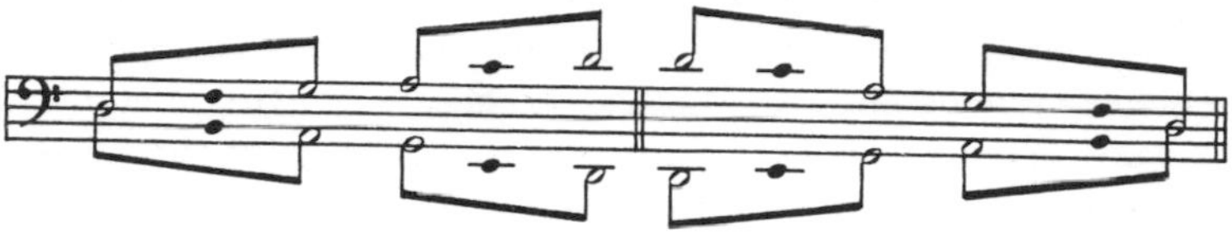

	30	36	40	45	54	60	18	20	24	27	30	36
Tonal Inverses	D	f b	G A	A G	c e	D	D	c e	A G	G A	f b	D
	6	:	8 ::	9	:	12	6	:	8 ::	9	:	12

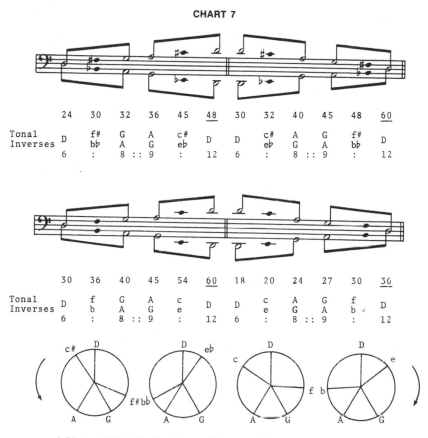

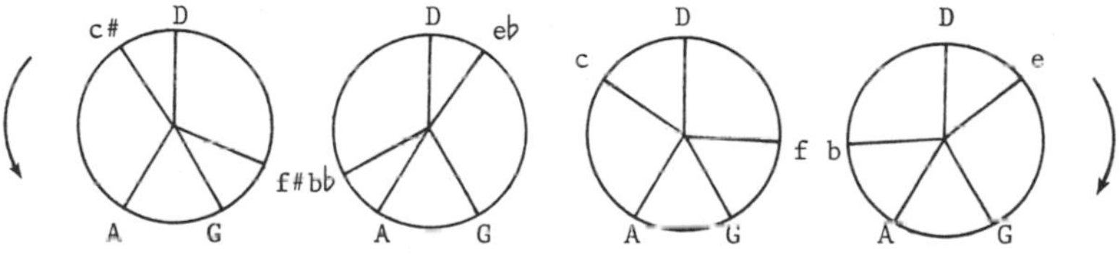

A Platonic "Wedding": Indra as Dancer and Lord of the Five Tribes

Numbers which define one pentatonic sequence are "friends" with the reciprocals of a second set, and the pair of number sets is related by the same ratios (4:3 mated with 5) to still another pair of similarly related sequences. These four patterns exhaust the musically useful marriages available under Plato's rules. The maṇḍala may be thought of as showing "Indra as Dancer" and "Lord of the Five Tribes."

is coupled with its reciprocal, b) every tetrachord is replicated in a second tetrachord which completes the octave, c) every octave is defined by a sequence of smallest integers, d) every integer set is "friends" with another integer set defining the same material from an opposite point of view (rising vs falling), and e) these four pentatonic (five-tone) sequences contain all of the diatonic-heptatonic material of Chart 3. The prime number 5 is generating pure major thirds of ratio 4:5 and complementary minor thirds of ratio 5:6 within the module of the perfect fifth, 2:3, shown in Chart 6. Later it will be shown that all of these new tones are "Aśvin twins," in the sense that they function as arithmetic and harmonic means in various derivative frames: f and f♯, for instance, are "twin means" within the module of the perfect fifth D:A, for 4:5:6 means A:F:D *and* D:F♯:A, as multiples of string length in the first case, and as divisors of it in the second. We are now well into the process of building up *alternative perspectives* on the same tonal material.

The *Ṛg Veda* is radically imbued with the conviction that no single perspective is conclusive, superior to all others. Its dogmatic adherence to this liberal attitude is the antithesis of that Western ideal which was profoundly influenced by Aristotle's effort to found philosophy on "first principles," continuing today in our efforts to develop a strictly logical foundation for mathematics. De Nicolás writes of the "radical skepticism" of the philosopher-poets of the Vedas and contrasts their attitudes with those of modern scholars whose analytical methods "make it almost impossible to attain a complete freedom in viewpoint changing." For him, "change of viewpoint is the gaining of Vedic viewpoint."[22] Our musical analysis must pursue many further contrasting viewpoints on the same tonal material in order to exercise the "Vedic imagination" which de Nicolás demands of us.

The constructions in Chart 7 are generated by the "*human* number " 5, and they are alternative pentatonic (five-tone) "octaves," *i.e.*, six-tone progressions spanning the ratio 1:2, so that first and last tones coincide. Indra, "the Dancer, is the Lord of men," (8.7.7), and he rules "the fivefold race of those who dwell upon the earth" (1.7.9). Note how his "horses" are harnessed: "Sixfold they bear him, or by fives are harnessed" (1.55.18). Dawn discloses "the pathways of the people" in "the lands where men's Five Tribes are settled" (7.79.1). "Five Bulls which stand on high full in the midst of mighty heaven" (1.105.10) allude to some still-unidentified constellation. There are "five regions" in the world "under thy Law" (9.86.29). Dīrghatamas, the supposedly blind poet of the most important Ṛgvedic creation hymn, unifies our pentatonic and diatonic constructions in a very interesting way:

> Upon this five-spoked wheel revolving ever
> all living creatures rest and are dependent.
> Its axle, heavy-laden, is not heated: the
> nave from ancient time remains unbroken.
>
> The wheel revolves, unwasting, with its felly:
> ten draw it, yoked to the far-stretching car-pole.
>
> *(1.164.13–14)*

Only ten children born of the "human number" 5 can be linked "chromatically" to the "car-pole" of the chariot we have been studying in Charts

3 through 7, and linked in "five-spoked" wheels, but we dare not assume that Dīrghatamas meant exactly what his words—taken out of context in a long creation hymn—seem to mean in the context I have given them. He is a man who knows *many* perspectives on creation, and his stress on a five-spoked maṇḍala will lead us to a variation in the next chart.

This protopythagorean attitude toward "5" seems to have survived in later Hinduism. According to Daniélou, "man is said to have been born of a ritual having five stages; hence in every ritual the fifth offering is called 'man.' "[23] Śiva became the dancing god, "ruler of the five directions of space, of the five elements, of the five human races, of the five senses and all that is ruled by the number 5," and he is represented as "five-faced."[24]

It is time now to assemble all the perspectives we have examined within one. This will be achieved by correlating all tones with *one sequence of smallest integers*, itself our guiding principle *in every perspective*.

FOOTNOTES

1. Allan Bloom, *The Republic of Plato*, (New York: Basic Books, 1968), 546a.
2. The atmospheric physicist Wendell Mordy offered this apt observation on the tone-maṇḍala.
3. Nicomachus, *Introduction to Arithmetic* (transl. by M. L. D'Ooge in *Great Books in the Western World*, vol. 11), Book I, Chapter III, 1. "Arithmetic, absolute quantity, and music, relative quantity."
4. Antonio T. de Nicolás, *Four-Dimensional Man: The Philosophical Methodology of the Ṛg Veda* (Bangalore: Dharmaram College Studies No. 6, 1971), p. 93.
5. *Ibid.*, p. 100.
6. *Ibid.*, p. 101.
7. Francis M. Cornford, transl., *Plato's Timaeus*, (New York: The Liberal Arts Press, 1959), 50b and 51a. "We may fittingly compare the Recipient to a mother, the model to a father, and the nature that arises between them to their offspring." This is Plato's explicit generalization of the function of sexual metaphor, and it is offered in the context of a dialogue in which the "World-Soul" itself is modelled on his Dorian scale.
8. de Nicolás, *op. cit.*, p. 109.
9. *Ibid.*, p. 101.
10. *Ibid.*, p. 93.
11. *Ibid.*, p. 148.
12. *Ibid.*, p. 149.
13. *Ibid.*, p. 148.
14. *Ibid.*, p. 114.
15. Plutarch, *De Iside et Osiride* (transl. by Frank Cole Babbitt in *Moralia*, vol. V), 373. He refers to the "human number 5" as the sum of the "female number 2" and the "divine male number 3."

16. *Timaeus*, 50d.
17. B. L. van der Waerden, *Science Awakening* (New York: John Wiley & Sons, 1963), p. 94.
18. Griffith, *op. cit.*, p. 412, and Alain Daniélou, *Hindu Polytheism* (New York, Pantheon Books, 1964), p. 43.
19. *Ibid.*
20. Griffith, *op. cit.*, p. 275.
21. *Republic* 546 and *Laws* 775.
22. *Four-Dimensional Man*, p. 15.
23. Daniélou, *op. cit.*, p. 72.
24. *Ibid.*, p. 210.

4

THE TONAL CALENDAR

360 "LIKE PEGS"

The smallest integers which can define the eleven tones of Charts 3 and 7 *in chromatic order* lie within the octave double 720:360, shown below and in Chart 8. The 360 internal subdivisions of this cycle (they are numerical units interpreted logarithmically on base 2, *not degrees*) correlate numerically with the idealized year of 360 days in the ancient calendar systems. Since the tones are distributed symmetrically around their "mean" on D, they can be correlated with the numbers in either a rising or falling order. Notice that the new tone numbers given here maintain the same ratios as those in Charts 3, 6, and 7. A change in numerosity is merely a change in context; the principle of smallest integers for a given context is never violated.

360	384	400	432	450	480	540	576	600	648	675	720	(integers)
D	e♭	e	f	f♯	G	A	b♭	b	c	c♯	D	(rising)
D	c♯	c	b	b♭	A	G	f♯	f	e	e♭	D	(falling)

The limiting number, factorial 6 = 720 (meaning $6! = 1 \times 2 \times 3 \times 4 \times 5 \times 6$), provides, however, for a total of eighteen tone numbers of the form $2^p3^q5^r$ (p, q, and r being integers), and all eighteen are shown in Chart 8. These eighteen can be regarded as the total "Indra tonal power"

CHART 8

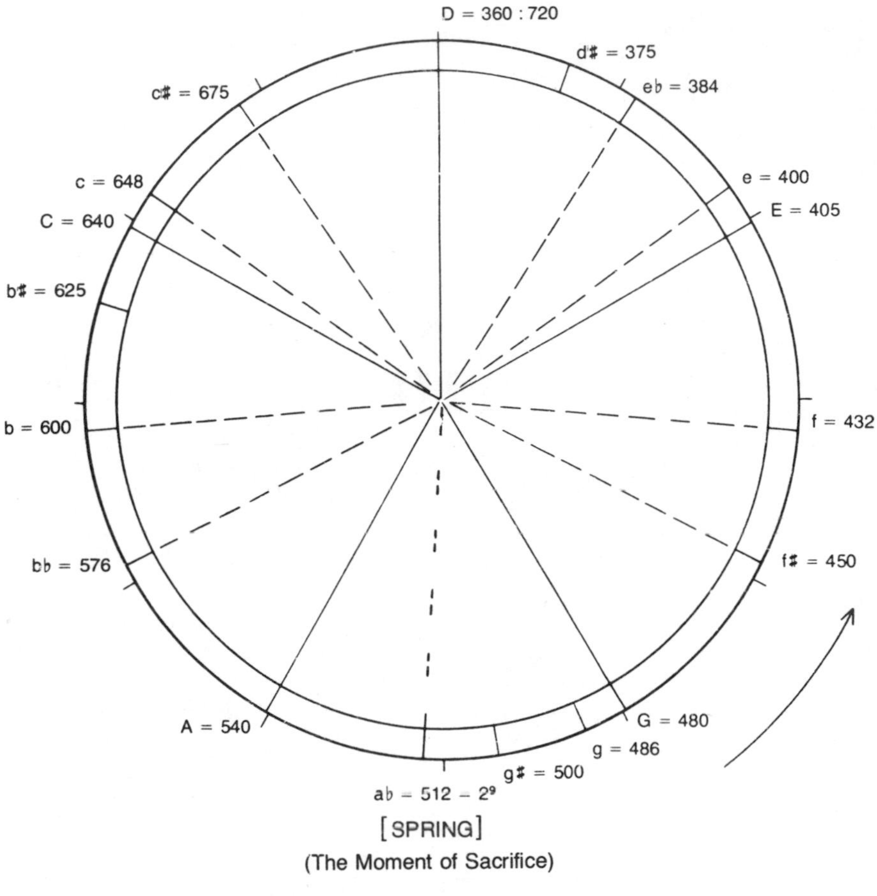

The Tonal Calendar: 360 "like pegs"

The eleven tones of Charts 3 and 7 acquire integer names in chromatic order within the octave double 720:360. A new pair of tone-numbers are now available for C and E, extending the perfect fifths of Chart 6 (G D A) to five tones (C G D A E) in "Pythagorean tuning." The total set exemplifies "Just tuning." Five additional products of 2, 3, and 5 lack reciprocals within this set, and play no role in establishing "months."

over Vṛtra (the chaos of the pitch continuum) up to the limit of 720, each tone number being a well-defined cut in the tone-maṇḍala. This particular maṇḍala is described in provocative detail in the famous Ṛgvedic creation hymn by the supposedly blind poet Dīrghatamas. His "Vision in Long Darkness" requires careful study of its *numerical* and *geometrical* detail.

VISION IN LONG DARKNESS (HYMN R.V. 1.164)

Twelve spokes, one wheel, navels three.
Who can comprehend this?
On it are placed together three hundred
and sixty like pegs;
They shake not in the least.

(1.164.48)

If the "twelve spokes" are the twelve tones of an octave tonal-zodiac, then the three "navels" may be powers of three prime numbers 2, 3, and 5, each rotating in a sense at its own speed, correlated by any terminating number which includes all three among its factors. The 360 "like pegs" which "shake not in the least" would seem to be the 360 subdivisions within the 720:360 octave matrix which correlates our reciprocal seven-tone scales. According to Dīrghatamas, the Sun has "seven heroes" for sons, and he rides a "seven-yoked chariot, one-wheeled":

A seven-named horse does draw this three-naved wheel,
Ageless and irresistible as well,
Which props all worlds.

Seven steeds draw the seven-wheeled chariot,
Wherein are placed the sacred notes seven. . . .

Who saw first this structured one when born?
What time was he born by the unstructured? . . .

Wise poets have spun a seven-strand tale,
Around this heavenly calf, the Sun.

(1.164.1–5)

Remembering that each diatonic tone-number in Chart 3 functions in two ways, we can understand why Dīrghatamas refers to "half-embryos seven" in verse 36. Since each tone-number functions not only as a "spoke" in the Sun's "single-wheeled" chariot but also as the center of a wheel (tone-field) in its own right, there are *alternative* viewpoints to be kept in mind. In fact, since the seven-tone diatonic constructions rest on the pentatonic foundation of Chart 7, the same poet is duty-bound to remind us of the five-spoked wheel drawn by ten men. Here is the Chethimattam-de Nicolás translation of verses 13 and 14 quoted earlier in Griffith's translation.

On the five-spoked wheel rolling are worlds supported;
Hardly grows its axle hot with a load immense as such;
Unbreakable it is from its very start,
As it is fitted right with its navel.

Drawn upward to self by the ten-yoked, it rolls on,
The undecaying wheel with its felly,
The Sun's eye by space enveloped,
On it are all worlds based.

Dīrghatamas refers directly to the limiting number, 720:

Never wears out the twelve-spoked wheel of Ṛta,
As it keeps turning over the heavens.
O Agni, there stand seven times hundred
And a score of sons in pairs.

The Father with five feet and twelve forms, some call him,
Affluent, residing in the far side of heaven.

(1.164.11–12)

Commentators pair days and nights to get 720 "sons in pairs"; musicians pair them in the special sense of 720:360 = 2:1, the octave matrix. The Father has "five feet" in the sense that pentatonic scales are basic, and "twelve forms" in the sense that our whole development aims at a "twelve-tone chromatic" year or zodiacal cycle. The best "five feet" are C G D A E.

If we examine Chart 8 from the "calendar" perspective, we see alternate loci for two tones, E-e and C-c. The "five pairs of twin sons" in Chart 3 are now six pairs in this enlarged number set. Notice the poet's description:

Besides the months in pairs is a seventh, born singly,
The six sets of twins are god-born rishis, they say,
Their sacrifices set in harmony with rules definite,
Alteration finds by arrangement.

Feminine though in truth, people tell me
they are masculine.
One with eyes sees indeed, the blind know not.

(1.164.15–16)

The "seventh son born singly" I take to allude to the reference mean on D, so that there are literally six sets of "twins" plus a thirteenth tone. Since most of these numbers are *even* they are tonally "feminine" in appearance while being actually "masculine" from the genetic viewpoint studied in Charts 4, 5, 6, and 7. No wonder, given the number of relevant alternative perspectives, Dīrghatamas alludes to his own blindness as to where absolute truth really lies. His hymn hurls successive alternatives at the hearer with no concern for "telling a good story," as de Nicolás points out.[1] Any coherent story about the logical derivation of the numbers and tones is our own invention; the *Ṛg Veda* is concerned with keeping alternative perspectives continually before us. Dīrghatamas alludes to all of the important alternative musical perspectives. He is confronting us with the *Sat* (the Existent)—from the root *as*, to exist—"in its existential dynamic form . . . and not in any conceptual and static form."[2]

De Nicolás makes the "radical" demand that we study the *Ṛg Veda* from within its own perspective, or "intentionality," meaning with a readiness to "sacrifice" every perspective the moment it is achieved in order to make room in our consciousness for equally relevant alternatives. For example, tonally speaking, 1 is equivalent to any power of 2, *e.g.*, 2^n, including $2^9 = 512 =$ a♭ near the bottom of the tone-maṇḍala in Chart 8. But it is equally legitimate to consider D = 360 = 720 at the top of the circle as "1" also, in the sense of the *geometric mean* whose "appearance" has been changed to avoid fractions. Now a♭ lies somewhat askew from the symmetrical twins we have been studying; it is near the locus of the square root of 2 which would have put the equal-tempered A♭ = G# precisely at the bottom of the circle, directly opposite D. It is in this region of the circle, I believe, that Indra will be born later as Indra-Agni, god of fire, not as a "point" in the circle but as a *segment* of the circle. The *Ṛg Veda* describes this birth as that of a kind of "breach baby": "Forth from the side obliquely will I issue" (R.V. 4.18.12). There is no *integer* at the locus in question. The great expansion of the number sets in later diagrams is motivated, I believe, by the effort to approximate as exactly as possible the *irrational* square root of 2 which is needed to locate a tone symmetrically opposite the mean on D, that is, precisely in the middle of our octave.

There appears to be a direct reference to our period of eighteen subdivisions in one of the hymns of another poet, Vāmadeva:

> Earth weareth beauties manifold: uplifted,
> licking her Calf of eighteen months,
> she standeth.
> Well-skilled I seek the seat of law eternal.
> Great is the God's supreme and sole dominion.
>
> *(R. V. 3.55.14)*

The eighteen chapters of the *Bhagavad Gītā* display an internal organization which parallels our eighteen tones, suggesting that this basic tonal "18" construction played a continuing role in Hindu imagery.[3] The Hindu theory of tuning today correlates better with Chart 8 than with Chart 3 shown earlier in the following way: while maintaining the same number of "major" and "minor" wholetones within the octave scale, the use of C and E now available (as opposed to c and e earlier) allows us to represent the pattern with the *major* wholetone lying *highest* in each tetrachord, the pattern normalized in Hindu theory.[4] In the table below, the octave scale is shown in both Hindu and Greek forms, together with our modern letter names.

The major wholetone of ratio 8:9 is worth about 204 cents; the minor wholetone of ratio 9:10 is worth only about 182. It is obvious, then, that our tones belong to different musical "castes," and Hindu musicologists have not hesitated to apply the caste names derived from the *Ṛg Veda*:

> The Brāhman was his mouth, of both his
>   arms was the Rājanya made.
> His thighs became the Vaiśya, from his
>   feet the Śūdra was produced.
>
> *(10.90.12)*

CHART 9

Correlation of Hindu and Greek Tuning Systems[4]

The traditional form of the Hindu diatonic scale is roughly equivalent in its interval progression to Didymus' diatonic tuning whose smallest integers lie in the 48:96 octave. This tuning is a subset of the calendrical octave 360:720 and is thus derivative from the tuning of the 30:60 "monthly" octave in Charts 1 and 3.

Hindu	śrutis	smallest integers	ratios	Chart 8 360:720	Tone
sa = ṣaḍja	4	48		540	A
			8:9		
ri = ṛṣabha	3	54		480	G
			9:10		
ga = gandhāra	2	60		432	f
			15:16		
ma = madhayma	4	64		405	E
			8:9		
pa = pañcama	4	72		720 / 360	D
			8:9		
dha = dhaivata	3	81		640	C
			9:10		
ni = nisāda	2	90		576	b♭
			15:16		
sa'		96		540	A
	total 22				

Hindu tuning theory assigns each tone from two to four possible loci, dividing the octave into twenty-two *śrutis* which are not defined mathematically. The *śrutis* are graphed below in correspondence with the Didymus tuning to suggest how the Hindu conception may have evolved from a once explicitly mathematical foundation. (Compare with the logarithmic scale of Chart 4.)

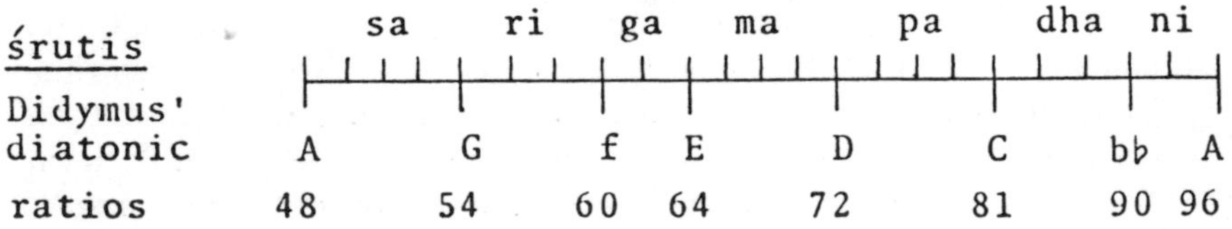

Tones of the "highest caste" (sa, ma, and pa) contain four *śrutis* (quartertones); tones of the second highest caste (ri and dha) contain three śrutis; tones of the third caste (ga and ni) contain two śrutis. Tones of the fourth class would contain only micro-intervals, such as the "comma" of ratio 80:81 between C and c or between E and e. Sourindo Mohun Tagore notes that the Sanskrit writers who first applied caste names to the tones,

> were prompted by no other motive than to distinguish their different classes; the principle being analogous to, if not the same with, that on which in Western music they are arranged under four heads; namely, the major tones, the minor tones, the semitones, and the artificial or chromatic notes.[5]

The interesting point is that the Hindu musical castes correlate with Plato's.[6] "Citizens of the highest property class" are generated by the "divine male number 3"; they are represented in Chart 8 by the tones C G D A E which, *taken alone*, could be defined either by $3^{0,1,2,3,4}$ or by 3^{-2}, 3^{-1}, 3^{0}, 3^{1}, 3^{2}. The "second caste" arises from the presence of the "human male number 5" among the generators, which generates some "minor wholetones" of ratio 9:10 as well as "major wholetones" of ratio 8:9.[7] Throughout the *Rg Veda* Indra is described as "Lord of the Five Tribes," generally understood as an allusion to the five Aryan tribes which overran India sometime between the fifth and third millenia B.C. Our five musical "Aryans" or "Brāhmins"—C G D A E—will extend their power over the whole tonal "region" in the diagrams which lie ahead. It seems impossible to disentangle Hindu "history" from Hindu "mathematical harmonics."

Tones of different musical "castes" perform different musical functions, each essential to the system as a whole. Only the highest caste can frame tetrachords; only the second caste can produce pure thirds; the third caste "semitones" are the "left-over" intervals within the tetrachords; the fourth caste "commas" are the micro-intervals which arise whenever the material of the preceding three castes exceeds the eleven-tone limits of Chart 3.[8] How the social caste system arose is a problem for anthropologists; but let it be noted that until the acceptance of equal-temperament musical theorists "needed" a system of social stratification.

> One to high sway, one to exalted glory,
> one to pursue his gain, and one his labour:
> All to regard their different vocations.
>
> *(R. V. 1.113.6)*

The musical castes are the consequences of the structural superiority of fifths and fourths over thirds within an invariant octave frame. It is the aim of attaining *purity* among both fifths and thirds which produces the "low caste" commas. The absolute "democracy" of equal-temperament had to abandon the conceptual purity of its two "highest castes." Indian musicians decline to follow that example; to them the eighteen tones in Chart 8 are distinctly different, and their refusal to mathematize relations according to our Pythagorean manner avoids the contradictions in terminology and in conceptual patterns which confront us. Since they use only seven tones in any one modal set, they do not need to define the exact differences which would arise, say, if all twenty-two *śrutis* were to be directly compared with each other. They would never perform all twenty-two seriatim, like we sometimes play our chromatic scale, as a "tour de force."[8]

It should be obvious by now that the subtlety of Hindu thought will force us into a variety of analyses of the tone-number field, none being absolute. Viṣṇu is a dramatic example. He is a minor deity in the *Ṛg Veda*, and one of the alternate names of the Sun. Known as the "Wide-Strider," his most significant quality is his ability to encompass heaven and earth in only *three* strides:

> Among the skillful Gods most skilled is he,
> who made the two world-halves which
> bring prosperity to all;
> Who with great wisdom measured both the
> regions out, and established them
> with pillars that shall ne'er decay.
>
> *(1.160.4)*

Now if the "world-halves" are tonal semicircles, mathematical reciprocity ensuring that they will be structured symmetrically, then the problem of defining the whole circle is the problem of defining either half of it satisfactorily. One half of the circle is a musical "tritone" of three wholetones. Viṣṇu can stride across both heaven and earth in three steps if he takes steps of the highest caste major wholetones of 8:9, as for instance, from D to E or D to C. However, three such consecutive wholetones will slightly exceed a semicircle (each is worth about 204 cents, and $3 \cdot 204 = 612$, not 600); he will force the "world-halves" apart, as the poets say. They will part in the region of the equal-tempered A♭ = G♯ near the bottom of the circle where Agni is due to be born. "Mortal men" do not normally move through three consecutive wholetones, the tritone "*diabolus in musica*" which was frowned on by the Church during the reign of "modal theory" in the West. Two such wholetones are all that can be contained within a tetrachord frame of ratio 3:4, leaving an undersized "semitone" *leimma* of ratio 243:256. (Note: $9/8 \cdot 9/8 \cdot 256/243 = 4/3$. We *add* intervals by multiplying their ratios expressed as fractions.) These acoustical facts suggest a basis for Dīrghatamas' reference to Viṣṇu:

A mortal man, when he beholds two steps
of him who looks upon the light, is
restless with amaze.
But his third step doth no one venture to
approach, no, nor the feathered birds of
air who fly with wings.

He, like a rounded wheel, hath in swift
motion set his ninety racing steeds
together with the four.
Developed, vast in form, with those who
sing forth praise, a youth, no more a
child, he cometh to our call.

(1.155.5–6)

Commentators suggest that Viṣṇu's "steeds, or spokes, are the days of the solar year, ninety in each of the four seasons."[9] Dīrghatamas, however, has given us much reason to suspect that he is intimately acquainted with our whole acoustical drama, and one of his verses can be read as a formula for Viṣṇu's basic "step":

Forming the water-floods, the buffalo hath
lowed, one-footed or two-footed or four-
footed, she,
Who hath become eight-footed or hath
got nine feet, the thousand-syllabled in
the sublimest heaven.

(1.164.41)

Now the number sequence 1:2:4:8:9 plays an important role in Plato's *Republic* where it generates exactly the kind of steps Viṣṇu would have to take to force the "world-halves" apart: 1:2:4:8 are cyclic identities, thus 9 means 9/8 or 8/9, a "major wholetone." In Chart 8, 9/8 × (D = 360) = E = 405, and 8/9 × (D = 720) = C = 640. Not until our "mother" matrix reaches the number 9 does it generate such wholetones, each worth about 204 cents instead of 200, so that three of them exceed half of the circle (cycle) by about 12 cents.

Curiously, although we do not know what Dīrghatamas knew about "tuning theory," he seems to lead us to all the interesting variant forms of the scale, albeit indirectly.[10] A musical cosmology which aimed to harmonize the fields of both visual and aural experience under the principle of *smallest integers* could scarcely avoid stumbling across or systematically developing the material we have presented in Charts 3 through 8. Since attention is being directed powerfully to number, we must look for some more convenient way of codifying algebraic operations than our tone-maṇḍalas have provided; they are convenient only for displaying the *metric* properties of tone-numbers. In the Hindu *yantras* to be studied next we shall see how simple pebble patterns codify all the algebraic aspects of musical number theory in triangular arrays which look like the mountains from which Hindu and Hebrew gods alike hurl thunderbolts at their enemies.

FOOTNOTES

1. Antonio T. de Nicolás, *Four-Dimensional Man: The Philosophical Methodology of the Rigveda* (Bangalore: Dharmaram College Studies No. 6, 1971), p. 125.
2. *Ibid.*, p. 131.
3. Antonio T. de Nicolás, *Avatāra: The Humanization of Philosophy* (New York: Nicolas Hays, 1976) chapter 6.
4. Arnold Bake, "The Music of India," in *The New Oxford History of Music* (London: Oxford University Press, 1957) pp. 195–227.
5. Sourindro Mohun Tagore, *Six Principal Ragas, with a Brief View of Hindu Music*, (Calcutta: Calcutta Central Press Company, 1877), p. 17.
6. See my essays on Plato, footnotes 4, 5, and 6 to Chapter 1.
7. Western harmonic theory eventually elevated the ratio 4:5 to the status of a "norm," a position it never held in Greek theory, and which equal-temperament now denies it. Hindu theory seems to have preserved it from such vacillations.
8. Ananda Coomaraswamy, "Indian Music," *The Musical Quarterly*, vol. III, April, 1917, p. 165.
9. Ralph T. H. Griffith, *The Hymns of the Rgveda* (Delhi: Motilal Banarsidass, 1973, New Revised Edition) p. 104.
10. I am indebted to Christopher George for pointing out to me that in the sixth Brāhmaṇa of *Śatapatha-Brāhmaṇa* (XI Kanda, I Adhyaya, 6 Brāhmaṇa, 1) the cosmic egg, or golden egg, floated in the sea of water "about as long as the space of a year" before producing Prajāpati, "Lord of Creatures." This could very well be a Hindu commentary on the 360:720 basic octave, the first 360 units being the preparatory period.

5

ALGEBRAIC YANTRAS

STAR HEXAGON AND DRUM OF ŚIVA

We turn now from tonal-maṇḍalas to algebraic yantras—arrays of counters—to develop a systematic view of the number field. We shall skirt uncertainties about early mathematical notation by restricting ourselves to patterns easily notated by an array of pebbles.[1] We have already shown in Chart 5 how pairs of successive integers define the "superparticular" ratios of interest to music theory, but the only such ratio which can be continued is that of the octave, through successive powers of 2: 1:2:4:8 etc. To build similar logarithmic equal-interval progressions with the "male" ratios 2:3, 3:4, 4:5, etc., we must discover "fathers" capable of producing two or more such ratios in succession. Nicomachus stated the rule which governed such operations during the ages when results had to be couched in "smallest integer" form:

> Every multiple will stand at the head of as many superparticular ratios corresponding in name with itself as it itself chances to be removed from unity, and no more nor less under any circumstances.[2]

The nested triangles of Chart 10a exemplify Nicomachus' rule: two consecutive perfect fourths of ratio 3:4 are "fathered" in *his* metaphor by $3^2 = 9$, "two places removed from unity," in the progression 9:12:16, while three are fathered by 3^3, "three places removed from unity," in the progression 27:36:48:64. The ratio 4:5 in the inner triangle of Chart 10a is similarly expanded to 16:20:25 and 64:80:100:125 in the outer triangles. So, too, is the ratio 3:5, for Nicomachus' rule applies not merely

CHART 10

Sacred Stones as Algebraic Yantras

o
o o
o o o
o o o o

a) Matrix for "Just tuning" (Charts 1 and 8) numbers $2^p3^q5^r$), model for logarithmic sequences generated by any three rational numbers (J, K, L) prime to each other. Reciprocation of *integers* by *unit* fractions (1/n) correlates with rotation by 180 degrees.

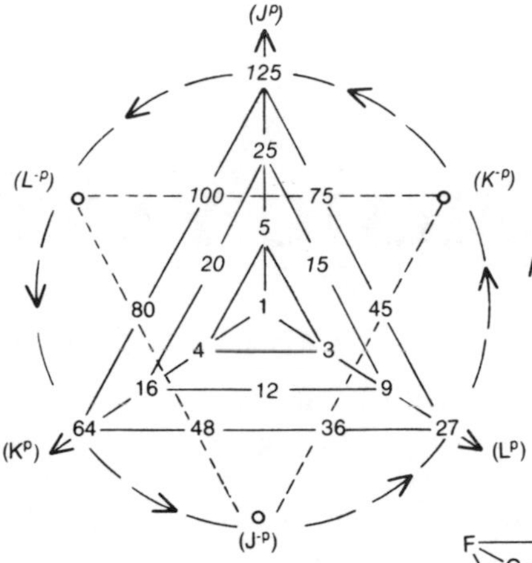

Puruṣa and Prakṛti in the Circular Field of Time

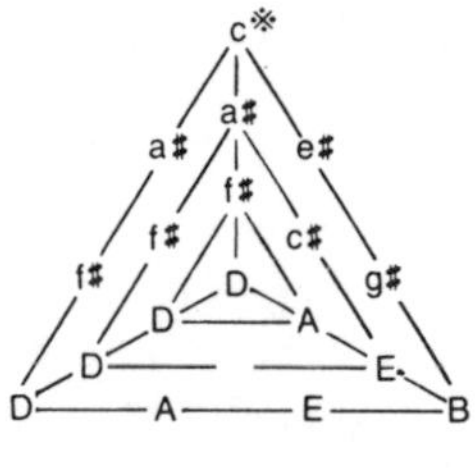

RECIPROCATION
Linga vs Yoni

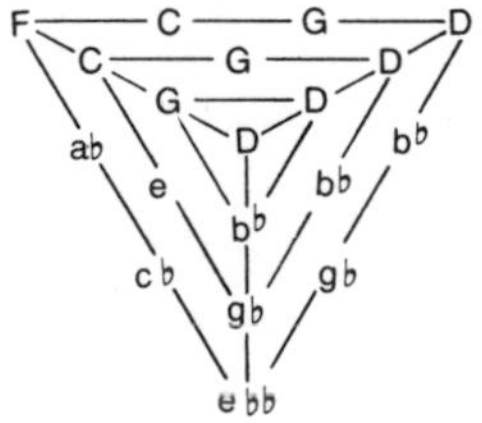

Tonal Interpretation

(b) Matrix for "Pythagorean tuning" (numbers 2^p3^q), model for logarithmic sequences generated from any two rational numbers (J, K) prime to each other.

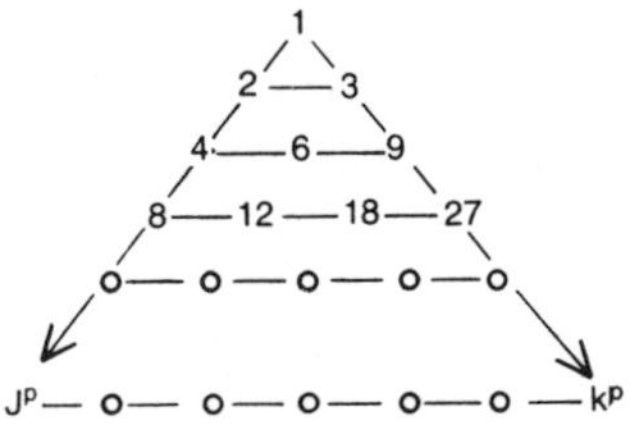

Nicomachean triangle

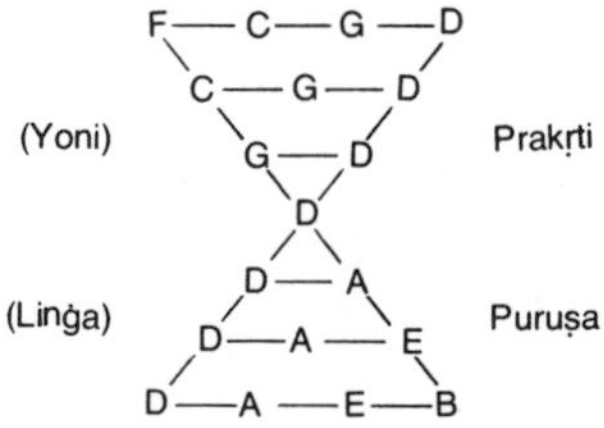

The Drum of Śiva

The "drum of Śiva" emerges as a subset in "Pythagorean tuning" from the star-hexagon matrix of "Just tuning."

to superparticular ratios but to any ratio of numbers *prime to each other* (having no common divisor except unity, 1). Nicomachus takes pains to emphasize that the numbers in his own triangular arrays function both as "multiples" and "submultiples," that is, as *integers* and as reciprocal "unit fractions," (1/3, 1/9, 1/27, etc.). It is the relevance of reciprocals which the interlocked triangles of the star-hexagon symbolize so beautifully. When those triangles are separated we see the male-female linga-yoni Hindu symbols. If we study the musical implications of the numbers in these sexually differentiated triangles, we can see the "drum of Śiva" containing only tones arranged by perfect fourths and fifths—*i.e.*, in "Pythagorean tuning"—emerging as a "subset" of the "Just tuning" being generated in the star-hexagon.[3] The tones in the "drum" can be rearranged in the pyramid according to the same rule of Nicomachus: it is immaterial whether we think of F–C–G–D as rising fifths of ratio 2:3 or as falling fourths of ratio 3:4, and whether the reciprocals D–A–E–B lie at opposite ends of the drum or along the base of a larger pyramid, "fathered" by 2^6 as six perfect fifths of ratio 2:3, or by 3^6 as six perfect fourths of ratio 3:4. By themselves the star-hexagon, pyramid, and drum do not produce scales: they produce the equal-interval progressions which tone-maṇḍalas "bend round into circles" (Plato's *Timaeus* metaphor), a context in which intervals overlap, and for which a new set of appropriate "smallest integers" must be found.

Nicomachus' rule needs only the ten pebbles of the Pythagorean "holy tetractys" to remind the operator that its "lawfulness" extends as far as the number field. The Pythagorean notion can be given a modern algebraic equivalent:

1 = point	o	$(n^0 = 1)$
2 = line	o o	A B
3 = plane	o o o	A^2 AB B^2
4 = solid	o o o o	A^3 A^2B AB^2 B^3

Today we equate the "zero power" of every number with 1, and our slide rules begin with 1 as the "point of origin" for their scales. The question of zero itself does not arise in the ratio theory being explored here; reciprocal meanings make 1 the geometric mean in the field of rational numbers from one point of view, while the necessity for presenting results in integer form, by the use of least common denominators, makes 1 the origin of number and its limit in the direction of decrease from another point of view. The triangles of Chart 10 embrace both points of view.

The star-hexagon answers Dīrghatamas' question:

> Ignorance of mine seeks knowledge from the seers,
> Longing to know what I know not yet;
> What is the Unborn One
> Who propped the six regions apart?
>
> *(1.164.6)*

The Unborn One is the unit, 1, which can mean either "whole" or "part," and which props "the six regions apart" by acting as the geometric mean for the reciprocal triangles of the star-hexagon.

The triangular yantra and its reciprocal give us a "six-spoked car" (verse 12) to go with those of 5, 7, and 360 which the same poet mentioned earlier, one which illuminates also his description of the Mother as "the Cow who wears all shapes in three directions" (1.164.9 and 12). The sacred cows of India and Egypt had a triangular pattern on their foreheads, and in the period between 4000 B.C. and 2000 B.C., when this mathematical system and its related mythology were being developed, all over the Middle East the equinoctial sun rose in Taurus, the Bull, whose horns form a triangle in the sky.[4] The triangle in the sky, like that in our star-hexagon which produces the material for our "tone-wheels," revolves about a center—the pole star:

> High on the forehead of the Bull one
> Chariot wheel ye ever keep,
> The other round the sky revolves.
>
> *(1.30.19)*

Agni (or Indra-Agni), incarnate savior and god of fire, is "the Steer with triple horn, the life-bestower" (5.43.13). In another verse we hear:

> The Bull who wears all shapes, the triple-
> breasted, three-uddered, with a brood
> in many places,
> Ruleth majestic with his triple aspect, the
> Bull, the Everlasting Ones' impregner.
>
> *(3.56.3)*

The Vedic calendar divided the year into six seasons, and the poets sing of "six divine Expanses" (10.128.5), of "six directions" (2.13.10), and of "the six expanses from which no single creature is excluded" (6.47.3). The star-hexagon establishes exactly six directions, three pairs of reciprocals.

If we are right in identifying the geometric mean on D = 1 as the "Mitra-Varuṇa linch-pin of the heavens," then the star-hexagon would seem to explain a curious verse to Varuṇa:

> On him three heavens rest and are
> supported, and the three earths are there
> in sixfold order. . . .
>
> Ruling in depths and meting out the
> region, great saving power hath he,
> this world's Controller.
>
> *(7.87.5–6)*

"As on a linch-pin, firm, rest things immortal: he who hath known it let him here declare it" (1.35.6). We have found the "linch-pin," I believe, which provides the most revealing perspective on the Ṛgvedic numbers to be studied later. Since all which exists does so by the power of Indra, he also rules "three earths" and "three heavens":

> Of thy great might there is a threefold
> counterpart, the three earths, Lord of
> Men, and the three realms of light.
>
> *(1.102.8)*

How "1" itself came into being is pure mystery:

> Existence, in the earliest age of Gods, from
> Non-existence sprang.
> Thereafter were the regions born. This
> sprang from the Productive Power.
>
> Earth sprang from the Productive Power;
> the regions from the earth were born.
>
> *(10.72.3–4)*

I find it hard to avoid the conclusion that the ten stones of the Pythagorean "holy tetractys" are the ubiquitous "press-stones" of the *Ṛg Veda*, ostensibly "pressing out" the mysterious "Soma juice" which fills the priests with intoxicating insight. "The loud speaking Pressing-stones" bring Indra "the sound of praise." It is the ten stones which are the "workers," "bulls," and "car-poles."

> 6. Like strong ones drawing, they have put
> forth all their strength: the Bulls,
> harnessed together, bear the chariot poles.
> When they have bellowed, panting,
> swallowing their food, the sound of their
> loud snorting is like that of steeds.

7. To these who have ten workers and a
 tenfold girth, to these who have ten
 yoke-straps and ten binding thongs,
 To these who bear ten reins, the eternal,
 sing ye praise, to these who bear ten
 car-poles, ten when they are yoked.

8. These Stones with ten conductors, rapid
 in their course, with lovely revolution
 travel round and round. . . .

11. Bored deep, but not pierced through with
 holes, are ye, O Stones, not
 loosened, never weary, and exempt from
 death,
 Eternal, undiseased, moving in sundry
 ways, unthirsting, full of fatness, void
 of all desire.

12. Your fathers, verily, stand firm from age
 to age: they, loving rest, are not
 dissevered from their seat.
 Untouched by time, . . .

13. This, this the Stones proclaim, what time
 they are disjoined, and when with
 ringing sounds they move and drink the balm.

(10.94)

Nicomachus would not have considered such praise extravagant: in his time the ten stones established the only pattern needed to carry a number theorist through the endless realm of ratio theory. For him, as for Plato before him, and presumably for the Vedic poets long before, to be "in proportion" meant to be "in the same ratio," therefore the most important rule for the operator is that which helps find smallest integers in all circumstances.

The poets link the Soma juice to the flowing streams of milk from the cows, to the life-giving rain from the clouds and waters from the rivers. It is by drinking whole lakes of Soma juice that Indra's powers expand. Those lakes, I suggest, are yantras, which lead to larger yantras. Increased insight comes from multiplication to larger sets. Soma is allegorical, if we believe our poets:

Of him whom Brahmans truly know as
 Soma no one ever tastes.

Soma, secured by sheltering rules, guarded
 by hymns in Bṛhatī,

49
STAR HEXAGON AND DRUM OF ŚIVA

Thou standest listening to the stones:
none tastes of thee who dwells on earth.

(10.85.3–4)

The "expanded consciousness" which Soma brings is first of all insight into musical experience = number theory. We are looking in particular for sets which remain invariant under reciprocation. "Men come not with one horse at sacred seasons; thus they obtain no honour in assemblies" (10.131.3). We want numbers which can be used either as "great" (multiples) or "small" (submultiples) like the 6:8::9:12 musical proportion in Chart 6, making the same *cuts* in the tone-maṇḍala (Vṛtra) either way.

Bring, O Soma, doubly-waxing wealth:
Thou in the worshipper's abode causest all
treasures to increase.

Set free the song which mind hath yoked,
even as thunder frees the rain. . .

Flow on, Sage Soma, with thy stream to
give us mental power and strength.

(9.100.2, 3, 5)

The god Soma is addressed: "O thou with stones for arms" (9.53.1). As for the singers, "While they at sacrifices fix the metres, they measure out twelve chalices of Soma" (10.114.5). In a sense, this essay will be finished when we understand how the Vedic poets arrived at the twelve "spokes" for the Sun's chariot within the number field generated by our yantras.

The Soma we care about is indeed a "triply-mingled draught" which "flows round into the worlds," for it is developed from three prime numbers, 2, 3, and 5, or from the "Pythagorean triple" 3:4:5 (9.86.46). These numbers are our "filters" for studying Hindu cosmological numbers (9.97.55). Numbers of the form $2^p3^q5^r$ are clearly a "triply-twisted thread" (9.86.32). But such mathematical insight cannot be shared with everyone. It is not so much the priestly desire for secrecy as the "weak-mindedness" of men which requires mathematical truth to be expressed in allegory:

To folk who understand will I proclaim it
—injure not Aditi, the Cow, the Sinless.

Weak-minded men have as a cow adopted me
who came hither from the Gods, a Goddess,

Who, skilled in eloquence, her voice uplifteth,
who standeth near at hand with all devotions.

(8.90.15–16)

It is the blunt words of the poets which justify de Nicolás' effort to discover a mathematical logic behind their metaphor. Without apology then, we shall reach now for a stronger grip on the number field, a slight transformation of the yantra which will rid us of all tonal duplication.

THE HOLY MOUNTAIN

The triangles of the star-hexagon, pyramid, and drum of Chart 10 have had a continuing life in Hindu symbolism, but the Ṛgvedic poets, I believe, possessed a stronger mathematical tool. In Chart 11 we see a kind of "stepped pyramid" yantra, shaped like a tent, or ziggurat, with a jagged side curiously like the "lightning" attributed to Indra—and with absolutely no tonal redundancy. It is merely the multiplication table for the prime numbers 3 and 5, cut off arbitrarily by some limiting number, or "index." The smaller triangle is limited to numbers $3^p5^q < 60$, needed for the diatonic scales of Chart 3, and the larger one is limited to numbers $3^p5^q < 720$, needed for the chromatic scale of Chart 8. Notice that even if the numbers had been placed directly over each other, making one corner into a right angle (converging on 1), limiting numbers of any size would still reduce such tables to a triangle with a jagged side. Since it will be argued later that the poets possessed such tables for their huge Kalpa, Brahmā, and Puruṣa numbers, and that the poems allude both to the limiting numbers and the exact size of the relevant tables, it is necessary to be perfectly clear how these curiously shaped figures in Chart 11 relate to the simplistic "Nicomachean" lawfulness of the triangles in Chart 10.

Any single triangle in the star-hexagon of Chart 10a can be located anywhere within the boundaries of the triangles in Chart 11. The horizontal arrays in the pyramid and drum are collapsed into a single line running through the new horizontal axis of Chart 11. We are dealing with logarithmic arrays which can be "translated" and "reciprocated" freely (*i.e.*, which can be moved up or down or to the right or left or rotated by 180°), so that we can easily observe *tonal invariance* while *arithmetic appearances* change freely. Along any horizontal row, tone-numbers belong to the same series of perfect fifths, ratio 2:3, or complementary perfect fourths, ratio 3:4. Numbers along one diagonal (/) belong to tones having the ratio of the pure major third, 4:5; numbers along the other diagonal (\) belong to tones having the ratio of the pure minor third, 5:6. When the same tone-letters occur in consecutive rows (as E and e, or C and c in Chart 11b), they are separated by the ratio of the syntonic comma, 80:81, discussed earlier. The numbers can be multiplied freely by the powers of 2 to define the same tones in linear scale order, starting on any tone, by integers of the form $2^p3^q5^r$ *within* some relevant "double" (such as 60:30

CHART 11

Musical Yantras

a) The "stepped pyramid" or "ziggurat" yantra for "Just tuning" as a multiplication table, 3^p5^q, eliminating the redundancies of Chart 10.

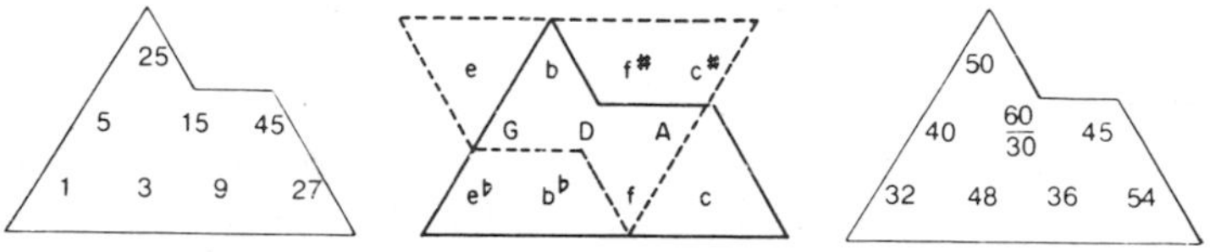

Irreducible integers — Tonal reciprocals — Diatonic scale order

The peculiar shape of the yantra results from the restriction to integers J ≤ 60. Multiplication by appropriate powers of 2 produces "tone-numbers" in the 30:60 "double" of Chart 3, but under the assumption of "octave-equivalence," or "reduction," the *male odd* numbers are sufficient, for all numbers are being interpreted according to a logarithmic scale on base 2.

b) The same yantra extended to the limit of 6! = 720 (factorial 6) required to name all eleven tones above in the *chromatic* order of Chart 8.

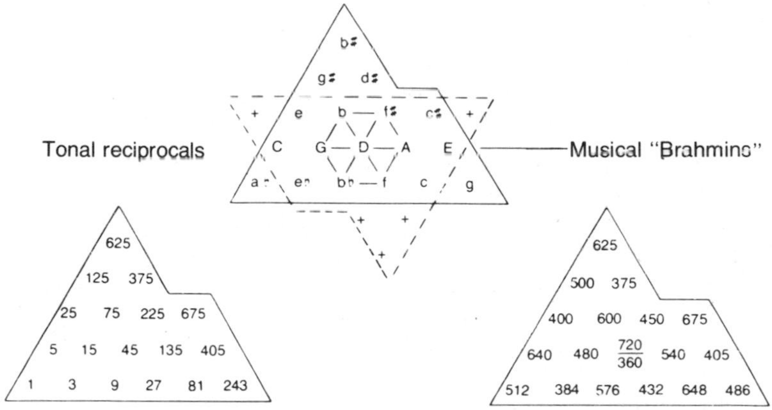

Irreducible integers — Chromatic scale order

Alternate tunings appear at C-c and E-e, differing by a "comma" of ratio 80:81. Five more tone-relatives of the form $2^p3^q5^r$ outside the common limits of reciprocal yantras do not participate in the perfect inverse symmetry around the central axis on D until the tone-number field is expanded to a larger limit.

Every horizontal array—when considered by itself—has the same meanings as the horizontal arrays in the drum of Śiva, Chart 10b. Every triangle has the same set of possible meanings as in the star-hexagon of Chart 10a.

and 720:360). Our reference tone D = 1 = n° is being transformed in "numerosity" by the use of new "least common denominators" so that we see it moved to the center of the triangle where it functions as a kind of "god on the mountain." When our multiplication table for 3 × 5 has grown to the size Vedic poets required, the table itself, taken together with its reciprocal, will acquire the "hourglass" shape associated with the later imagery of the "holy mountain," Mt. Meru, or Sumeru.[5,6]

We need not wait, however, for these later confirmations to sense the relevance of our yantra. Notice that in Chart 11 the only tonal meanings which remain invariant under reciprocation are those along the central horizontal axis. The creation hymn R.V. 10.129 is explicit in its reference to this relation:

> 4. Sages who searched with their heart's
> thought discovered the existent's kinship
> in the non-existent.
>
> 5. Transversely was their severing line extended;
> what was above it then, and what below it?
> There were begetters, there were mighty
> forces, free action here and energy up yonder.
>
> 6. Who verily knows and who can here declare it,
> whence it was born and
> whence comes this creation?
> The Gods are later than this world's production.
> Who knows then whence it first came into being?
>
> 7. He, the first origin of this creation, whether
> he formed it all or did not form it,
> Whose eye controls this world in highest
> heaven, he verily knows it, or perhaps
> he knows not.

If the "primal seed" grows in the way suggested by the star-hexagon, then it produces the "transevering axis" of Chart 11 containing the tones which symbolize "Sun gods." Since only five are present (C G D A E), they are outnumbered by other creatures "above" and "below" distinguished by having either an excess or deficiency of powers of 5 in their genetic make-up. "The Gods are later than this world's production" in the sense that our number field must grow systematically to some larger limit in order to produce twelve tones along this axis.

It is appropriate to display some diffidence about "whose eye controls this world," and whether he "knows it" or not, for we have already witnessed a multitude of ways in which it might be said to achieve Existence. From one perspective, the generating unit 1 is still present at the lower-left corner of the triangle. From another perspective, the tone-number at the top of the triangle, always some power of 5, in a sense "looks down" on all the others and sees them, in each row, as successive powers of 3. But from a *central* perspective, god = 1 = geometric mean has been transformed to *least common denominator* for the tones represented in the diagram here, 720, and sends his rays through the table in all directions. ALL PERSPECTIVES ARE EQUALLY RELEVANT.

It is important to understand that genetically there are only three "Brāhmins" in Chart 7 (G, D, and A) and only five in Chart 8 (C, G, D, A, and E). Only these numbers retain invariant tonal meanings under reciprocation so that it can be said of them:

> Neither the right nor left do I distinguish,
> neither the east nor yet the west.
>
> *(2.27.11)*

Only along this central horizontal axis does "the delight of the Gods spread out transversely" (10.70.4). Contempt is expressed for "those men who step not back and move not forward" (10.71.9), that is, who do not participate in the to-and-fro ritual dance of the Brāhmin priests, a ritual movement assumed by the chorus on the Greek stage.

In these five "Brāhmin" tones we have discovered, I suggest, the tonal-arithmetical correlatives of the "Five Aryan tribes," and in later diagrams we shall watch them extend their power over the "Land of Seven Rivers" without ever being able to separate fact from fancy. We are immersed in a symbolism which revelled in its power to express a cosmic unity, invented by men whose mathematical rigor matched their musical and poetic feeling, and in whom reverence was mated with humor.

The upright triangle 3^p5^q appears to be the Vedic "mountain of god," and the inverted triangle is apparently the Vedic "rain cloud."[7] The more it "rains" from above, forcing us to ever larger common denominators to integrate reciprocals in integer sequences, the deeper will be the waters below our "transevering axis" which functions as an "earth" separating the two waters. Curiously, it is the acoustical facts which require us to pursue such increases through a triangle of fourteen steps, and the moon which "increases" or waxes for fourteen days is linked in the Vedic mind with our "press-stones" whose male-female implications produce our insight: Soma the drink and Soma the Moon owe their powers to "the Singers" who create this whole universe "with their minds."

ORIGINS OF GEOMETRY

The algebraic yantras and tone-maṇḍalas presented here were known in India, Mesopotamia, and Egypt probably in the third or fourth millenium

B.C., judging by further arithmetical evidence discussed in Chapters 10 and 11. The essential geometrical symbolism, however, like the musical bow, drum, and panpipes, is far older. Carl Boyer has pointed out that Neolithic man (tenth to fourth millenia B.C.) "paved the way for geometry" by the drawings and designs in his pottery, weaving, and basketry that "show instances of congruence and symmetry, which are in essence parts of elementary geometry."[8] Simple sequences like the following, he says, "suggest a sort of applied group theory, as well as propositions in geometry and arithmetic."[9]

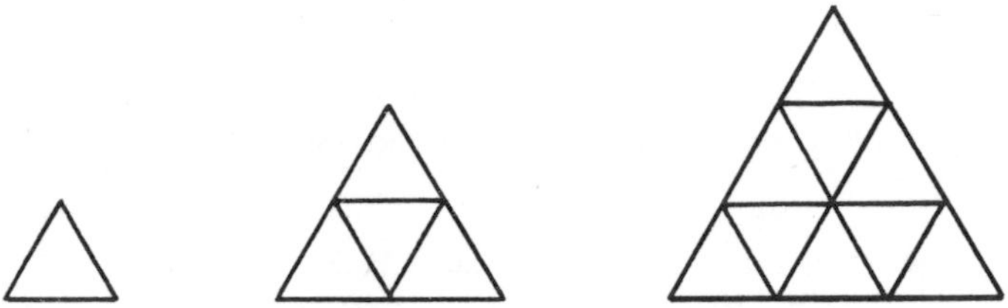

In *Earliest Civilizations of the Near East*, James Mellaart presents painted pottery patterns from Hacilar and Çatal which clearly reflect Boyer's "group" motifs.[10]

The pottery of pre-Vedic India abounded in the use of such geometric patterns. The Harappan culture made extensive use of "repetition patterns . . . that can be repeated indefinitely in any direction," including circles, semicircles, triangles, hatched triangles, crosses, and swastikas.[11] Many of the same patterns emerged in Europe at a far earlier time. Marija Gimbutas has documented the existence of geometric imagery similar to our yantras, for instance, in the fifth millenium B.C. The figure below from a Vinca mound, c. 4000 B.C., is inscribed on the back with typical yantra-like elements.[12]

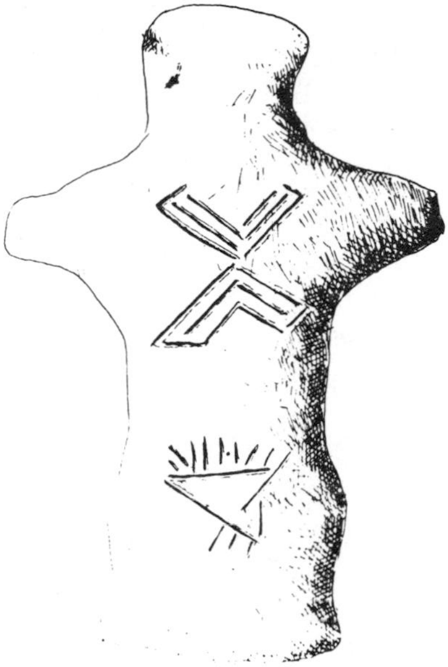

By the third millenium B.C., V. Gordon Childe says that India confronted Egypt and Babylonia "with a thoroughly individual and independent civilization of her own, technically the peer of the rest."[13] Nevertheless, direct commercial intercourse that existed between India and Mesopotamia even before 2350 B.C. makes it impossible to decide whether common elements, like a concern for similar geometric patterns, are linked by diffusion or are technically independent.

Out of Boyer's nested triangles, hexagons emerge, leading to circular maṇḍalas. His points of intersection can symbolize numbers in a Nicomachean triangle; his largest design, for example, is isomorphic with the Pythagorean tetractys and with the plotting of ratios along three axes within the "group" of rational numbers, hexagonal patterns being an approximation to a circle and, in the case of tone-numbers, also relevant to the octave-maṇḍala as well as to a rotating yantra-maṇḍala.

Mary Danielli states that "numbers in early times are almost invariably associated with the symbolism of the maṇḍala."[14]

> Anthropologically, the maṇḍala is concerned among other things with increase and growth, keeping these within the natural pattern, so that they do not disintegrate into fragments.[15]

The maṇḍala is "a wordless symbol" which "speaks for itself."[16] It is a model "discovered by man *in himself*," and "no one knows how early he became conscious of it." The maṇḍala has "several systematisations" attached to it simultaneously; it represents "restraint, organisation, harmony, and the cultivation of the individual as a creative person."[17] In brief, "Man is the maṇḍala." Professor Danielli's analysis of the technical characteristics of a maṇḍala is summarized in six points that are applicable to all of the maṇḍalas in this book:

1) The maṇḍala is concentric around a center (applicable both to tone-circles and reciprocal yantras).
2) The maṇḍala is symmetrical around three axes (illustrated by all tonal yantras); alternately, 2^n axes may appear.
3) The mandala is self-replicative (*i.e.*, its patterns can be "translated" arithmetically and "transposed" tonally and "rotated" and "reflected" geometrically).
4) The maṇḍala is three dimensional in fact, although often represented as a two-dimensional base plan (*i.e.*, most of the yantras in this book are multiplication tables for the prime numbers 3 and 5, hence "two-dimensional," but powers of 2 constitute a "third-dimension" relevant to any tonal realization and must be supplied mentally).
5) Every part communicates with every other part (*i.e.*, musical intervals overlap within the confines of the octave and provide alternate channels of "communication" between any two tones).
6) Every line, every junction, and every space has a meaning (*i.e.*, every junction is a number and a tone, every space is a tonal interval and a ratio, and every line is a route of connection).

In *Earliest Civilizations of the Near East*, James Mellaart presents two white and red painted pottery pieces from the Middle Neolithic sites of Slatin and Kremikovci (Sofia region, Bulgaria), late sixth millenium B.C.[18] They are ornamented with triangles and dots exactly like those patterns of counters essential to finding "smallest integer solutions" to problems in Nicomachean ratio theory (*i.e.*, within the "group" of *rational numbers*, under the *operation* of *multiplication*).

Mellaart also finds, this time in Çatal Hüyük (in present-day Turkey) a symbol painted on the wall of a shrine which a thousand years or more earlier anticipates the whole mathematical theory being presented here.[19]

Harappan seals of the third millenium are incised with approximately 400 different signs of a script that cannot yet be deciphered. The writing is from right to left, but where there is a second line, it is from left to right. On a large number of seals multiple strokes occur, suggesting numbers. Rarely more than twelve strokes are used, and some accompanying signs may prove to be those for larger numbers.[20] Walter Fairservis suggests that one possible source for this still puzzling Indian script may be the potters' marks of northern Baluchistan.[21] His examples can be read as allusions to relations in our tonal yantras, mute evidence of a concern for patterns which mathematical harmonics found essential.

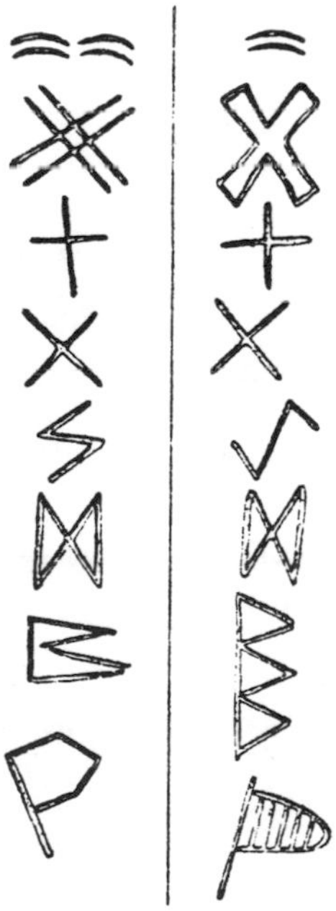

Baluchistan potters' marks

Harappan script (undeciphered)

The pottery designs which "paved the way" for geometry led also into a theory of numbers, a theory of music, and—in ways yet to be understood—a related mythology. In the words of Giorgio de Santillana:

> Number gave the key. Way back in time, before writing was ever invented, it was *measures* and *counting* that provided the armature, the frame on which the rich texture of real myth was to grow.[22]

My own study of ancient mythology aims at demonstrating that what was being measured and counted from an indeterminate but early time included the lengths of pipes and strings. The key to the meaning and development of mathematics and mythology in ancient civilizations is music—musical harmonies and musical invariances.

FOOTNOTES

1. "Inscriptions from the earliest period at Mohenjo-Daro show at first simple vertical strokes, arranged into groups." Carl B. Boyer, *A History of Mathematics* (New York: John Wiley & Sons), p. 234. Nothing more complicated is actually required for our tables. If nothing better was available, it is easier to appreciate the great air of mystery in the poems.
2. Nicomachus, *Introduction to Arithmetic* (transl. by M. L. D'Ooge in *Great Books in the Western World*, Vol. XI) Book II, Chapter 3, 1.
3. Alain Daniélou, *Hindu Polytheism* (New York: Pantheon Books, 1964), pp. 350–361.
4. E. A. Wallis Budge, *Amulets and Talismans* (New York: University Books, 1968), p. 85.
5. The so-called "Pascal triangle"—a triangular table of the coefficients of the expansion $(a + b)^n$—was known as "Mt. Meru" to Pingala, c. 200 B.C. The sums of numbers in successive rows are 2, 4, 8, etc., showing that 2 is again the female matrix number in this new context. Now since the example 3:4:5 is the root of two related expansions—continued geometric progression in the tables of Nicomachus, and the "binomial" expansion $(2 + 3)^n = 5^n$—triangles could be read in either way, through the field of limitless expansion. Since Mt. Meru is shown with an "hourglass" shape, however, it seems more likely to have been associated more intimately with the "Nicomachean" patterns we are graphing in this study. See A. N. Singh, "On the Use of Series in Hindu Mathematics," *Osiris*, Vol. I, January 1936, pp. 606–628.
6. How "Heaven and Earth" emerge from the splitting of the primal unity is discussed eloquently by Stella Kramrisch in "Two: Its Significance in the Ṛgveda," *Indological Studies in Honor of W. Norman Brown* (New Haven: American Oriental Society, 1962), pp. 109–136. The imagery of the "bowls" or "world-halves," the importance of "twins," the plethora of alternative explanations, the role of the uncreated "seed" and the "kiss" of heaven and earth I read as a commentary on the triangles of Charts 10 and 11.

7. I suggest that the upright triangle be considered the "mountain of god," and the inverted triangle be thought of basically as a "rain-cloud." S. Gandz has pointed out that ancient Babylonian, Arabic, and Hebrew words for "diagonal" mean also "falling raindrops," and reasoned that the only experience with things which fell diagonally was with the rain. All of the diagonals in our yantras are metaphorical "raindrops," I believe.
8. Boyer, *op. cit.*, p. 6.
9. *Ibid.*
10. James Mellaart, *Earliest Civilizations of the Near East* (New York: McGraw-Hill, 1965), p. 109.
11. V. Gordon Childe, *New Light on the Most Ancient East* (New York: Grove Press, 1957), pp. 172–188.
12. Marija Gimbutas, *The Gods and Goddesses of Old Europe 7000–3500 B.C.* (Berkeley: University of California Press, 1974), p. 86.
13. Childe, *op. cit.*, p. 183.
14. Mary Danielli, *The Anthropology of the Maṇḍala* (Amherst, N.Y.: The Center for Theoretical Biology, 1974), p. 16.
15. *Ibid.*, p. 12.
16. *Ibid.* In the first thirty-six pages of her book, Mary Danielli has effectively summarized the psychological, anthropological, and philosophical implications of the maṇḍala, with particular reference to the culture of India.
17. *Ibid.*, p. 36.
18. Mellaart, *op. cit.*, p. 117.
19. James Mellaart, *Çatal Hüyük* (New York: McGraw-Hill, 1967), Figure 40.
20. Walter A. Fairservis, Jr., *The Roots of Ancient India* (Chicago: The University of Chicago Press, 1975), pp. 273–282.
21. *Ibid.*, p. 201.
22. Giorgio de Santillana and Hertha von Dechend, *Hamlet's Mill* (Boston: Gambit, 1969), p. ix.

6

EXPANSION OF THE TONE NUMBER-FIELD

THE BṚHASPATI AND PRAJĀPATI CYCLES OF 3,600 AND 216,000 "YEARS"

The Bṛhaspati cycle of $60^2 = 3{,}600$ "years" and the Prajāpati cycle of $60^3 = 216{,}000$ "years" are symmetric expansions of the basic material defined by 60 in Charts 1 and 11. Notice in Chart 12 that the "Five tribes" along the "transevering axis" of the Bṛhaspati yantra (C G D A E) have grown to "Seven Rivers" in the Prajāpati yantra (F C G D A E B). These sets are the only ones which remain invariant under reciprocation (= "rotation" by 180°). The five-tone set is immortalized in the Chinese pentatonic system.[1] The seven-tone set is immortalized as the ancient Greek Phrygian mode (*i.e.*, one of the two modes Plato admitted in his ideal city of the *Republic*), and as "Modus Protus" in the modal theory of Christendom (*modern* Dorian mode). When these seven tones are arranged in symmetric scale order—rising or falling—they are bounded by the numbers which dominate Hindu cosmology:

ratios	432	486	512	576	648	729	768	864
rising	D	E	F	G	A	B	C	D
falling	D	C	B	A	G	F	E	D
components 3^n	3^3	3^5	3^0	3^2	3^4	3^6	3^1	3^3

We shall meet the numbers required for this most precious "octave-double" $1:2 = 432:864$ repeatedly in the larger yantras which lie ahead. They

CHART 12

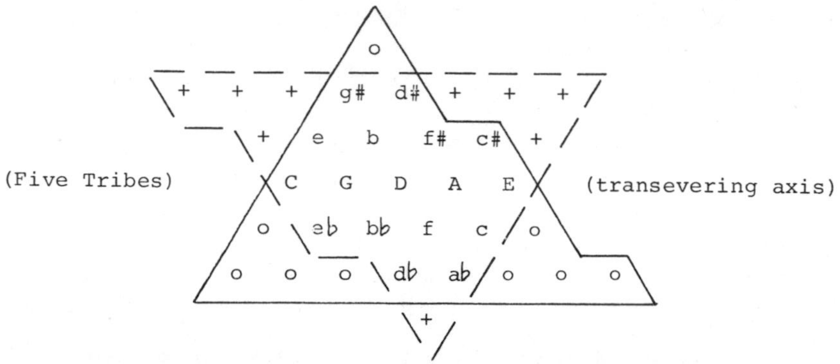

a) The Bṛhaspati Yantra for numbers $3^p5^q < 60^2 = 3600$

The yantra is first of all the multiplication table for 3 × 5, with powers of 3 along the base and powers of 5 along the diagonal, /. Tone names have been given only to those elements which possess a reciprocal "twin" around the center of symmetry on D. All numbers can be multiplied by 2^n without increasing the number of cuts in a tone-maṇḍala, hence all can be represented *within* the "double" 3600:1800 = 2:1.

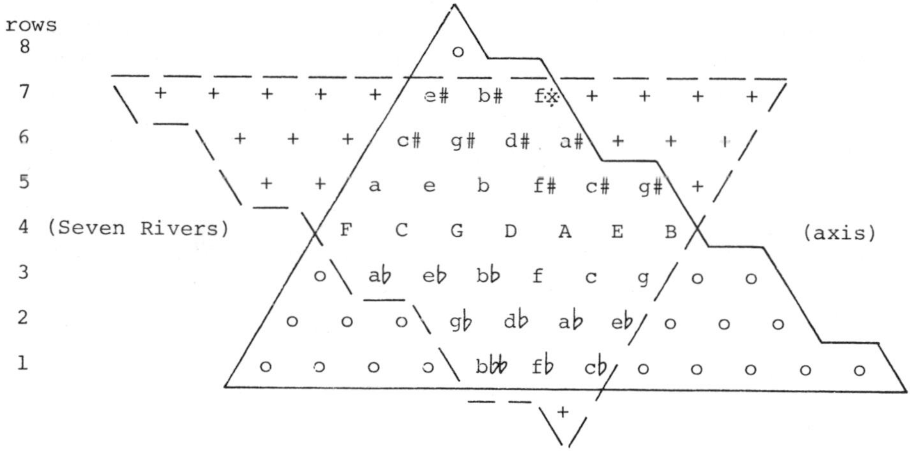

b) The Prajāpati Yantra for numbers $3^p5^q < 60^3 = 216{,}000$

The same multiplication table for 3 × 5, extended to a larger limit within which seven tones, F C G D A E B, remain invariant under reciprocation. From one perspective the table grows upward and to the right; from another, it grows symmetrically around the Mitra-Varuṇa "linch-pin" on D.

play profoundly significant roles in the later temples of Angkor Wat.[2] By the very simple device of "translating" this well-known scale into its older Pythagorean integer form, we are stumbling, I believe, into some of the deepest secrets of religious mysticism, "secrets" merely because of our own failure to study ancient ideas with ancient tools. All musicologists are familiar with this scale, but no one uses monochord "integer arithmetic" any more—cents prove to be so much more convenient—and Hindu practice preserves so many variant tunings that this one has attracted no special attention. It will remain, however, the focus of our attention; it consists of seven very good chariot "spokes" and our future efforts will be devoted to finding five more from this same "Brāhmin" class.

Hindu "days" and "years" are euphemisms: we are studying an abstract number theory with a concrete musical application. One of the continuing problems of translators is that the *Ṛg Veda* is so casual about indicating what its numbers actually represent that spokes, days, cows, tones, and gods have to be supplied by the imagination. In the Hindu astronomical treatises of the sixth century A.D., "days" actually mean *degrees*; "the Hindu 'days' are simply sexagesimal fractions of a sidereal year."[3] In our more ancient text, however, the numbers can be interpreted as sexagesimal fractions which have been cleared by a least common denominator. For instance, if our basic scale (in the 30:60 octave) were interpreted according to the Babylonian sexagesimal "place-value" habits, the numbers would have stood for multiples or submultiples of $60^{\pm n}$, *according to context*. Thus D = 1 = 60 would have remained 1 during the expansion through the Bṛhaspati and Prajāpati expansions graphed above:

$$D = 60 = 1 \qquad = 60^2 = 1;0 \qquad = 60^3 = 1;0;0$$

We see here an interesting blending of Babylonian sexagesimal habits with Hindu decimal habits. Both systems seem to be profoundly musical.[4] Musicians, however, while pressing the claims of music on the attention of historians, must respect Otto Neugebauer's warning:

> We stand today only at the beginning of a systematic investigation of the relations between Hindu and Babylonian astronomy, an investigation which is obviously bound to give us a greatly deepened insight into the origin of both fields.[5]

We do not know when 360 "days" actually became 360 *degrees*, just as we remain ignorant of when 3:4:5—of fundamental importance to "tuning theory"—became the "sides" of a Pythagorean right triangle.[6] Until historians untangle the web of the past, musicians can feel free to suspect that their own art had an elementary scientific basis at the very dawn of civilization.

It is not clear whether or not the numbers $60^2 = 3{,}600$ and $60^3 = 216{,}000$ actually occur in the *Ṛg Veda*, but since they are subsets of all the important larger cosmic numbers we must study them with some care. The number $60^2 = 3{,}600$ may be given in "poetic form" in the verse in which we hear that the Aśvins (the arithmetic and harmonic means) who pull Indra's chariot travelled three days and three nights in "three cars, hundred-footed, with six horses" (1.116.4).

3	cars(?)
6	horses(?)
00	hundred-footed(?)
3600	

Perhaps "thrice-sixty Maruts waxing strong"—"Men of Heaven" and companions of Indra—should be read as $60^3 = 216{,}000$ (8.58.8). Perhaps there is a hidden allusion to the progression 60, 60^2, 60^3 in Hymn 1.34 where we read that the same Aśvins journey round the heavens "thrice by day" and "thrice by night." "Thrice in the selfsame day" they "banish want," "vouchsafe us store of food, with plenteous strength," and come to our home bringing "abundant wealth" and "heavenly medicines." Since each larger set includes the previous smaller ones, and since 60^3 is a set necessary for some important acoustical lessons, these three powers of 60 provide a possible answer to a question in verse 9 of the same hymn:

> Where are the three wheels of your triple
> chariot, where are the three seats thereto
> firmly fastened?

We might try to justify linking Bṛhaspati, "teacher of the gods," to 60^2 on the grounds that this cycle encompasses the fundamental arithmetic (Charts 1 through 11), and linking Prajāpati, "lord-of-progeny," to 60^3 on the grounds of its being, in several important respects, a culminating metric unit. What is more important here, however, is that we understand *how* these cycles exhibit some of the central concerns of the poets, and *what* specific acoustical lessons they encode.[7]

Dīrghatamas describes two birds sitting on the world-tree, one singing and the other a passive spectator.

> 20. Two birds, close-knit friends,
> Find the same tree for their perch;
> The one eats sweet berry;
> The other just looks on, not eating.
>
> 21. Here the birds sing without cease,
> In the wise assembly of the draught of immortality . . . .

22. On that tree where the honey-sucking birds roost and breed,
The sweet berry grows at the top.
Who knows the Father not at all,
Hardly ever reaches the top.

(R.V. 1.164)

De Nicolás observes that what separates these two Vedic birds is "their identification with a particular philosophical perspective."[8] The two birds, we suspect, are the reciprocal yantras being introduced here to explain Hindu cosmic numbers, only one of which can "sing" at a time. The shift in viewpoint, from numbers as multiples to the same numbers as submultiples, is a taxing conceptual exercise from which the operator is rescued only by moving to a still larger frame within which the relations of interest possess a common denominator (as they do only *within* the common boundaries of our reciprocal yantras). It is with great relief that we discover those number sets which remain identical in meaning under reciprocation, as for instance the musical proportion 6:8::9:12, and the diatonic scale in "Pythagorean tuning" within the 864:432 "double," and the chromatic scale in "Just tuning" within the 720:360 "double." In Hymn 1.29 the poet pleads:

3. Do thou, O Indra, give us hope of beauteous
horses and of kine,
In thousands, O most wealthy One.

4. Lull thou asleep to wake no more, the
pair who on each other look.

"Put to sleep the two reciprocally looking," is Wilson's literal translation.[9] Reciprocals are "put to sleep" by larger common denominators, and in accordance with Nicomachus' rule. Our yantras permit the operator to recognize reciprocals at a glance: the center of symmetry rises one row for each factor of 5 in the limiting number, and moves one place to the right for each factor of 3. We are suppressing, of course, the repeated doubling which allows any number 3^p5^q in the whole table to become the terminating number $2^p3^q5^r$; the yantras, in short, can be "hinged" any way the operator desires so that the same acoustical science which the Hindus encode so very elegantly and systematically can also be encoded by cosmological numbers of different but comparable size in other ancient cultures.

Reciprocity is one of the great concerns of the *Ṛg Veda*, and its meaning in ratio theory is that every *integer* functions as both "great" (multiple) and "small" (submultiple).

Glory to Gods, the mighty and the lesser,
glory to Gods the younger and the elder!

(1.27.13)

The poets challenge a musician with their riddle:

> Resolve for me, O singer, this my riddle:
> The rivers send their swelling water backward.
>
> *(10.28.4)*

Our "rivers" do flow backward as readily as forward when number sets like 6:8::9:12 and the others just cited *make the same cuts* in a tone-maṇḍala whether read as "mighty" multiples or "lesser" submultiples. The poet who invented the riddle gives his own clue to its solution in a later verse:

> The great will I make subject to the little.
>
> *(10.28.9)*

The "great" is subject to the "little" only *within* the common boundaries of our reciprocal yantras. In the yantra for 60^3, Chart 12b, there are exactly thirty-three "pebbles" common to our reciprocal diagrams about whom we could justifiably say:

> Not one of you, ye Gods, is small, none
> of you is a feeble child:
> All of you, verily, are great.
>
> *(8.30.1)*

"Thirty-three gods" play a central role in the *Ṛg Veda.* In Hymn 8.28 they are described as "guardians in the west, and northward here, and in the south, And on the east." In our yantras, for reasons to be discussed later, east is on the right, the direction our transevering axis will grow in the yantras for still larger numbers. The "three times eleven" deities of Hymn 8.35 are closely associated with the Maruts, "men of heaven" who aid Indra. The ten verses of Hymn 8.39 laud "the Thrice Eleven Deities" and repeat the refrain: "Let all the others die away."

Why the thirty-three "great" gods of the Prajāpati cycle are so important to acoustical theory can be understood best if we project them into a tone-maṇḍala, as in Chart 13. There we can see at a glance that the *metric* properties of numbers $2^p3^q5^r \leqq 60^3$ are becoming *visually* and *aurally* indistinguishable; their "angular values" are beginning to coincide when interpreted according to a cyclical or "circular" logarithmic scale on base 2. To understand how nearly certain pairs of numbers agree in meaning, we must actually perform the calculations; two kinds of near coincidences are interesting, and computing them will test the usefulness of our yantra 12b.

1) There are near coincidences between respectively e♯ and b♯ in row 7 and the tones labelled f♭ and c♭ in row 1, and between all tone-numbers similarly spaced in larger yantras. In modern equal-temperament e♯ and

CHART 13

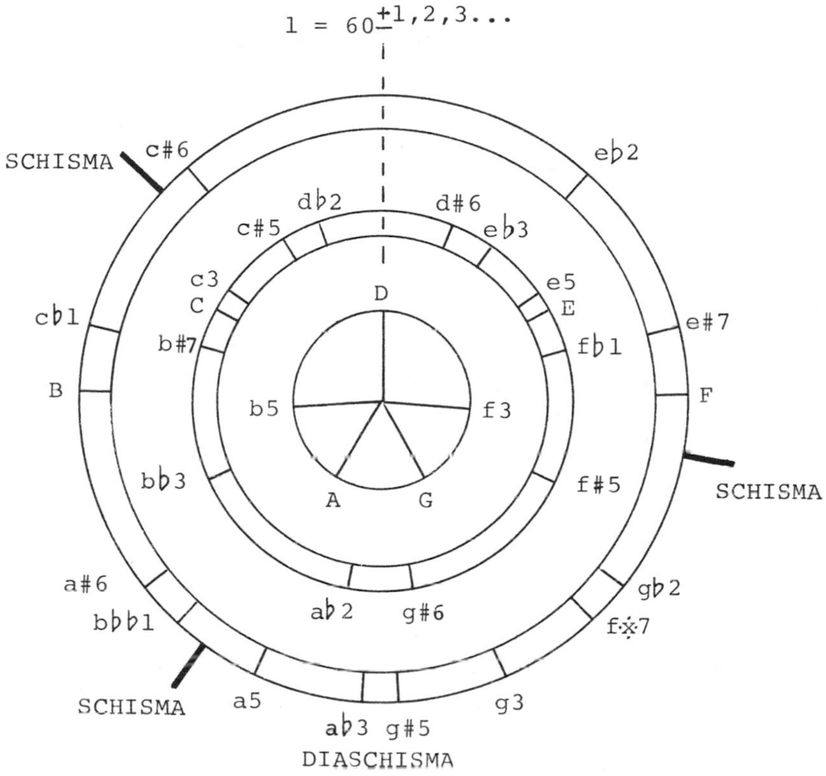

Maṇḍala of the Thirty-three Gods in 60³

The reciprocals within the successive octave doubles bounded by 60, by 3600, and by 216,000 are shown here in an effort to suggest a possible musical basis for the notion of "Thirty-three gods." Each of the larger sets includes the members of the smaller sets, but only the new pairs of "twins" are shown to simplify the drawing. Numerical exponents refer to rows in Chart 12b. Very near coincidences occur at three loci, the pairs of tones forming a *schisma* being only about 2 cents or half a degree apart. (These tones are neither shown nor labelled here as their reciprocals would require a still larger number set.) Near-coincidences in the tone-maṇḍala means that differences in pitch are becoming subliminal. The discrepancy between a♭ and g♯ at the bottom of the maṇḍala is the *diaschisma* of ratio 2025:2048.

f♭ would be separated by a semitone, and b♯ and c♭ similarly, but the "pure" ratios of natural numbers used here distort the meaning of our letter notation, there being a cumulative error (surplus) of 2 cents in each interval counted *to the right* and a deficiency of 14 cents in each interval counted *upward* along the right diagonal (/). Since e♯ lies six places above the reference 1 at the lower left-hand corner of the triangle, it is $6 \times 14 = 84$ cents flat with an idealized equal-tempered value, while f♭ lying five places to the right is $2 \times 5 = 10$ cents sharp compared to another equal-tempered value, hence $84 + 10 = 94$ cents cumulative error means that these two tones are within 6 cents (less than two degrees) of agreement. Still using the yantra, let us calculate the problem again with integers: counting six places upward along the side (/) to reach e♯ means that we have reached $5^6 = 15{,}625$, while counting five places to the right to f♭ carries us only to $3^5 = 243$. This last number must now be doubled and redoubled until we are *within* an octave double of 15,625.[10] Six successive doublings carry us to $2^6 = 64 \times 243 = 15{,}552$, at which point the ratios can be compared directly (or translated again into musical logarithms).

$$\frac{e\sharp}{f\flat} = \frac{5^6}{2^6 \times 3^5} = \frac{15625}{15552} = 1.0046$$

The discrepancy, about one part in 200, lies at the threshold of accuracy in tuning and cannot be discriminated in a purely melodic context.

2) There is a much closer agreement between the reference 1 at the lower-left corner of yantra 12b and the ninth "pebble" in the row above, and between all "pebbles" with a similar planimetric spacing in this and in larger yantras. We shall compute the problem first in cents and then again in integers directly from the yantra. Counting eight places to the right involves $8 \times 702 = 5616$ cents, an excess of 16 cents in the chain of perfect fifths; counting one place upward along the diagonal (/) involves 384 cents, a deficiency of 14 cents in the major third; but $5616 + 384 = 6000$ cents, and the octave identity $5 \times 1200 = 6000$ cents. This remarkable agreement can be checked by the integer calculation: counting eight places to the right of our reference tone in the corner takes us to $3^8 = 6561$, and counting one place upward along the diagonal (/) is a multiplication by 5 to $5 \times 6561 = 32{,}805$. We must now return to the reference unit in the corner and double it repeatedly until we are within an octave range of 32,805. Fifteen doublings are required, carrying us to $2^{15} = 32{,}768$. The ratio $32{,}805/32{,}768 = 1.0011$, known in acoustical theory as a *schisma*, is at the threshold of accuracy for even our best piano turners. Cents approximation hides this discrepancy.

We have reached, so it would seem, the practicable limits of "tuning theory." The further accuracy which we seek is of primarily theoretical interest to musicians; only astronomers really need more accurate "angular" measures. In the ancient Egyptian temples—functioning as "telescopes" by admitting light through a very long and narrow chamber—far more accurate angular measures could easily be made, for the heavens cooperate in forming a grid.[11] The old Babylonian arithmetic which functioned by about 1800 B.C. employed standardized tables of reciprocals limited to three places, meaning to values which could be expressed via $60^3 = 216{,}000$ as a common denominator; later Babylonian astronomy needed ten or more places—powers of 60—to express the greater accuracy it was able to observe.[12] The *Ṛg Veda* pursues another path, specifically musical, I believe, and more primitive mathematically. Therein lies part of its claim to greater antiquity.

It would be foolish to insist that we have correctly identified the important "thirty-three Gods" of the *Ṛg Veda*; later we shall meet a number set in which the central axis contains eleven "Brāhmins," and since "earth" and "heaven" are reciprocal reflections of events taking place in "mid-air" it is possible to imagine other sets of thirty-three. Yet this set has a special claim on our interest: 60^3 is a valid tonal limiting number, and its yantra "puts to sleep" thirty-three reciprocals, seven with invariant meanings along the central axis plus thirteen pairs in the rows above and below. Hymn 8.30 can be read as a tribute to this construction:

1. Not one of you, ye Gods, is small, none
   of you is a feeble child:
   All of you, verily, are great.

2. Thus be ye lauded, ye destroyers of the
   foe, ye Three-and-Thirty-Deities,
   The Gods of man, the Holy Ones.

3. As such defend and succour us, with
   benedictions speak to us:
   Lead us not from our fathers' and from
   Manu's path into the distance far away.

4. Ye Deities who stay with us, and all ye
   Gods of all mankind,
   Give us your wide protection, give shelter
   for cattle and for steed.

It is interesting that 3,600 was the Sumerian šár, meaning "universe."[13] We shall meet this number again in the numerology of several cultures.

FOOTNOTES

1. Virtually all articles on Chinese music emphasize the fundamental importance of five tones from the same series of musical fifths, usually given as C D E G A (scale order) rather than in the tuning order of Chart 10a. Fritz Kuttner reports that "near-complete lithophone sets" dating about 900 B.C. and representing a twelve-semitone scale were "tuned at incredible precision to the so-called 'Pythagorean' scale," and that "these sets also contain the interval

of the major third in just (acoustically pure) intonation side by side with the wider 'Pythagorean' interval." ("The Music of China: A Short Historical Synopsis Incorporating the Results of Recent Musicological Investigations," *Ethnomusicology* 8 (2), May, 1964, pp. 121–127.) The lines of possible influence between India and China are not well understood in this ancient period, but it appears that "tuning theory" was well understood in both countries long before it was developed in Greece.

2. Perhaps the most rigorous recent pursuit of the numbers 432 and 864 in the architecture of Angkor Wat is that by Eleanor Morón in *Angkor Wat: Meaning Through Measurement* (Ann Arbor: Xerox, 1974). By converting actual temple measurements to a system of proportion, Morón has uncovered a considerable network of interrelated numbers which can be tied directly to the arithmetic of the scale. In her system, 432 measures the width of the temple moat, hence the length of the bridges into the temple compound. (See pp. 60–72 especially.) For both temple and scale, 432 is the "entrance" number.

3. Otto Neugebauer, *The Exact Sciences in Antiquity* (New York: Dover Publications, 1969), p. 173. (Neugebauer is referring to the astronomical treatise Pañca Siddhāntikā by Varāha Mihira, sixth c. A.D.)

4. The Old Babylonian tables of reciprocals were generally limited to " 'regular' numbers whose reciprocals can be expressed by a sexagesimal fraction of a finite number of places." (Neugebauer, *op. cit.*, p. 33) This means, in effect, a restriction to products of three primes, 2, 3, 5, and their reciprocals, the same restriction which governs "Just tuning." The *tonal* effect is to limit the system to those numbers factorable by 2, 3, and 5 to the limit of 81 together with their reciprocals. See Chart 29 for a tonal interpretation of Neugebauer's set of sexagesimal multiplication tables. Chapter 10 will develop the Babylonian materials more fully.

5. Neugebauer, *op. cit.*, p. 173.

6. Carl Boyer writes, "It is not known just when the systematic use of the 360° circle came into mathematics, but it seems to be due largely to Hipparchus in connection with his table of chords. It is possible that he took over from Hypsicles, who earlier had divided the day into 360 parts, a subdivision that may have been suggested by Babylonian astronomy." *A History of Mathematics* (New York: John Wiley & Sons, Inc., 1968), p. 180. Both authors wrote in the second century B.C. As for the Pythagorean right triangle with sides of 3, 4, and 5 units, so often credited to the Egyptians, Boyer writes that "there is no hint of this in the papyri that have come down to us" (p. 18). The ancient Babylonians, however, were fluent with the Pythagorean theorem (pp. 42–43).

7. The Bṛhaspati and Prajāpati numbers are among those quoted by James Adam in *The Republic of Plato* (Cambridge: Cambridge University Press, 1902 and 1965), p. 303. His source is an article by Martin in *Rev. Archeol.*, XIII, pp. 286–287. They are important to Platonism because of Plato's expansion *through them* to the fourth power of 60 = 12,960,000 in his "marriage allegory" (*Republic* 546).

8. Antonio T. de Nicolás, *Four-Dimensional Man: The Philosophical Methodology of the Ṛg Veda* (Bangalore: Dharmaram College Studies No. 6, 1971), p. 53.

9. Ralph T. H. Griffith, *The Hymns of the Ṛgveda* (Delhi: Motilal Banarsidass, 1973, New Revised Edition), p. 17.

FOOTNOTES

10. This doubling of the basic unit to reach a desired product is one of the curious features which permeates "Egyptian" calculation. Such archaic methods, however, are all that acoustical arithmetic really required; together with the addition and subtraction of unit fractions, it would easily produce all of the material in any of our yantras and maṇḍalas. Since Egyptian calculation is based on "the arithmetical fact that every (positive whole) number is uniquely representable as a sum of powers of 2," we see here another reason for regarding 2 as a universal "matrix" number. See *Mathematical-Physical Correspondence* by Stephen Eberhart, Number 11, Easter 1975, p. 2, and Boyer, *op. cit.*, pp. 15–16.

11. J. Norman Lockyer was particularly fascinated by temples oriented to certain stars so that they became outdated within a few hundred years, requiring either a change in the temple orientation or a lapse of time until a new star came into focus. His drawings of the ground plans of Egyptian temples show both how the pillars were arranged to block disturbing light from the sides, and how temple alignment was changed (four times at Luxor) to correct for change in amplitude. See *The Dawn of Astronomy* (Cambridge: The M.I.T. Press, 1964), pp. 155–166.

12. Neugebauer reports that in the Seleucid period (fourth to third c. B.C.) some tables of reciprocals ran to as high as seventeen places. *Op. cit.*, pp. 29–34.

13. *Ibid.*, p. 141.

7
COSMIC CYCLES

THE FOUR YUGAS

Hindu cosmology knows four Yugas, or "ages of the world," numbers which I have graphed in Chart 14 as yantras of the form 3^p5^q. They are another form of "ten-ness," in which our Kali Yuga "dark age" of 432,000 "years" is the unit.

	Kali Yuga	=	1	=	432,000
	Dvāpara Yuga	=	2	=	864,000
	Tretā Yuga	=	3	=	1,296,000
	Kṛta Yuga	=	4	=	1,728,000
total:	Mahā Yuga	=	10	=	4,320,000

Notice that the only set of invariant tone-numbers within these limits belongs to seven tones, F C G D A E B, whose symmetric scale order (D E F G A B C D rising or D C B A G F E D falling) commences with 432, a number which has been multiplied by 1,000 to give the Kali Yuga unit, and by 10,000 to give the Mahā Yuga total. Notice also the hexagonal symmetry *within* our Kali Yuga set: there is exactly enough material along the six axes radiating from D for the star-hexagon of Chart 10. That is, for a point-line-plane-solid progression through powers of 2, 3, and 5 (or 3, 4, and 5) and their reciprocals, showing "ten-ness" in the microcosm, with a similar expansion "backwards" in Mahā Yuga, showing "ten-ness" in the macrocosm.

Ancient commentary on these numbers is interesting: for Berossos, the last priest of Marduk (c. 300 B.C.), 432,000 was the Babylonian "Great

CHART 14

The Yugas

Mahā Yuga	4,320,000	= 10
Kṛta Yuga	− 1,728,000	= 4
	= 2,592,000	
Tretā Yuga	− 1,296,000	= 3
	= 1,296,000	
Dvāpara Yuga	− 864,000	= 2
Kali Yuga	= 432,000	= 1

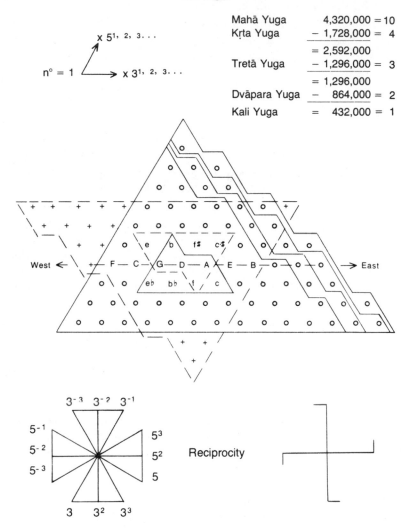

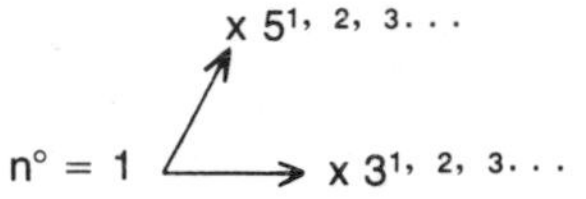

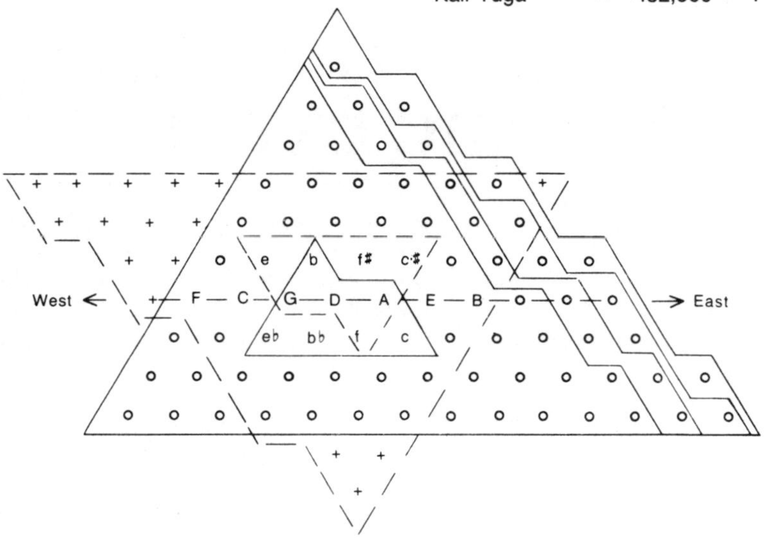

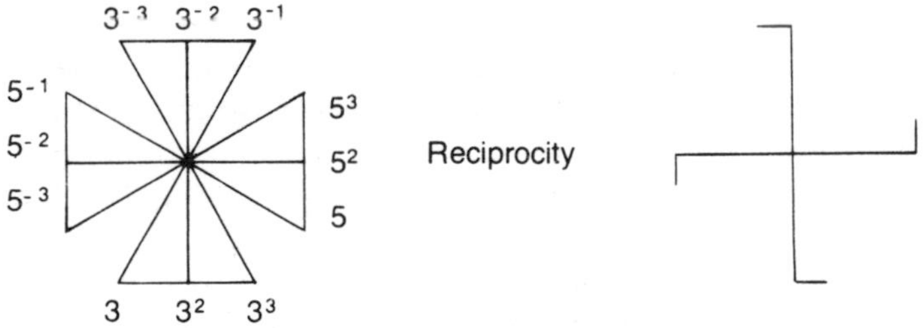

"Male" odd numbers, 3^p5^q, are shown in triangular arrays appropriate to periods of decreasing "radiation," together with our "dark age" Kali Yuga reciprocals. This "field of contest" consists entirely of "friends and relatives," with the highest caste along the horizontal axis, and with supporting castes above and below. The seven tones which remain the same under reciprocation (F C G D A E B) are the "Pythagorean" team from Chart 12b. Yantras of the cross and swastika suggest routes traversible by "Egyptian" operations (using doubling, halving, and unit fractions). Every triangular subset has the same relations as in the star-hexagon of Chart 10.

Year"; for the authors of the *Grimnismal*, 432,000 was the number of fallen warriors whom the Valkyries carried to Valhalla and who ride forth to do battle for Odin on the last day of its existence.[1,2] In the *Ṛg Veda*, whose 10,800 stanzas average forty syllables per stanza, 432,000 is the total number of syllables.[3] In Babylonian sexagesimal notation, 432,000 is merely another form of the female matrix number 2, written as 2;0;0;0 in Neugebauer's modernized form and meaning 2×60^3. For Ptolemy, 432,000 was least common denominator for his monochord fractions.

I cannot find these Yuga numbers within the *Ṛg Veda*, but they may yet come to light there, possibly among the many allusions to the complex metric schemes of the poets, or in numerical passages whose meanings now vex translators. Dīrghatamas may be giving us the indirect clues in one of his hymns:

> Let not the wood ten times up-piled
> consume me, when fixed for you it bites
> the ground it stands on. . . .
>
> Dīrghatamas the son of Mamatā hath
> come to length of days in the tenth age
> of humankind.
>
> *(1.158.4–6)*

The stones are "ten times up-piled" within the Mahā Yuga limit (the "peak" of our yantra represents $5^9 = 1{,}953{,}125$, the largest power of 5 *within* 4,320,000), and the poet himself belongs to our own "dark" age, "the tenth age" in the sense that division by 10 produces the Kali Yuga 432,000.

Commentators have assumed that the extravagant powers of 10 attributed to Indra's forces were simply generous tributes to the god, but numbers—*factors*—of the form 10^n are actually a part of the essential arithmetic. Again and again Indra is addressed as "Lord of a Hundred Powers." (Hymn 1.30.6 is one of many examples.) "Help us, O Indra, in the frays, yea, frays, where thousand spoils are gained" (1.7.4). We hear that Indra slew "ten thousand Vṛtras" (1.53.6). Or Indra won "ten thousand head of kine," and ten thousand other "gifts" (8.6.47 and 8.8.2). It is by such extravagant multiples of 432 and 864—the bounding numbers of our basic "Pythagorean" scale—that we have arrived at the Yuga numbers themselves, and a similar multiplication by 10^3 carries us to the still larger Kalpa and Brahmā numbers to be studied next.

Before going ahead, however, let us look back a moment at the *smallest integer* form of the five tones, C G D A E, which were the only invariances in Chart 8 and its allied yantra in Chart 11.

ratios	72	81	96	108	128	144
rising	D	E	G	A	C	D
falling	D	C	A	G	E	D

Notice that 72 begins this symmetric pentatonic scale form, and $10 \times 72 = 720$ defines the "Just" limits within which it arises. These digits play a prominent role in Hindu, Hebrew, Christian, and Chinese arithmology. "Ten-ness" is a curiously revealing aspect of "Pythagorean" musical arithmetic.

KALPA AND BRAHMĀ CYCLES

One thousand Mahā Yugas constitute a Kalpa of 4,320,000,000 "years," and its "double" is Brahmā—the "Immense Being"—a cycle of 8,640,000,000 "years." The only invariances in either set belong to the same seven tones—F C G D A E B—which we first met in Charts 12, 13, and 14, tones which in scale order, rising or falling, are bounded by $432:864 = 1:2$, numbers which recur in Chart 15 multiplied by $10^7 = 10{,}000{,}000$ (a thousand myriads). And to what purely scientific purpose? The seventh pebble in the bottom row is a remarkably close approximation to A♭ = G♯ = $\sqrt{2}$ *in this context*; the top pebble, standing alone in the fifteenth row, is its reciprocal. The demonstration is in *smallest possible integers*: division of the larger Brahmā number by 2 cancels nine products of the form 3^p5^q, among them 3^05^{14} at the peak of the triangle; division by 3 would erase the left side of either yantra (/ = F and B) and division by 5 would lower the "transevering axis" by one row, thus eliminating the important seventh item now in the bottom row. We see here, I believe, one of the most elegant constructions in mathematical harmonics ever devised, at least so early in history. There are important lessons in acoustical theory, in integer arithmetic, in Ṛgvedic imagery, and in wider religious symbolism to be gleaned from these yantras.

Notice that within the Kalpa limits there are ten tones along the "transevering axis": F C G D A E B F♯ C♯ G♯. Under reciprocation these become B E A D G C F B♭ E♭ A♭ ≠ G♯! In other words, our "Brāhmins" produce an internal conflict between the extreme tones of their axis. Counting from left to right and taking A♭ as the "first" or "leader" in this particular perspective, its "twelfth disciple" (to borrow a Christian metaphor) = 3^{12} = G♯ "betrays" it by the so-called "Pythagorean comma" of ratio 531,441:524,288, approximately 74:73, or about 24 cents. MORAL: We cannot exceed *eleven* tones even by the very best integer methods without meeting a "fourth caste" comma which must be "sacrificed" in one way or another, being worth only about an eighth of a tone, subliminal to the

CHART 15

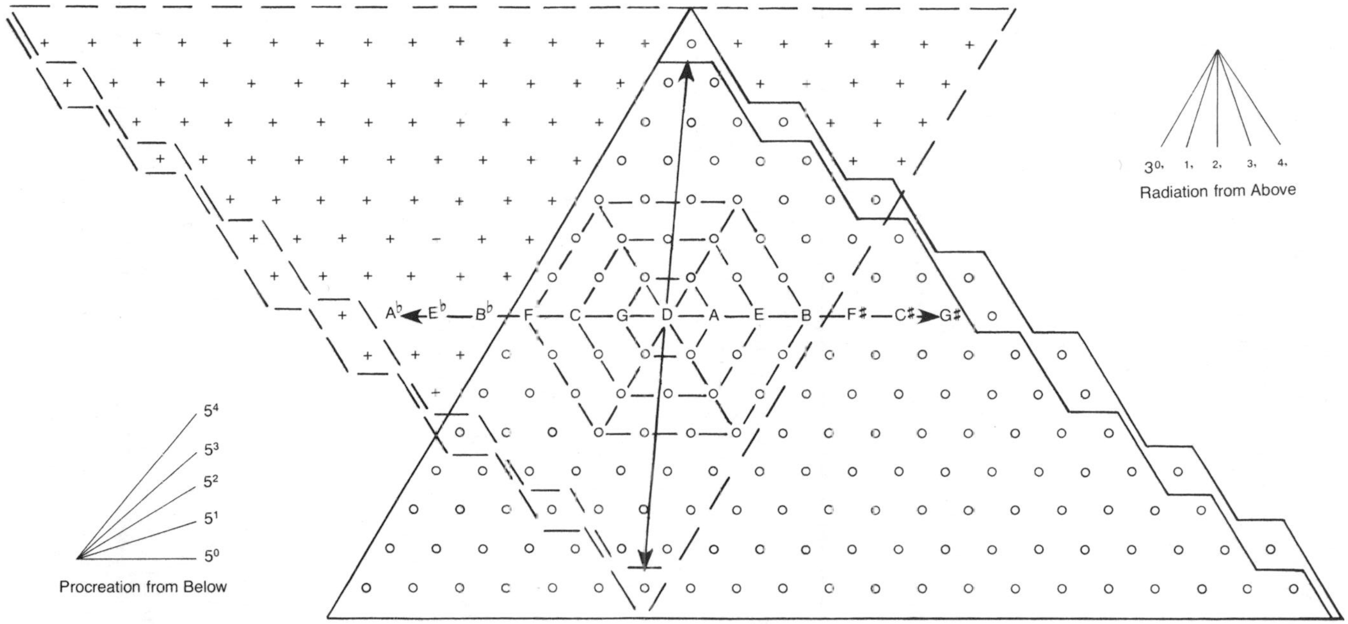

Yantras for Kalpa and Brahmā Periods

Vedic Cosmology: Algebraic array of integers 3^p5^q in Kalpa = 4,320,000,000 and Brahmā = 8,640,000,000.
Hexagons define "sexagesimal" subsets, $1 = 60^{\pm 1,2,3}$. Limits of the central cross $\approx \sqrt{2}$: $A\flat \neq G\sharp = (9/8)^3$ (horizontal) and $\dfrac{5^7}{2^{11} \times 3^3}$ (vertical).

ear in a melodic context although quite audible during a monochord demonstration. Notice that this "sacrifice" arises among the most prestigious powers of 3, the "divine" number. (To compute the comma merely notice that the twelfth interval will be defined by $3^{12} = 531{,}441$; raise the reference tone from 1 through repeated doubling to the nearest power of 2, $2^{19} = 524{,}288$, and then compare directly, $531{,}441/524{,}288 = 1.0136^{+}$, a discrepancy whose tonal implications can be more easily understood if the ratios are converted to *cents*. Remembering that every perfect fifth of ratio 3:2 is worth about 702 cents instead of 700, it is easy to see that twelve intervals along any row of our yantra will carry us to a thirteenth "tone-value" which is 24 *cents wider* than it should be for perfect agreement within the tone-maṇḍala.)

To appreciate both the necessity for "sacrifice" and the elegance of the Kalpa and Brahmā yantras it will help to examine the various approximations to A♭ = G♯ = $\sqrt{2} = 1.414^{+}$. We have never used 7/5 = 1.4 which looks so very convenient; its reciprocal would require our "cosmological numbers" to be multiplied by 7, and to no advantage, for the ratio 45/32 (= 720/512) = 1.40625 is closer to $\sqrt{2}$ and has been with us since Chart 8. Our new "Brāhmin" G♯ computed directly from the reference D, our "linch-pin," gives the ratio 729/512 (*i.e.*, 3^6 divided by the nearest power of 2) = 1.423, a slightly worse value, and its reciprocal will require a still larger yantra to be "put to sleep" in integer form. At the bottom of the Kalpa yantra, however, and in its reciprocal at the peak of the Brahmā yantra, we reach a remarkably close approximation to the square root of 2. Notice that these values can be reached either by moving three places to the left of the reference tone on D and then seven places upward along the diagonal (/), or by moving three places to the right and then seven places downward (/). Seven places along the diagonal (/) are equivalent to multiplication or division by $5^7 = 78{,}125$; three places along the horizontal axis are equivalent to $3^3 = 27$, a number which must be doubled and redoubled until it reaches $2^{11} \times 27 = 55{,}296$ (*i.e.*, within an "octave" of $5^7 = 78{,}125$), at which point the numbers can be compared directly.

$$78{,}125/55{,}296 = 1.4128$$

The yantras prove convenient for a calculation in cents. Starting from the reference pitch, D, three moves to the left are the modular equivalent of a *counter-rotation* in the tone-maṇḍala by 3 × 702 = 2,106 cents, while seven moves upward along the diagonal (/) are the modular equivalent of a *rotation* by 7 × 386 = 2,702 cents (*i.e.*, three perfect fifths to the left, and seven pure thirds upward). The difference, 2,702 − 2,106 = 596 cents, falls just 4 cents short of the equal-tempered A♭ = G♯ = $\sqrt{2}$ = 600 cents (about one *degree*).

79
KALPA AND BRAHMĀ CYCLES

The rather spectacular "numerosity" of the Kalpa and Brahmā yantras arises from the self-imposed requirement that 78,125/55,296 and its reciprocal be "put to sleep" (Ṛgvedic metaphor) or be made "conversable and rational" (Platonic metaphor) by the use of a common denominator which allows both members of the pair to be expressed in smallest integers. We are now looking, I believe, at a direct confrontation between "god on the mountain" = 5^{14} = Viṣṇu at the peak of the Brahmā yantra, and his "twin" reciprocal, the "dragon in the deep," seventh pebble along the base of the yantra. That seventh pebble represents $3^6 = 729$, and it must be doubled and redoubled by the "whirling" of Vṛtra until it reaches $2^{23} \times 729 = 6{,}115{,}295{,}232$, at which point it can be compared directly with "god" = $5^{14} = 6{,}103{,}515{,}625$.

$$6{,}103{,}515{,}625 \div 6{,}115{,}295{,}232 = .998$$

The discrepancy is about two parts in a thousand, like the schisma, and is acoustically negligible.

It must have been impossible to separate strict science from an exuberant number mysticism when confronted with such elegant constructions, at least in an age which was just discovering what real power lies in number. Notice how the scale numbers seem to have imposed these expansions on us. The numbers 60 and 720 were required for "Just tuning" in smallest integers earlier, and now the numbers 432 : 864 so appropriate to "Pythagorean tuning" are recurring as if by necessity during these expansions by powers of 10 up to 10^7. Notice that 7, which we have not needed for a ratio number, is actually the limiting number of very many important sets. The Hindu mind has always revelled in number theory, in ways mysterious to the West. It is pure *rationality*, not mysticism, which discovered these relations. That the poets understood everything we have discovered—and more—is an inference from imagery in which they seem to allude not only to the Kalpa and Brahmā numbers but to the specific yantra patterns developed here.

A possible allusion to the Kalpa number can be heard in verses 2 and 3 of hymn 4.58:

> So let the Brāhman hear the praise we utter.
> This hath the four-horned Buffalo emitted.
>
> Four are his horns, three are the feet that
> bear him; his heads are two, his hands
> are seven in number.
>
> Bound with a triple bond the Steer roars loudly:
> the mighty God hath entered in to mortals.

My interpretation suggests that some kind of "place marker" must have been available to the Hindus as early as the composition of this verse:

4	"horns"
3	"feet"
2	"heads"
0000000	"hands" (= 10^7 "fingers")
4,320,000,000	"years" in Kalpa

The "triple bonds" would appear to be the powers of three prime numbers: $2^{11} \times 3^3 \times 5^7 = 4{,}320{,}000{,}000$. "Like rivers our libations flow together" (verse 6). "The streams of oil flow pure and full of sweetness. The universe depends upon thy power and might within the sea, within the heart, within all life" (verses 10–11). Both the *number* and its *function* are described poetically.

A somewhat less complete allusion to the Kalpa number can be read in another verse:

> The rich new car hath been equipped at morning;
> four yokes it hath, three whips,
> seven reins to guide it:
>
> Ten-sided, friendly to mankind, light-winner,
> that must be urged to speed with
> prayers and wishes.
>
> *(2.18.1)*

The Kalpa number is "ten-sided" perhaps in having ten digits, and it is led by four "yokes" and three "whips," and its seven "reins" can be read as another allusion to 10^7 (seven "hands"). In verses 4, 5, and 6 this same poet counts Indra's horses: 2–4–6–8–10–20–30–40–50–60–70–80–90–100. "Now may that wealthy Cow of thine, O Indra, give in return a boon to him who lauds thee" (verse 9).

The Brahmā number can also be found in "poetic" form if it is legitimate to use some imagination:

> Horses of dusky colour stood beside me,
> ten chariots, Svanaya's gift, with mares
> to draw them.
>
> Kine Numbering sixty thousand followed after.
> Kaksīvān gained them when the days were closing.
>
> Forty bay horses of the ten cars' master
> before a thousand lead the long procession. . . .

An earlier gift for you have I accepted
eight cows, good milkers, and three
harnessed horses.

(1.126.3–5)

8	"cows, good milkers"
60000	"kine"
40	"bay horses"
0000000000	"chariots"
8,640,000,000	"days and nights in the life of Brahmā"

We risk inventing nonsense by such free interpretation, but very many other verses seem to allude to the Kalpa and Brahmā yantras, specifically to the number of "pebbles" outlining depth and height and the extent of the "transevering axes."[11] Across the base of both yantras, twenty-one pebbles symbolize the powers of 3 from 3^0 to 3^{20}. "Shout twenty forth the hymn of praise" could be an allusion to this array, the first of its kind among any of our cosmological numbers (1.80.9). "Daughter of Manu" (progenitor of men), "Parsu bare a score of children at a birth"[4] (10.86.23). Parsu means "rib," and our lowest rib in the yantra emanates from 1×2^n at the lower left corner and "bears" twenty children all at once at the Kalpa limit. At Indra's moment of triumph over Vṛtra we hear that his thunderbolt pierced "thrice-seven (=21) close-pressed ridges of the mountains" (8.85.2). Indra brings about the downfall of twenty-one "tribes" (7.18.11). "Thrice-seven libations" are drunk to the gods (1.20.7). "The names borne by the Cow are three times seven" (7.87.4). There are "three times seven Milch-kine in the eastern heaven" (9.70.1). The "Three Times Seven pour out the milky flow" of Soma, the sacred juice, "pressed out with stones" (9.86.21–23). "The three-times-seven bright sparks of fire have swallowed up the poison's strength." (1.191.12) There are "thrice-seven mystic things contained within" Agni, incarnate Savior, and "thrice-seven wandering Rivers, yea, the mighty floods" (1.72.6 and 10.64.8).

Our Brahmā yantra is fifteen steps high. The *Ṛg Veda* tells us "the fifteen lauds are in a thousand places: that is as vast as heaven and earth in measure" (10.114.8). The same hymn tells us that "the Chariot's majesties are fourteen others," a possible allusion to the height of the Kalpa yantra, and adds that "seven sages lead it onward with their voices," a possible allusion to the seven invariances along the central axis (10.114.8). "Fifteen-fold strong juices" are prepared for Indra (10.27.2). For the marriage feast the same hymn which assigned Parsu, the "rib," twenty children seems to have fifteen priests preparing twenty bulls for the sacrifice: "Fifteen in number, then, for me a score of bullocks they prepare" (10.86.14).

There are hints that this yantra is not peculiar to the Hindus. A Hebrew myth describes the digging of the temple foundation to a depth of fifteen "cubits," and fifteen psalms (numbers 120–134) are labelled "A Song of Ascents."[5] In Egyptian mythology fourteen steps lead upwards to the throne of Osiris, and in his judgment hall the deceased's heart is weighed in the balance—against "the feather of the law"—while forty-two judges look on from the side: they are seated in two rows of twenty-one each, like the top and bottom rows of our reciprocal yantras in Chart 15.[6]

It is the central horizontal axes of our yantras, however, which command the most attention, for it is there that invariance arises. Now the only rows which participate directly in the twelve-tone division of the octave have been the "transevering axis" itself and the adjacent rows above and below. In the Brahmā yantra note that there are eleven elements in the axis, ten in the row above, and thirteen in the row below, for a total of 10 + 11 + 13 = 34. We read of Indra that "with four-and-thirty lights he looks around him, lights of one colour though their ways are divers" (10.55.3). In the hymn to the "Cosmic horse," whose ritual sacrifice was an especially important event, we read:

> The four-and-thirty ribs of the swift
> Charger, kin to the Gods, the slayer's
> hatchet pierces.
> Cut he with skill, so that the parts be
> flawless, and piece by piece declaring
> them dissect them.
>
> *(1.162.18)*

Notice that in the Kalpa yantra there are only ten elements in the central axis, with nine and eight respectively in the rows above, and notice also that within the common boundaries of the yantra and its reciprocal there are seven elements in many rows, including that below the axis. With this in mind we read:

> Seven heroes from the nether part ascended,
> and from the upper part came
> eight together.
> Nine from behind came armed with
> winnowing-baskets: ten from the front
> pressed o'er the rock's high ridges.
>
> One of the ten, the tawny, shared in
> common, they send to execute their
> final purpose.
> The Mother carries on her breast the
> Infant of noble form and soothes it
> while it knows not.
>
> *(10.27.15–16)*

This last verse, with "one of the ten" elements in the central axis being sent "to execute their final purpose," invites us to look specifically at the "final purpose" of our whole arithmetical expansion, a purpose which can be achieved only by a sacrifice of perfect accuracy in the location of the twelfth tone or spoke. In Ṛgvedic metaphor, we must examine the birth of Agni, incarnate savior, in the flames of sacrifice.

THE BIRTH OF AGNI, INCARNATE SAVIOR

We have gone to extravagant arithmetical lengths to look for A♭ = G♯ = $\sqrt{2}$, a tone which would complete our circle of 12 while maintaining perfect inverse symmetry, D:A♭::G♯:D′. Whether or not our poets knew that this value was "irrational" or "incommensurable" with their integer system may be open to debate, but they at least knew that we are being saddled with an unconscionable "numerosity," while still missing our goal. Remembering that it is the duty of Brāhmins, and only Brāhmins, to sacrifice, and that their ritual requires a to-and-fro dance, notice that the tenth element in the central axis of the Kalpa yantra is a "Brāhmin" G♯ whose reciprocal A♭ disagrees by the interval of the "Pythagorean comma," too small for use as a melodic interval, so nearly subliminal under most circumstances as to invite our glossing over it, yet painfully present to an awakened consciousness in search of absolute truth. Here is an "original sin" among the powers of the "divine number 3" for which neither men nor gods are responsible.[7] This discrepancy, worth about 24 cents, is far worse than that between "god" = 5^{14} at the peak of our yantra and its reciprocal, the "dragon" in the bottom row, worth only about 4 cents, but if we can live with it and accept the consequences we can escape having to work with ten-digit numbers, which still are not absolutely free from the same kind of "error."

It is in this locus, I suggest, that Agni is born as Indra-Agni, god of fire. This "child of three mothers" (de Nicolás catalogues "three heads, three stations, three tongues, three bodies, three dwellings, three kindlings," etc.) is simultaneously the child of 45/32 and its reciprocal, 729/512 and its reciprocal, and 78,125/55,296 and its reciprocal.[8] In Chart 16 I have tried to graph the loci of these ratios in the tone-maṇḍala, among the eleven other "Brāhmin" tones, tones in "Pythagorean tuning" by perfect fourths and fifths, defined by numbers 2^p3^q.

The "wedge" in the tone-maṇḍala of Chart 16 is the area in which the "friction" between alternate approximations to the square root of 2 produces the "flames of sacrifice." The circle, remember, is the womb of Uṣas, daughter of the Sun. The *Ṛg Veda* is filled with frank sexual humor (which Griffith, being a nineteenth century English gentleman, translated into Latin rather than English) concerning the condition of male and female

CHART 16

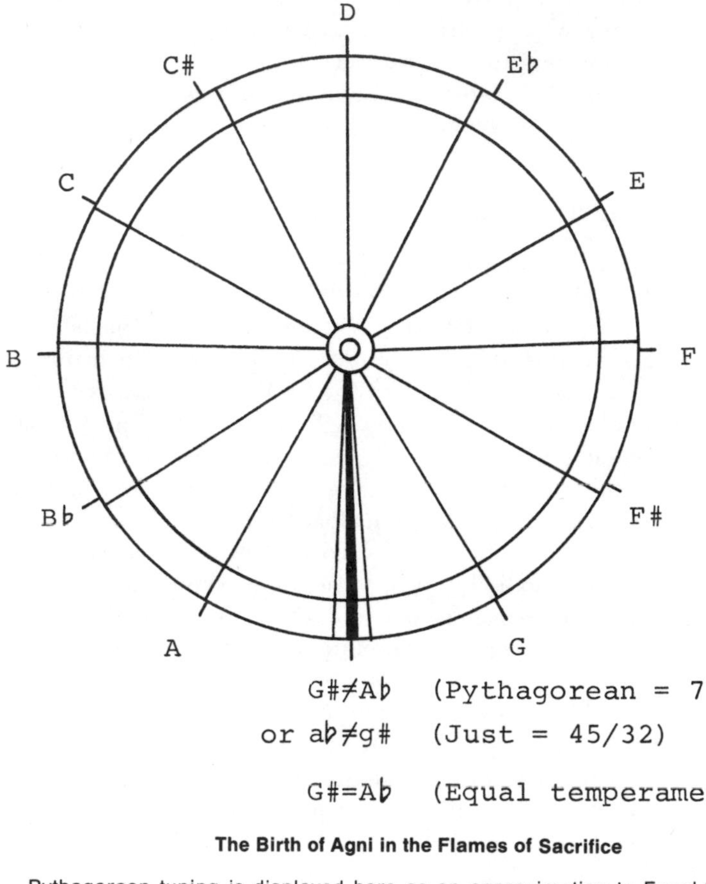

G#≠A♭ (Pythagorean = 729/512)

or a♭≠g# (Just = 45/32)

G#=A♭ (Equal temperament = $\sqrt{2}$)

The Birth of Agni in the Flames of Sacrifice

Pythagorean tuning is displayed here as an approximation to Equal-temperament. The cumulative discrepancy of 2 cents in each perfect fifth or fourth reaches a crisis in the middle of the octave at A♭ ≠ G♯. The Viṣṇu/Vṛtra ratio of 78125/55296 nearly closes this gap. The difference between the Pythagorean 729/512 and the Just 45/32 is too small to graph. (*i.e.*, The excess of 24 cents in "Pythagorean tuning" just about matches the defect of 22 cents in "Just tuning.")

organs during intercourse.[9] Since the "Brāhmin" A♭ and G♯ *overlap* in the circle, they rather naturally "stretch" the "vagina," our "world-halves." Our "wedge" even looks something like the Indian plough, "a big thorn-piece of wood or metal," called a *śepaḥ*, "penis" (Latin *cippus*, "stake, post").[10] Our whole construction arises from the interplay of "male" and "female" Nicomachean triangles, and the "commas" which arise are a kind of "genital friction." In *Indian Erotics* Ivo Fišer explores Vedic sexuality, and he reminds us that a verse was conceived as *yoni* (womb) of the melody that originated from it. "In the act of procreation, the woman is to be looked upon as a place of sacrifice," with her pubic hair as the grass, her skin as the "soma-press," and the labia as "the fire in the middle."[11] The mathematical origins of Vedic sexual imagery appear to have been as neglected as Plato's sexual humor, which is based on the fact that "male" odd numbers "procreate" on each other in a homosexual fantasy. The latter, we suppose, has nothing to do with Plato's convictions about sex.

The overlap between the "Brāhmin" A♭ and G♯ is probably related to the lotus position in which the legs are crossed over each other during meditation. The concentration on the single syllable *OM* must certainly be derived in some way from the lack of unity in the integer approximations to the square root of 2. Hindu mythology seems to have aimed at and achieved a total unity between the physical and the metaphysical, with number theory providing the ground for an absolute certainty of viewpoint.

We have now achieved, I believe, the material we need for another look at the chariot of the gods, "fashioned mentally."

THE CHARIOT OF THE GODS

We have watched our tone-number sets expand from the smallest possible to the largest necessary for an acoustical theory restricted to the "pure" intervals of "superparticular" ratios, and have discovered good reasons for restricting that theory to the products of the prime numbers 2, 3, and 5. In our yantras the pebble at the lower-left corner always represents 1×2^n; the pebble at the lower-right corner represents 3^n (or in some cases, 2×3^n); the pebble at the top represents 5^n. The Mitra-Varuṇa "linch-pin" on D represents the reference tone around which the tone field unfolds symmetrically; it has the role of "1" = *geometric mean* in the *field of rational numbers*, but since we are always clearing fractions by common denominators, its "numerosity" is continually changing. Chart 17 is an effort to schematize the whole development we have witnessed as a "Chariot of the Gods, fashioned mentally" (4.36.1–2). The "car-pole" demands careful attention. The tenth tone along the "transevering axis" is G♯ (counting F C G D A E B F♯ C♯ G♯). The next tone in the axis, D♯, available only in the Brahmā set, plays the major role in the birth of Agni, I believe. It is eleventh in order but ONLY SEVEN PLACES FROM THE LINCH PIN on D and so is to be regarded as "eighth hero" in the hymn which follows. (Remember that F C G are the reciprocal meanings of A E B, and are thus superfluous numbers *if* all those to the right of *D function* reciprocally.)

CHART 17

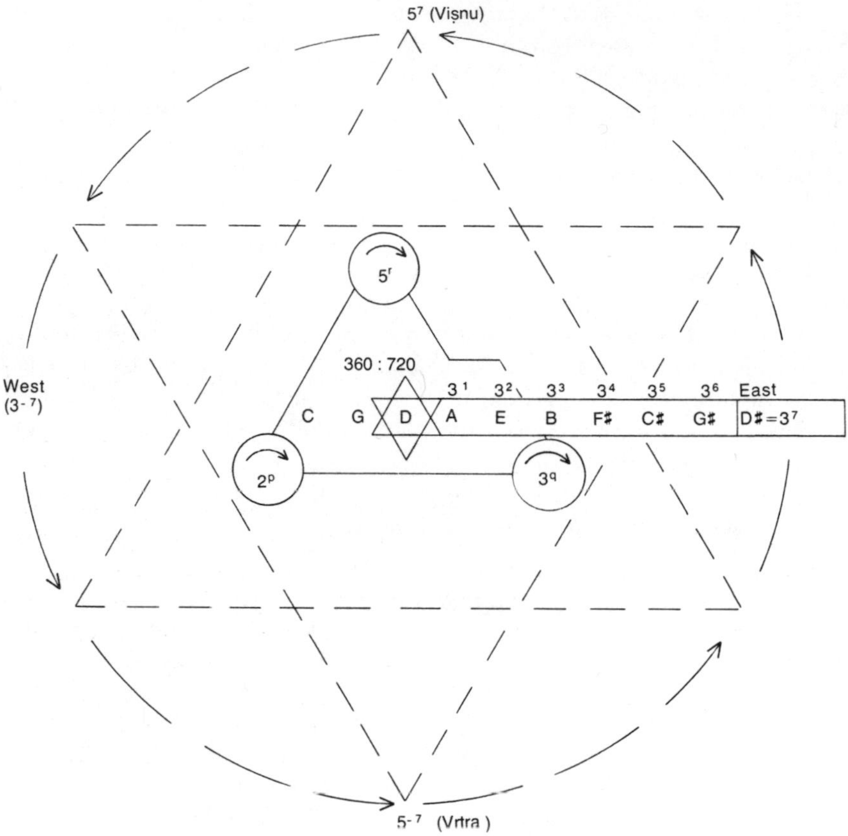

The Chariot of the Gods, "Fashioned Mentally"

7. The Chariot's majesties are fourteen others:
   seven sages lead it onward with their voices.
   Who will declare to us the ford Āpnāna,
   the path whereby they drink first draughts
   of Soma?

8. The fifteen lauds are in a thousand places:
   that is as vast as heaven and earth in measure.
   A thousand spots contain the mighty thousand.
   Vāc spreadeth forth as far as Prayer extendeth.

9. What sage hath learned the metres'
   application? Who hath gained Vāc,
   the spirit's aim and object?
   Which ministering priest is called eighth Hero?
   Who then hath tracked the two Bay Steeds of Indra?

> 10. Yoked to his chariot-pole there stood the
> Coursers: they only travel round earth's
> farthest limits.
>
> *(10.114)*

The "eighth hero," I suggest, is an allusion to seven *as exponent*. It is when the reciprocal yantras of the star-hexagon integrate $5^{\pm 7}$ with $3^{\pm 6}$ that we reach the Kalpa-Brahmā limits and the lessons they encode. The number 3^7 from D, which occurs only in the Brahmā set, is a kind of bonus we did not ask for and do not need, but we do need 7 as exponent to put "Viṣṇu" in the heavens as "Sun" where he can look down on his reciprocal in the deep. The abstract pebble notation for ratio theory makes every pebble an exponent for whatever set of ratios is involved.

We would seem to have reached a logical stopping place. We have a "wheel-less car, fashioned mentally, one-poled but turning every way" (10.135.3). It is also a "twelve-spoked car," "three-seated" if we care to view it that way, and "fashioned by singers with their lips." If some mathematical perfection must be sacrificed to achieve it, the loss is not great. In Hymn 1.191 the poet addresses "venomous" creatures, "biters of shoulder or of limb" (v. 7), with confidence that "the three-times-seven bright sparks of fire have swallowed up the poison's strength" (v. 12). What has actually been "swallowed up" is the slight discrepancy between the *real* number we need, the square root of 2, and its nearest *rational* approximations via the most primitive "Egyptian" arithmetic, or most severe limitation to the products of only three prime numbers. That hymn ends, so I would like to believe, with the singer's evaluation of the slight inaccuracies introduced by this sacrificial Ṛgvedic "tempering":

> Scorpion, thy venom is but weak.

But we are not finished. There are always more numbers. Daniélou points out that Brahmā, our "Immense Being," is not especially worshipped in Hinduism, and he quotes an interesting reason from the *Skanda Purāna* why he is not: "He was condemned by Śiva never to be worshiped by mortals because he lied, pretending he had reached the summit of the *linga* of light."[12] There is an even bigger number to be examined, one that will throw even more light on the *Ṛg Veda*.

THE DURATION OF THE UNIVERSE

Why the "duration of the universe" should be exactly 155,520,000,000,000 $= 2^{16} \times 3^5 \times 5^{10}$ "years" can probably be deduced from the yantra in Chart 18a. The limits of invariance under reciprocity are the eleven tones we began with in Chart 2—a "father and ten sons" in "Just tuning," now

CHART 18a

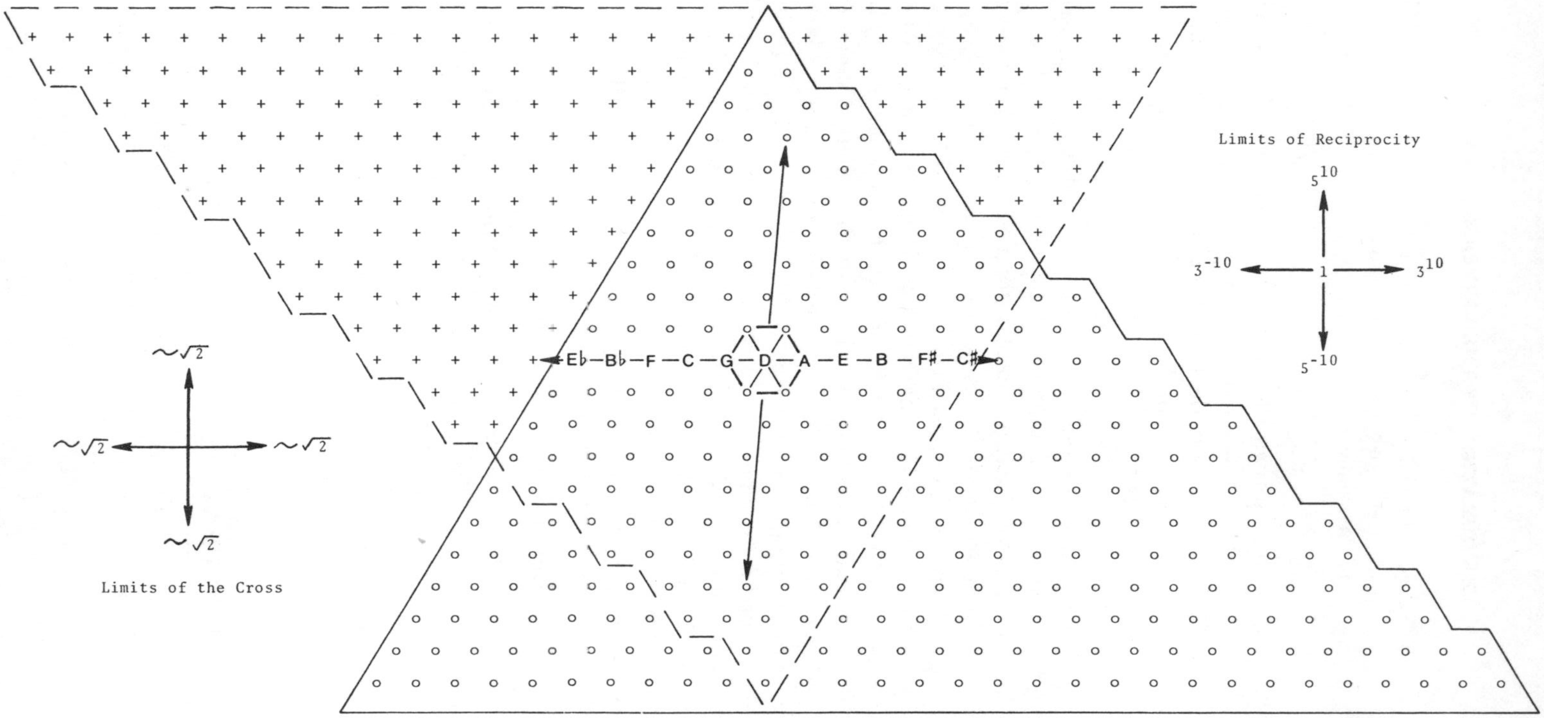

The "Duration of the Universe" or "life of Brahmā" = Puruṣa, "MAN"

Yantra for numbers $3^p5^q < 155{,}520{,}000{,}000{,}000 = 2^{16} \times 3^5 \times 5^{10}$ "years." The Hebrew Tetragrammaton YHWH = 10–5–6–5 may allude to this construction, for the "male" genetic elements in the index are exhausted by the formula $5^{10} \times 6^5$. (Count upward along the diagonal, /, ten places to 5^{10} = E♭, then to the right 5 places to 6^5 = D.)

"improved" as a "father and ten sons" in "Pythagorean tuning," that is, generated exclusively by the "divine male number 3." The limits of the yantra, however, taken together with its reciprocal, show that the "world-egg" has developed from our central D both right and left to the limit of $3^{\pm 10}$ and up and down to the limit of $5^{\pm 10}$. What more handsome culmination to Ṛgvedic "ten-ness" could we find?

The eleven invariances can be arranged as reciprocal diatonic scales in the basic Hindu-Greek mode within the octave double 384:768, familiar to Plato scholars as the *Timaeus* model of the "World-Soul."

ratios	384	432	486	512	576	648	729	768
falling	D	C	B♭	A	G	F	E♭	D
rising	D	E	F♯	G	A	B	C♯	D

The computation of the "duration" number is described in detail by Daniélou. (His source is *Mārkaṇḍeya Purāṇa* 46.22.) He begins with the four Yugas of Chart 14, whose sum is the Mahā Yuga, 4,320,000.

> One thousand cycles of the four Yugas make one day of Brahmā (*i.e.*, the Kalpa number); 360 such days make a year. Brahmā's life lasts for one hundred years. When this period is ended Brahmā himself ceases to exist. He and all the gods and sages and the whole universe are resolved into their constituent elements.[13]

4,320,000	=	sum of the four Yugas (Mahā Yuga)
× 1,000	=	
4,320,000,000	=	Kalpa ("one day of Brahmā")
× 360		
1,555,200,000,000	=	"one year of Brahmā"
× 100		
155,520,000,000,000	=	"life of Brahmā"

I cannot find this number in the *Ṛg Veda*, but several passages can be read as allusions to its yantra. All of the quotations cited earlier concerning the twenty-one elements in the base of the Kalpa-Brahmā yantras apply now to the twenty-one layers in the vertical dimensions of this yantra. A reference to Indra's lightning striking "obliquely" makes better sense if the twenty-one rows of this yantra are the "twenty-one mountains" it pierces. A reference to sixteen priests employed in sacrifices (Hymn 1.15.5) makes sense out of the sixteen elements here in the "transevering axis." A reference to twenty-one "layers of fuel" in the following hymn makes sense only in respect to this yantra and justifies our labelling it *Puruṣa*, "Embodied Spirit," or "Man."

1) A thousand heads hath Puruṣa, a thousand
eyes, a thousand feet.
On every side pervading earth he fills a
space ten fingers wide.

2) This Puruṣa is all that yet hath been and
all that is to be;
The Lord of Immortality which waxes
greater still by food.

11) When they divided Puruṣa how many
portions did they make?

14) Forth from his navel came mid-air; the
sky was fashioned from his head;
Earth from his feet, and from his ear the
regions. Thus they formed the worlds.

15) Seven fencing-sticks had he, thrice seven
layers of fuel were prepared,
When the Gods, offering sacrifice, bound,
as their victim, Puruṣa.

(R.V. 10.90)

There are three factors of 1,000 in our "Puruṣa" number (heads? eyes? feet?). Its yantra fills a space ten units (fingers?) in all directions, and its number includes a factor of 10^{10}. The "navel" is on D, and "heaven" and "earth" are symmetric opposites above and below. The seven "fencing-sticks" are the diatonic, heptatonic scales we have studied continuously, and "thrice-seven layers of fuel" are in plain view.

How much human blood, we wonder, has been spilt to make not only the Hindu culture but many others "incarnate" the lessons of this yantra? Any "point" within it is a "one" from which a new universe can emerge; every element in the "body" is sacred. Our search for invariance is complete.

Many readers will have encountered the still larger Hindu number of 311,040,000,000,000 years, exactly double my number in Chart 18a. Heinrich Zimmer calls the Puruṣa number a "Brahmā century," after which everything vanishes, "resolved into the divine, primeval Substance." This state of absolute silence prevails for another Brahmā century, "after which the entire cycle of 311,040,000,000,000 human years begins anew."[14] I have refrained from graphing that absolute silence.[15]

* * * * *

My book was intended to end here, with this study of Ṛgvedic numerology, but in the course of our dialogue de Nicolás and I caught many

CHART 18b

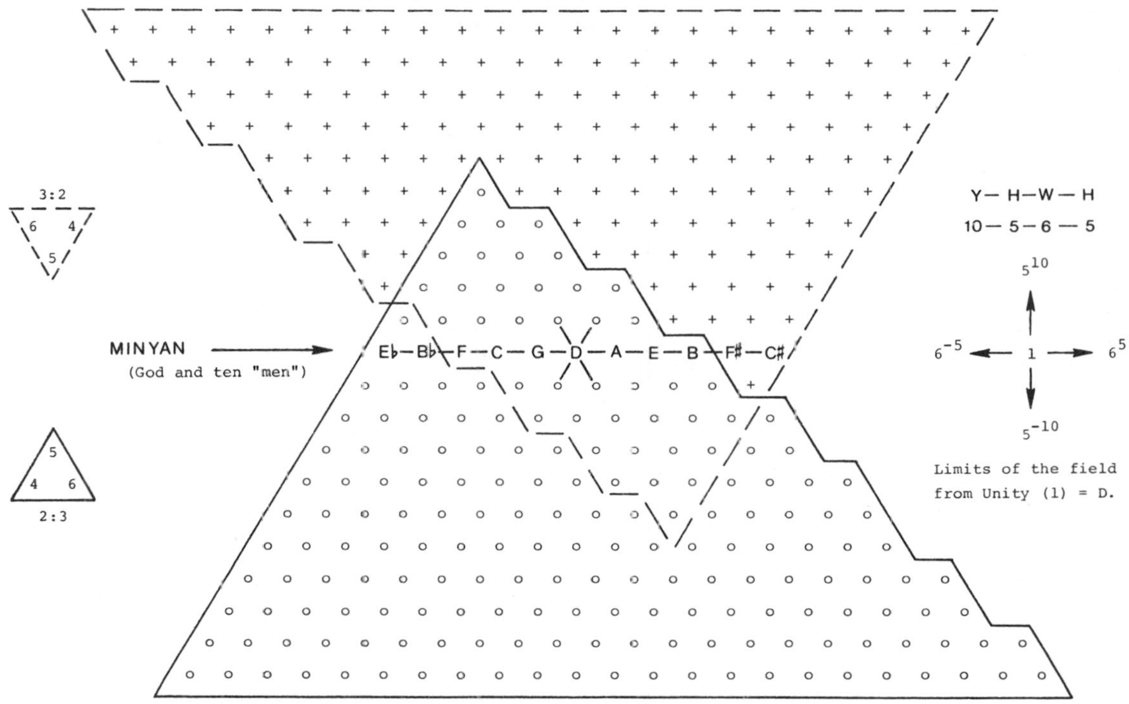

The Hebrew tetragrammaton YHWH, meaning 10–5–6–5, is interpreted here as $5^{10} \times 6^{5} = 75{,}937{,}500{,}000$. The vertical extension of the yantra, the "waters" above and below the "dry land" of the axis, is the same as in the Hindu Puruṣa yantra, while the "minyan" along the axis shows diatonic and chromatic limits free from any need for "sacrifice," due to its own self-limitation. Notice that the formula 10–5–6–5 alludes both to the shape of the yantra and to its limiting "index."

glimpses of possible wider meanings in the mythologies of other peoples. For instance, consider the Hebrew Tetragrammaton YHWH, the unpronounceable name of God whom Christians know as Jehovah. The numerical values of the Hebrew letters are 10–5–6–5, and if we read them as $5^{10} \times 6^5$ they carry us right to the "linch-pin" of our Puruṣa yantra in Chart 18a. (Starting from the unit, 1, in the lower-left-hand corner of the yantra, count upwards along the diagonal, /, ten places to 5^{10} in the axis, and then count to the right five places to 6^5, where the "index" locates the "linch-pin.") Could the tetragrammaton YHWH secretly allude to this once all-encompassing Hindu construction? Notice furthermore that there are seventy pairs of reciprocals within the Puruṣa limit, lying above and below the eleven tones of the central axis. Now Jacob descended into Egypt with seventy men, while Moses ascended a mountain to look into the promised land with another seventy men, and seventy men made identical Greek translations of their sacred Hebrew texts. These are interesting coincidences. We cannot leap to the conclusion that we have established any causal connections between the *Ṛg Veda* and the Old Testament, but our Vedic analysis is opening new possibilities which invite further exploration. (See Chart 18b.) Chapter 8 will review systematically the numerology which the scale and the calendar share in common, and the following three chapters will explore foundational images in Christian, Babylonian, Hebraic, and Egyptian religions and in Plato's political mythology, testing rigorously the power of our Vedic methodology.

FOOTNOTES

1. James Adam, *The Republic of Plato*, Vol. 2 (Cambridge: Cambridge University Press, 1902 and 1965), p. 303.
2. Giorgio de Santillana and Hertha von Dechend, *Hamlet's Mill* (Boston: Gambit, 1969), p. 162.
3. *Ibid.*
4. Ralph T. H. Griffith, *The Hymns of the Ṛg Veda* (Delhi: Motilal Banarsidass, 1973, New Revised Edition), p. 598.
5. There are "seven palaces in upper Eden," and seven others in "lower Eden," and "a soul dwelling in a particular 'palace' of the lower Eden contemplates the same divine aspect as a soul dwelling in the corresponding 'palace' in the upper Eden." Leo Schaya, *The Universal Meaning of the Kabbalah* (London: George Allen & Unwin Ltd., 1971), p. 76. This could be said of Chart 15.
6. E. A. Wallis Budge, *The Gods of the Egyptians* (London: Methuen & Company, 1904; New York: Dover Publications, Inc., 1969), p. 418.
7. "Plutarch's main interest is, as he does not try to conceal, an ethical one. He wishes to find in Plato some explanation of the evil in the world which will avoid making God responsible for it." A. E. Taylor, *A Commentary on Plato's*

Timaeus (Oxford: Clarendon Press, 1928, 1962), pp. 115–116. Taylor is summarizing Plutarch's attitude in *Generation of the Soul of the World in the 'Timaeus,'* without suspecting the nature of Plato's mathematical argument—purely "Ṛgvedic"—or the accuracy of Plutarch's concern. To the best of my knowledge, no Plato scholar takes Plutarch seriously when he describes, quite accurately, the "sexual" character of the numbers 3, 4, and 5, hence Platonism remains naïve both about Plato's musical mathematics and the ethical lessons he derived from it analogically.

8. Antonio T. de Nicolás, *Four-Dimensional Man: The Philosophical Methodology of the Ṛg Veda* (Bangalore: Dharmaram College Studies No. 6, 1971), p. 133.

9. Griffith, *op. cit.*, pp. 652–654.

10. Ivo Fišer, *Indian Erotics of the Oldest Period* (Praha: Universita Karlova, 1966), p. 91. See pp. 33–36 and 85–86 for extensive commentary on phallic worship.

11. *Ibid.*, p. 109.

12. Alain Daniélou, *Hindu Polytheism* (New York: Pantheon Books, 1964), p. 235.

13. *Ibid.*, p. 249.

14. Heinrich Zimmer, *Myths and Symbols in Indian Art and Civilization* (New York: Harper & Row, 1962), pp. 13–19.

15. H. P. Blavatsky, *The Secret Doctrine* (Adyar, Madras: The Theosophical Publishing House, 1938), Vol. 2, pp. 84–95, treats this larger number at some length. She calls it the Mahā Pralaya "Night," and allows that even it can be doubled "in the case of the lucky Jīvanmukta who reaches Nirvāna at an early period of a Manvantara" (p. 86). Madame Blavatsky considers that last doubling "long enough to be regarded as eternal, if not endless."

8

MUSIC AND THE CALENDAR

With our "mathematical harmonics" now established in the language of smallest integers, and according to the principle of symmetry, and pursued to fifteen-digit numerosity, we can turn our attention to the correlation of music with astronomy. Since there is at least as much confusion about the early history of astronomy as about the early history of music, we will bypass historical questions and examine for ourselves the correlations in numbers and in maṇḍala graphs between the simplest forms of the scale and the calendar which "tunes" Sun and Moon to each other. We shall restrict enquiry to the most obvious relations, that is, to correlations likely to have been noticed in antiquity when mathematical theory still "played the major role" in both astronomy and music theory.[1]

In the *Ṛg Veda* "the moon is that which shapes the years" (10.85.5). The month of thirty days and twelve-month schematic year of 360 are tied to the scale, as shown in Chapters 2, 3, and 4, by the diatonic scale in smallest integers in the 30:60 octave, and by its derivative chromatic scale in the 360:720 octave. It remains to be shown now that the musicians' commas which arise in these calendrical tunings are analogous to the calendrical discrepancies of lunar and solar cycles. Finally, by studying the tonal possibilities in the Hindu precessional period, we shall see how the yantra for the number 25,920 and its related maṇḍala encode a brilliant summary of the musical concerns of the *Ṛg Veda* and render superfluous—for practical purposes of "tonal cosmology"—the huge numbers we have been studying.

In Chart 19 we see the tonal correlatives for a) the calendrical deficiency in the 354-day period of twelve lunations, b) the calendrical excess in the $365\frac{1}{4}$ day solar year, and c) a related deficiency in the Hebrew 50-year Jubilee cycle. All three maṇḍalas focus attention on the locus of the square root of 2, opposite the reference *mean* on D, that is, on the point where perfectly coordinated cycles theoretically *begin*. It is always this "beginning" which is in doubt, and our poets decline to credit even God with knowing:

> The Gods are later than this world's production.
> Who knows then whence it first came into being?
>
> He, the first origin of this creation, whether
> he formed it all or did not form it,
> Whose eye controls this world in highest heaven,
> he verily knows it, or perhaps he knows not.
>
> *(10.129.6–7)*

In Chart 19a, a subset of the "calendrical" maṇḍala for 360:720 in Chart 8 (Just tuning), we see that the nearest approximations to $\sqrt{2}$ are a♭ ≠ g♯. They are separated from each other by the ratio 125:128 (=500:512 in Chart 8), the musician's *diesis*, worth about 41 *cents* or $3/10 \times 41 = 12.3$ degrees. Twelve "lunations" of 29.5 days total 354, and fall short of the solar year by $11\frac{1}{4}$ days, hence by roughly the same portion of a maṇḍala. Since these tones are separated by three pure thirds of ratio 4:5, each embracing four semitones (a♭–C, C–e, and e–g♯), they maintain a twelve-tone link with the twelve months of the year.

In Chart 19b we see that the pure fourths and fifths of Pythagorean tuning—a better approximation to equal-temperament—lead to the Pythagorean comma of ratio 531441:524288, the ratio by which A♭ and G♯ *overlap*, worth about 24 cents or $3/10 \times 24 = 7.2$ degrees. This "solar" tuning—generated by the "divine male number 3" and using only numbers 2^p3^q—thus has a maṇḍala excess roughly comparable to the excess of the $365\frac{1}{4}$-day solar year over the 360-day calendar base. Any tuning by the "pure" ratios of integers would lead to tone spirals rather than tone cycles, comparable to those in Just and Pythagorean tuning, and the infinite complexity of the heavens would allow us to find correlatives there for any "commas" which arose in our tuning system. We shall stop here, however, at those commas which have been most obvious.

In Chart 19c we see what would happen if the ratio 7:5 were employed as an approximation to $\sqrt{2}$ *in a tonal context.* Symmetry leads us to the double 35:70 so that multiplication by 7/5 and 5/7 both enjoy integer products; here we meet a comma of ratio 49:50, worth about 34 cents or $3/10 \times 34 = 10.2$ degrees.

CHART 19

Tonal and Calendrical "Commas"

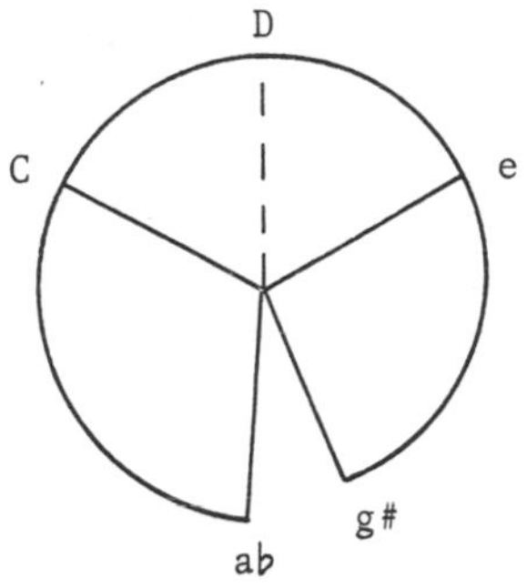

a) Deficiency in 354-day period of twelve lunations (each musical third symbolizing four semitione "months")

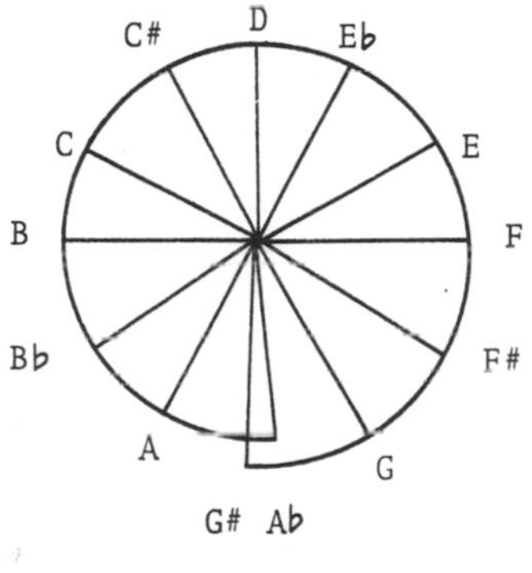

b) Excess of the solar year over the calendar base

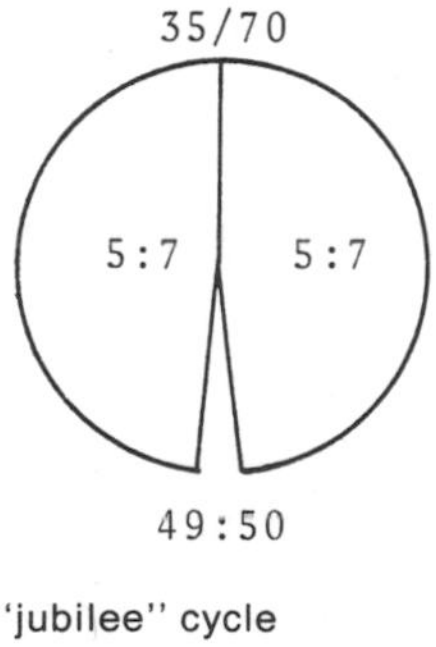

c) "Barren" 50th year in the "jubilee" cycle

1:2

35 : 49::50 : 70

5:7 5:7

Plato emphasized these ratios in the *Republic*, in ways to be discussed in Chapter 11. Leviticus decrees that after "seven weeks of years," or forty-nine years, the fiftieth year "shall be a jubilee" for the Hebrews, a year in which no crops are to be planted or reaped and all debts must be cancelled (25:8–13). It is tempting to try to read a possible allusion to these numbers in the *Ṛg Veda*.

In one of the hymns to the Maruts, "storm-gods," "healers," and "Indra's helpers," they are numbered forty-nine: "The mighty ones, the seven times seven, have singly given me hundred gifts" (5.53.17). A square with sides of 5 units would have a rational approximation to its diameter in $\sqrt{49} = 7$, and a square with sides of 7 units would have a rational approximation to its diameter in $\sqrt{100} = 10$, hence 5, 7, 10, 49, and 100 are locked together in this fundamental problem, as shown in Chart 20. "Replace the dislocated limb" might be read as a prayer to the Maruts to help us find our footing in "Indra's dance," as an extension of Chart 7 (8.20.26). Śiva, for instance, is shown dancing on one leg, as if he had surmounted the problem we are having here. These "men of Heaven," we are told, "were born together, of themselves," a possible allusion to their being the "square" of 7 (1.64.4). And since the ratio 7:5 is a wondrously simple approximation to $\sqrt{2}$ wherever it can be safely employed, we can understand why "forty-nine Maruts" were "no thieves, but helpers, splendid to behold" (5.52.12). These curious deities have "no eldest and no youngest in their band, no middlemost" (5.59.6). They "stretch their thighs apart, like women when the babe is born" (5.61.3). And "they make the world-halves tremble with their greatness" (7.58.1). But we are indulging poetic fancy; the Maruts remain as problematical as they have been for some millenia. Our study must be grounded on more complicated numerical problems.

The discovery of the "precession of the equinoxes"—a slow westward motion of the equinoctial points along the ecliptic—is generally credited to Hipparchus in 127 B.C. De Santillana and von Dechend suggest that Hipparchus' discovery was actually the rediscovery of a fact "known some thousand years previously."[2] Hipparchus, and later Ptolemy, underestimated the annual precession, which now is computed as 50.3757 seconds of arc per year. It is not clear when Indian astronomers finally came to accept 25,920 years as the total precessional period; that number is not in the *Ṛg Veda*, and it would be pointless to become embroiled here in the

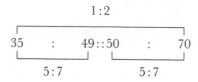

CHART 20

Approximations to the Tritone = $\sqrt{2}$

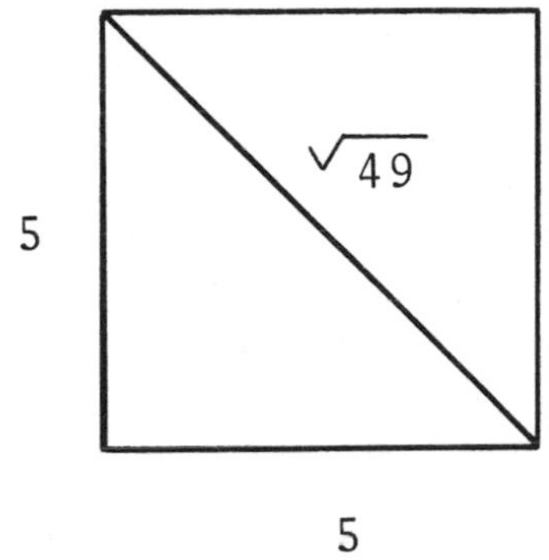

a) Platonic cabala for $\sqrt{2}$. The number 4,800 is "one hundred rational diameters of the five, lacking one for each," meaning 100 × (49 − 1 = 48). (*Republic* 546c. See *The Republic of Plato*, James Adam, ed., Vol II, pp. 285–286.)

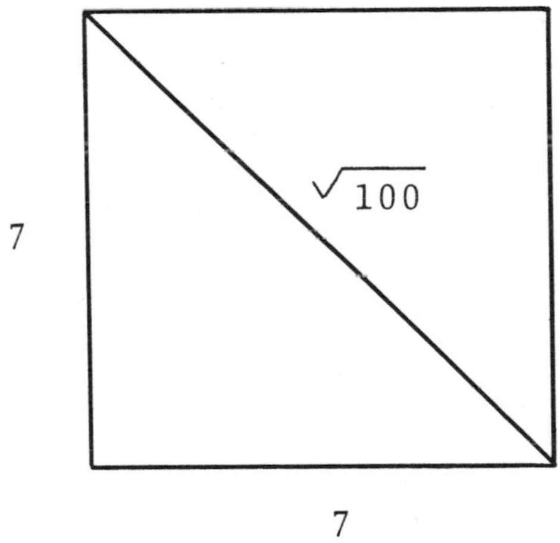

b) Suggested Ṛgvedic cabala for $\sqrt{2}$. "The mighty ones, the seven times seven, have singly given me hundred gifts" (5.52.17). Both examples concern the nearest rational approximation for an irrational diagonal.

argument as to whether the precession was actually known in Vedic India.[3] The important point is that the number 25,920 (Western writers usually say "about 26,000") leads us to a yantra and a related maṇḍala which summarize the musical lessons of the *Ṛg Veda* and hence unify music and astronomy in a quite surprising way. The number gives a musical theorist the kind of victory the Sumerian hero Gilgamesh once won over the giant

Humbaba ("Hugeness"); it establishes a complete tuning system, with perfect inverse symmetry, with numbers of only five digits.

In *Oriental Mythology* Joseph Campbell calculates the precessional cycle, which he believes may have been known to the ancient Babylonians, as follows: the slight annual lag of about 50 seconds amounts to 1 degree in 72 years ($50'' \times 72 = 3{,}600'' = 60' = 1°$) and in 2,160 years amounts to 30 degrees, which is one sign of the zodiac, hence in 25,920 years ($12 \times 2{,}160$) it would be 360 degrees, one complete cycle of the zodiac, often referred to as a "great year," or a "Platonic year," although the number has little to do with Plato.[4] Campbell observes that, although this number is attributed to the sixteenth c. A.D. (sic!), 25,920 divided by 60 (a standard Babylonian "unit") yields 432 (our "standard" *Ṛg Veda* digits), digits which occur in the 432,000 years which Berossus, the last priest of Marduk (c. 290 B.C.) gave as the sum of the reigns of the ten antediluvian kings. The precessional number is thus embedded, not far below the surface, in the normal "sexagesimal arithmetic" of Babylon; the Hindus habitually clear sexagesimal fractions by a least common denominator, but build their cosmology on the same base. The number 432,000 measures the diameter of Ptolemy's "great circles"; he takes 60 as the "unit" of the radius so that the diameter is "double" at 120, and he subdivides this diameter into 60 minutes of 60 seconds each ($120 \times 60^2 = 432{,}000$). Since he describes Greek tuning systems with sexagesimal fractions rather than with Hindu whole numbers, we overlook his direct linking of Eastern and Western musical thought. In short, we remain totally confused as to when and where and by whom our system was invented, and quite uncertain how much knowledge should be attributed to the ancient cultures which knew the numbers we are using. About all that we can say for certain about the precessional number 25,920 (which is astronomically slightly too large, according to modern measures) is that it fits beautifully into the cosmology of those people who never tried to break the original bonds between music, mathematics, and astronomy.

In Chart 21 we see our standard yantra form for integers $3^p5^q < 25{,}920$. Along the "transevering axis" we meet again our invariant seven tones—F C G D A E B—whose *scale order* beginning on D requires 432 as the first digit in either a rising or falling direction. The only reciprocity within the set of integers $2^p3^q5^r \leqq 25{,}920$ belongs to the elements in this axis and in the two neighboring rows, which are mutually reciprocal.[5] Taken by themselves, each of these rows consists of seven tones from the same sequence of perfect fourths or fifths; taken together, however, each row is displaced from its neighbor by the ratio of the syntonic comma, 80:81. The twenty-one tones can be viewed as a "transposition system" for the calendrical *Just* tunings we studied in Chapters 2, 3, and 4; taken by themselves

CHART 21

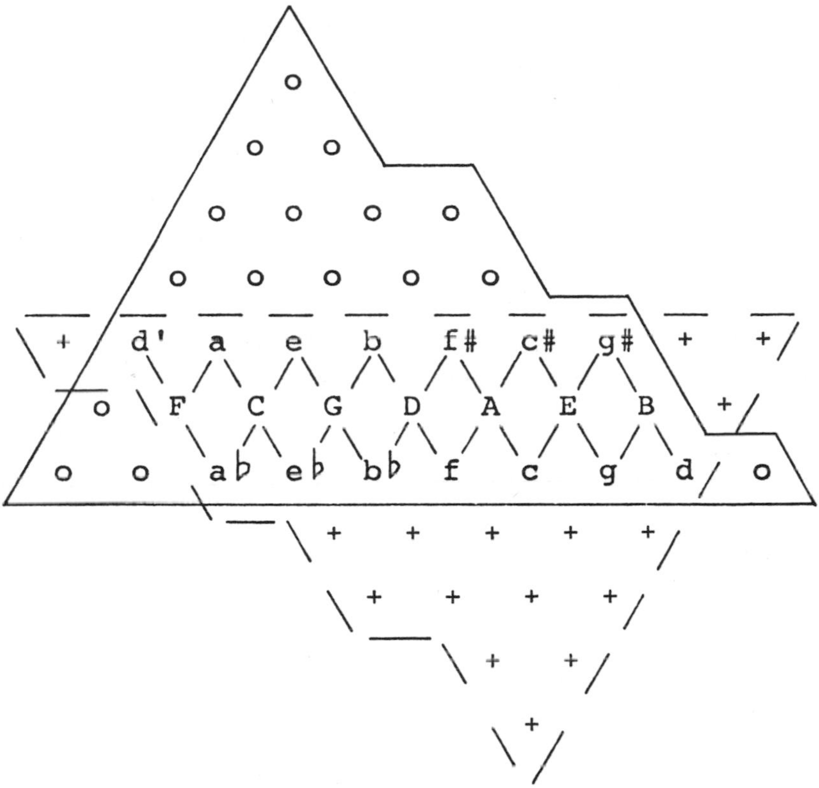

Yantra for the Precessional Cycle of 25,920 Years

Every triangular subset of contiguous elements has the genetic ratio 3:4:5 or 4:5:6. Only those elements common to reciprocal yantras can be paired symmetrically within the octave. The twenty-one elements given tone names constitute a transposition system for "Just tuning."

the seven "gods" along the axis can be viewed as a permutation system for the standard modal scales in *Pythagorean* tuning. The zig-zag lines added to the yantra indicate how Western musicians now group these tones into major ∧ and minor ∨ triads of ratios 4:5:6. In ancient times the same tones were grouped into "male" △ and "female" ▽ triads of 3:4:5.

In Chart 22 the twenty-one tones of the yantra which enjoy reciprocity are projected into a maṇḍala. The tone-maṇḍala is a visual projection of the aural problems which arise in Just tuning. The commas of ratio 80:81 which accompany the seven standard tones (F C G D A E B) must

CHART 22

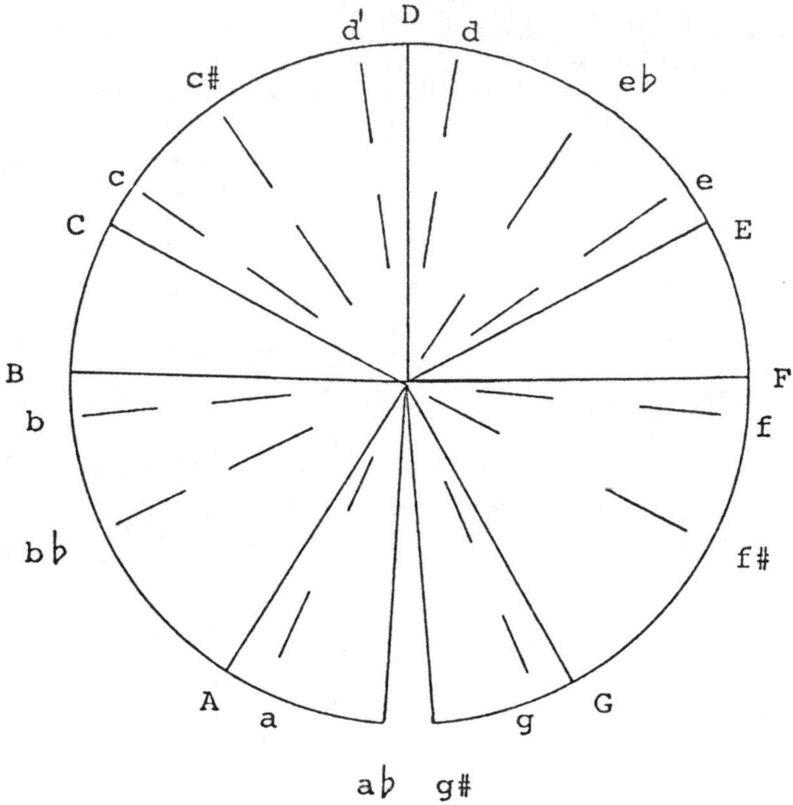

Maṇḍala for the Precessional Cycle of 25,920 Years

Diatońic semitones (such as D to e♭) have the ratio 15:16, chromatic semitones (such as e♭ to E) have the ratio 24:25, while two "Pythagorean semitones" at E to F and B to C have the ratio 243:256. The small discrepancies between capital and small letters are syntonic commas of ratio 80:81. The gap between a♭ and g# is a diaschisma of ratio 2025:2048. The maṇḍala makes visual the aural discrepancies which arise when transpositions are attempted in "Just tuning" and integrates tuning theory with the calendrical problems of astronomers.

somehow be glossed over by the performer's art. The "linch-pin" D which remains the center of symmetry in this tone-field takes all the "mathematical sins" of this world on himself in the poetic sense that the "tonic" *must* remain invariant. Indian music most often has a drone accompaniment to keep one tone fixed while all others move. The gap which remains between a♭ and g# at the bottom of the circle is now narrowed to a *diaschisma* worth about 20 cents or $3/10 \times 20 = 6$ degrees, wondrously close to the $5\frac{1}{4}$-day shortage between the ancient calendar base of 360 days and the true solar year of $365\frac{1}{4}$. (The ratio results from the reciprocal meanings of 45:32, which measures the distance of both a♭ and g♯ from D. $45^2 : (2 \times 32^2) =$ 2025:2048 is slightly smaller than the Pythagorean and syntonic commas.)

The maṇḍala accurately reflects the musicians' problems with a tuning theory based on the "perfect" relations of integers, and symbolizes the astronomers' problems in defining celestial cycles from the platform of an earth which "wobbles" on its axis while viewing planets which "wander" by about the distance of our commas from the plane of the ecliptic. Is it possible to be "unmoved" by such coincidences?

CHART 23

Tone Numbers for the Precessional Octave

Within the octave double ratio 1:2 = 12,960:25,920, only the following tones and numbers are symmetrically paired. Since the smaller number is to the lower limit as the larger limit is to the larger number and the products of means and extremes are equals, the product of any pair of "twins" or "friends" is 335,923,200 (*i.e.*, 12,960 × 25,920).

		(80:81 from D)
d and d′	13,122 and 25,600	
		243:256
e♭ and c♯	13,824 and 24,300	
		24:25
e and c	14,400 and 23,328	
		80:81
E and C	14,580 and 23,040	
		243:256
F and B	15,360 and 21,870	
		80:81
f and b	15,552 and 21,600	
		24:25
f♯ and b♭	16,200 and 20,736	
		15:16
G and A	17,280 and 19,440	
		80:81
g and a	17,496 and 19,200	
		24:25
g♯ and a♭	18,225 and 18,432	
		2025:2048 (*diaschisma*)

The tonal zodiac of Claudius Ptolemaeus (fl. A.D. 127–48) is of particular interest both on account of its antiquity and because it clearly implies the acceptance of temperament. As shown in Chart 24, Ptolemy correlated the twelve signs of the zodiac with the fifteen tones of the Greek Greater Perfect System in a way which makes the Ram stand both for the ground tone, *Proslambanomenos*, and for the limiting tone, *Nete hyperbolaion*, two octaves higher.[5] Each sign, then, rules the area of a wholetone, and the wholetone is thus graphed as 1/12th of the circumference of a two-octave

CHART 24

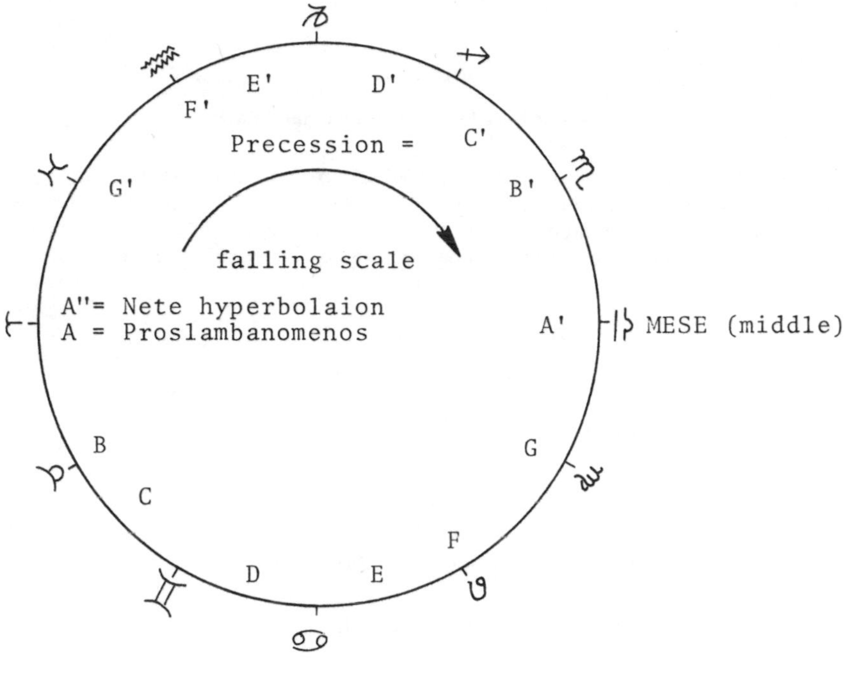

Ptolemy's Tonal Zodiac

The twelve signs of the zodiac are correlated with the thirteen tones of the two-octave Pythagorean scale on which was established the so-called Greater Perfect System of ancient Greece. The ground-tone of the monochord string, *Proslambanomenos*, and the highest tone, *Nete hyperbolaion*, two octaves above, coincide. I have substituted the usual modern letters for Ptolemy's Greek names for the tones. Since each wholetone is 1/12th the circumference of the circle, his zodiacal signs actually correlate with a wholetone scale in equal-temperament (after Ingemar Düring).

Standard tetrachords A G F E D C B

circle, meaning that it correlates with 30 degrees and with 2,400/12 = 200 cents, its value in modern equal-temperament, rather than with the standard Pythagorean value of 8:9 = 204 cents (a tempering of a little more than one degree). I have substituted the standard modern letter names for the Greek labels of the tones. I do not mean to imply that Ptolemy was advocating equal-temperament. I believe that he was merely using the standard Pythagorean scale as a convenient approximation. His accompanying discussion assigns the standard ratios of the tonal intervals (octave 1:2, fifth 2:3, etc.) to appropriate sections of the circumference. It is very likely that there were older precedents for Ptolemy's procedure for the ratio 8:9 is very nearly one sixth of an octave, and it was the most convenient musical interval to associate with six or twelve equal divisions of a maṇḍala. Compared to the theorists who followed him, Ptolemy is strangely modern. It is evident that he considered tuning to be cyclic.

If the *Ṛg Veda* today is a "text out of context," as de Nicolás writes, it is partly because Indian musicians at some ancient time abandoned tone-numbers—so I suggest—and took "all the sins" of the tone-world on themselves. In the fourth century B.C. Plato used similar tone-models for a political theory in which numbers symbolized citizens who, for the sake of the community, must never demand for themselves "exactly what is owed." In the same century Aristotle and Aristoxenus declared that the ear alone, not number, rules the universe of tone. Theirs was the century when Greek mathematicians conquered the irrational, but it was also the century Alexander conquered Babylon and India and released a flood of numerology into the West, a numerology which gave a renewed lease to the vigor of the old "Pythagorean" integer arithmetic, at least among philosophers. Within a few centuries there arose the Christian solution to the problem of sin: rational number was enthroned again, the irrational banned, and God took all the sins of the world *on himself*! The next chapter must try to show how Christian numerology is a variation on Ṛgvedic themes, that is, how the Christian West kept alive Ṛgvedic musical materials while the Hindu East progressed beyond them—until a new crisis in the sixteenth century caused the whole acoustical drama to be re-enacted, this time in the West.

FOOTNOTES

1. Otto Neugebauer, *The Exact Sciences in Antiquity*, 2nd ed. (New York: Dover Publications, Inc., 1969), p. 97.
2. Giorgio de Santillana and Hertha von Dechend, *Hamlet's Mill* (Boston: Gambit, 1969) p. 66.
3. Sukumar Ranjan Das, in "Scope and Development of Indian Astronomy," *Osiris* II, 1936, pp. 197–219, points out that only the Sun and Moon are

certainly mentioned in the *Ṛg Veda*, that possible allusions to planets are questionable but probable, and that the precession was unknown. He also points out that the names of the planets "are peculiar and of purely Indian origin," that the axis and daily rotation of the Earth were known, and that it was known also that "the sun never rises nor ever sets." He quotes Max Muller's opinion that the first astronomical treatise "has a practical object which is to convey such knowledge of the heavenly bodies as is necessary for fixing the days and hours of the Vedic sacrifices," and Diksit's opinion that the Vedas date from about 3000 B.C., and concludes that "Vedic astronomical facts are not strictly accurate," as the writers were more directly concerned with their religious rites. He also quotes Bentley's opinion that "there had been a great destruction of manuscripts" belonging to the period between the Vedas and the fifth century A.D. when Indian astronomy began to flower.

4. Joseph Campbell, *The Masks of God*: *Oriental Mythology* (New York: The Viking Press, 1962), pp. 129–130.
5. Ingemar Düring, "Ptolemaios Und Porphyrios Über Die Musik," from Book III of Ptolemy's *Elements of Harmony*, (*Goeteborgs Hoegskolas aarsskrift*, 1934:1), p. 125.

9

REVELATION: THE MEETING OF EAST AND WEST

The Book of Revelation concludes the Bible with apocalyptic visions of judgment on the enemies of God, victory for the faithful, a second resurrection and—at the end of time—the descent from the clouds of the sinless city of "New Jerusalem." Bible scholars have long been troubled that Revelation has "many mythological features which in themselves are neither Jewish nor Christian."[1] Some imagery has been traced to Persia, Babylon, Egypt, and Greece.[2] Numerological details intrude with no apparent sense: there are seven "angels with trumpets," twenty-four "elders with harps," and a choir of 144,000 male virgins rescued from death at the first resurrection to "sing a new song" around the heavenly throne, a song "no one could learn" but themselves. There is a divine mother with twelve stars in her crown who must hide in the wilderness for 1,260 days, chased by a beast whose number for those who know how to "reckon" it is 666, and who "exercises authority" for forty-two months ($= 42 \times 30 =$ 1,260 days). When New Jerusalem finally appears it proves to be a cube, with a "wall" of 144 units, a length, breadth, and height of 12,000, and a volume of 1,728,000,000,000. Bible scholars complain that "there is too much unassimilated second-hand material, and often it is employed pointlessly."[3] It has even been doubted that the author himself—ostensibly the same John who wrote the fourth Gospel—"really understood all that he wrote."[4]

The problematic mythology and numerology of Revelation appear to be a musical variation on a Ṛgvedic theme. Only the "intentionality" is new: God now absorbs all "the sins of the world" on himself. The true believer is rescued from the nightmare of inevitable discrepancies which ancient mathematics, astronomy, and music separately and together had shown to be integral to experience. When Hipparchus discovered the precession of the equinoxes in the third century B.C., Greek scientists knew how the sun offered man one certain measure of time for all the variegated cycles of the heavens, and Plato's faith in the basic perfection of all celestial cycles—his denial that the sun, moon, and planets *really* "wandered"—must have seemed justified. Five times in Revelation the number 1,260 is alluded to cabalistically; that number measures the greatest distance of the sun and the minimum distance of Mars in earth radii in the planetary system Ptolemy developed from Hipparchus' material.[5] That same number—$1{,}260 = 2^2 \times 3^2 \times 5 \times 7$—shows a musical theorist *how* the sacred number 7 *generates* along *with* the "human" 5 and the "divine" 3, thus it reveals a basic lesson in mathematical harmonics suppressed in the *Ṛg Veda* except by allusion, yet essential to the understanding of "Ten-ness" in all ancient cosmology.

In the third century B.C. the Buddhist king Ashoka established direct contact with Syria, Egypt, and Macedonia so that we cannot rule out the possibility of some direct link between Vedic and Christian cultures.[6] Plato, however, had already made extensive use of similar mathematical mythology in the *Republic*, *Timaeus*, *Critias*, and *Laws*, hence the most important source materials had been available in Greek, the language of the New Testament, for five centuries. Since the same mathematical harmonics appears to have been known in Babylon and Egypt much earlier, there is no reason to suppose that Old Testament Hebrews were ever unfamiliar with such material. Questions concerning the exact sources of Revelation imagery must still wait; for the present it is enough to know that the whole Middle Eastern cultural complex had been alive with this same mathematical-musical imagery for many centuries. Ptolemy, fortunately, documented Greek tuning theory in a way which allows the "new song" in Revelation to be studied against the contrapuntal context of its own age.

If Revelation was written within a century of the crucifixion, as is now supposed, then it was written in the century of Plutarch, Ptolemy, and Nicomachus on whose musical and mathematical clues we have based our entire study of the *Ṛg Veda*, and in the century of Philo Judaeus who applied a similar "Pythagorean" analysis to Old Testament numerology and mythology. In interpreting Revelation musically we are merely pursuing methods its own age took for granted. The risk is that musical imagination may be so atrophied that we exercise it incautiously. What follows is an experiment in thinking through the meaning of the "new song" which Revelation advertises and its numerology encodes. Irrespective of its Christian validity, our digression from the *Ṛg Veda* to the cabala of Revelation provides an important lesson in the function of 7, and establishes a contrasting perspective from which the archetypal nature of Hindu mathematical harmonics can be viewed in bolder relief.

NEW JERUSALEM: THE WALL OF 144 UNITS

We have developed "Ṛgvedic musicology" on a sexagesimal base tied to a diatonic scale *in smallest integers* in the 30:60 octave. The basic Hindu-Greek scale has thus been associated with a set of numbers whose *numerosity* increases as we ascend the scale; in modern terms, the numbers are ratios of frequency. To define that same scale as string-length ratios on the monochord requires in terms of smallest integers a set of Platonic "friends" in the 72:144 octave. Thus New Jerusalem's "wall" of 144 cubits is musically inseparable from the *Ṛg Veda*'s opposite limit of 30; anyone concerned with numerical sequences which *increase* and *decrease* symmetrically had to know both the basic Hindu set and its "Christian" transformation.

Christian	72		80		90		96		108		120		135		144
Hindu	60		54		48		45		40		36		32		30
ratios		9:10		8:9		15.16		8:9		9:10		8:9		15:16	
rising	D		e		f♯		G		A		b		c♯		D
falling	D		c		b♭		A		G		f		e♭		D

Both number sets apply to both rising and falling scales, numbers always functioning, as Nicomachus insisted, as both "multiples and submultiples" in ratio theory.

We may note in passing that thirty is the age when Jesus, like a Platonic "guardian," assumed his ministry, and it is the number of pieces of silver for which he was betrayed. The number 72 which begins our "translation" from Vedic to Christian numerology is the legendary number of translators of the Septuagint, that is, the number of scholars who produced identical Greek versions of the Hebrew Bible during the years 278–270 B.C.

Since both Hindu and Christian numerals point to the same basic scale pattern, and since the reciprocal meanings in *either* set require the "calendrical double" 360:720 for common denominators (see Chart 8), the numerology associated with both religions must be intimately related, whatever variations develop.

THE CHOIR OF 144,000

The original Greek text of Revelation makes clear that the choir of 144,000 redeemed from the earth at the first resurrection to "sing a new song before the throne" are *male celibates* who "have not defiled themselves with women" (Rev. 14:4).[7] The number 144,000 is mentioned three times in Revelation, and that this number has a musical meaning is emphasized in the author's reference to the "new song": "No one could learn that song except the hundred and forty-four thousand who had been redeemed from the earth" (14:3). I assume that the restriction to "male virgins" points to an awareness that Vedic-Platonic mathematical harmonics can be reduced to the study of how odd, hence *male*, numbers behave in the octave matrix. In the neo-Pythagorean milieu of the Revelation period, 1 and 2 were not considered numbers at all, but rather "the principles of number," hence 3 was indisputably the "first number." Since the only prime factors of 144,000 are 2, 3, and 5, we can study any song such male celibates could sing by constructing a yantra for the male numbers $3^p5^q < 144{,}000$ and noting its tonal possibilities. Noticc that the digits

CHART 25

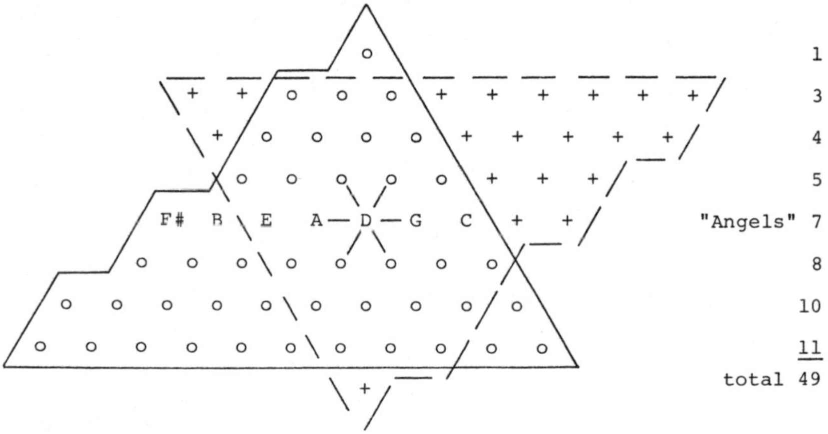

Yantra for the Celestial Choir of 144,000 "Male Virgins"

In mathematical harmonics 144,000 "male virgins" reduce to exactly forty-nine *odd* numbers 3^p5^q, of which seven belong to "Pythagorean tuning" along the central horizontal axis and forty-two belong to "Just tuning" only. Each row is displaced from the next by the ratio 4:5, thus "angels" differ from "men" bearing the same tone-names by the syntonic commas of ratio 80:81 which make "Just tuning" highly impracticable. Much of the imagery in Revelation can be read as an interpretation of this yantra within the larger context of the next one in Chart 26. (Right and left have been reversed in comparison with earlier yantras, for reasons discussed in the text.)

in the wall (144) are multiplied by 1,000 for the choir; a New Testament rationale for such recurrences can be found in the notion of "one day with God being as a thousand years" (2 Peter, 3:8).

The yantra for numbers $3^p5^q < 144{,}000$ has twenty-four elements in its *perimeter* to correlate with "twenty-four elders, clad in white garments" seated "*around* the throne" (4:4), "each holding a harp" and singing the "new song" (5:8–9). The horizontal axis contains seven tones in "Pythagorean tuning"— C G D A E B F♯—to correlate with "seven angels with trumpets" (8:2). If Christian angels correlate with Vedic gods and Platonic "citizens of the highest property class," then the replacement of F by F♯—programmed by the use of 144,000 as terminating number—is our clue to the "new song." (*i.e.*, $144{,}000 = 2^7 \times 3^2 \times 5^3$ contains only two factors of the "divine male number 3," hence the reference D on which reciprocal yantras hinge is only two places, two rising fifths or falling fourths, removed from the beginning of its row.) The "new song" can be interpreted either as a *transposition* of the basic seven-tone Vedic-Pythagorean set (F C G D A E B) or a *modulation* (change of mode) or *both*, according to one's preferred point of view. As a sequence of musical fifths, the standard Vedic "leader" on F is displaced by a "follower" on F♯, generated by a higher power of 3. (I have reversed right and left on the Revelation yantras to gain further correlations with the imagery, hence the *first* tone of the Christian set, C, is to the *right* of the others. This arrangement conforms to the pattern of Hebrew writing from right to left, and to later habits with the abacus and with our "place value notation" where numerical value increases to the left and decreases to the right.)[8]

Vedic set	F	C	G	D	A	E	B	
"Angels with trumpets"		C	G	D	A	E	B	F♯
"Divine" numbers 3^p	3^0	3^1	3^2	3^3	3^4	3^5	3^6	3^7

Since any set of seven consecutive musical fifths generated by the "divine male number 3" possesses the same seven modal permutations, the "new song" can be viewed from seven different positions. If the *middle* tone of the set is taken as beginning and end of a model octave, then our two sets can both be defined *in scale order* within the standard Vedic limits of 432:864, applicable to both rising and falling tonal progression (in modern terms, a change of key).

Tone numbers		432	486	512	576	648	729	768	864
Christian	rising	A	B	C	D	E	F♯	G	A
set	falling	A	G	F♯	E	D	C	B	A
Hindu	rising	D	E	F	G	A	B	C	D
set	falling	D	C	B	A	G	F	E	D

This is the Greek *Phrygian* mode, renamed *Dorian* in the eighth century by a Christian supposedly confused by the Greek names. Whatever his reasons, he assigned the prestigious Dorian label to the only internally symmetric scale so that Christianity's *modus primus* inherited both the standard Vedic numbers and the best name Greece could offer. It is more than merely amusing that 432 A.D. is the legendary beginning of Saint Patrick's Christian mission in Ireland; Irish monks were among the first propagators of the Gregorian chant and would have known these numbers well. They belong to Plato's Timaeus scale, the one scale whose numbers were never lost to history, and to Archytas' scale, though that has not been recognized.

There are forty-nine elements in our yantra for 144,000, of which forty-two generated by the "human number 5" belong to sequences of musical fifths displaced from that of the angels by successive commas of ratio 80:81. (Study Chart 11b if this is not clear. Remember that successive rows in the yantras are 14 cents closer together than they would be in equal-temperament, and the elements in each row are 2 cents further apart. In my yantras the distance between two numbers with the same tone names is one row, 14 cents, plus four places = 2 × 4 = 8 cents, the total of 22 cents being the syntonic comma.) If these commas symbolize musically the "sins of the world," then they must be "purged" before all 144,000 can sing their "new song" in tune with the angels. Revelation describes a series of purging plagues visited on mankind before the second resurrection; the "beast" is allowed to "exercise authority" for forty-two months (13:5), sparing neither God nor his dwelling, and the holy city itself "is given over to the nations" to trample for forty-two months (11:2). Curiously, the next fifteen centuries of the Christian era, in which *only* "Pythagorean tuning" was employed, carried out exactly the purging described in Revelation, for chromaticism was vigorously restrained so that no commas could arise. Hindu readiness to accept as valid many points of view or many "tunings" was transformed into a Christian acceptance of just one, harmonized to the precise limits of perfection, whether among concepts or among tones and numbers. "Just tuning" remains an *unrealizable ideal.* For us, Plato is the clearest link in the transition between the Hindu gradual evolution of the gods as numbers increase and the Christian yearning for an end to all disorder *in the process.* Plato generated the "world-soul" in *Timaeus* solely from numbers 2^p3^q, Pythagorean tuning, with barely a hint there of any flaw in creation, and this section of the dialogue (in Cicero's Latin translation) remained almost the only Plato material known to Christians, who venerated it almost as much as the Bible, for the next thousand years. Not until the new "chordal" harmonies of the sixteenth century made the "human number 5" (in the triad ratios of 4:5:6) a factor to be reckoned with did "Just tuning" and its plague of commas intrude again on Western thought. (For instance, most textbooks and dictionary entries on acoustics generate the major scale via three triads of ratio 4:5:6 on C:e:G, F:a:C, and G:b:D and then show that they can be given integer names in the octave 24:48:

C	D	e	F	G	a	b	C
24	27	30	32	36	40	45	48

Notice that such a scale *lacks* the *similar tetrachords* which were standard in ancient Greek tunings, the whole tones of 8:9 and 9:10 = 24:27:30 being reversed to 9:10 and 8:9 at 36:40:45. This is virtually the only numerical sequence most music students ever study; it is quite appropriate for the sixteenth century but totally useless in introducing anyone to ancient Pythagorean habits.)

Much of the imagery of Revelation can be read, I believe, as a commentary on the yantra for 144,000 and on the "cube" of New Jerusalem (in the next yantra) which encloses it.

NEW JERUSALEM AS THE CUBE OF 12,000

In interpreting the "holy city" as a cube *number* I am assuming that the author, like Plato, is following a precedent set by Pythagoras, at least for the Greek world, and that he is calling attention to a "point-line-plane-solid" progression by which he arrives at the number which teaches the lesson he cares about via a process which disguises a form of "ten-ness."

1	(point)	12	"tribes," "gates"
2	(line)	12,000	side (= 12 × 1000)
3	(plane)	144,000,000	area = $12{,}000^2$
4	(solid)	1,728,000,000,000	volume = $12{,}000^3$
10			

I propose to study intensively the data encoded in the yantra for $12{,}000^3$. Chart 26 shows all numbers $3^p5^q < 12{,}000^3$, with the yantra for the 144,000 singers centered on the same reference tone, D, and with the Vedic dragon and his celestial counterpart indicated by the vertical arrows extending seven rows above and below the central axis. A possible justification for interpreting the thirteen elements in the axis, a sequence of fifths or fourths in "Pythagorean tuning," as a "leader and twelve disciples" ($3^0 = 1$ to 3^{12}) or a "savior and twelve angels" (Rev. 21:12) can be found in the curious appendix to the fourth Gospel, also by John. There the resurrected Jesus shows himself to *seven* disciples who had gone fishing during the night. "Just as day was breaking, Jesus stood on the beach" (John 21:4). Notice the "leader = F" on the axis of the horizon, with the "mountain of God" or "sky" on *his* right and the "sea" beneath on *his* left. *Seven* "disciples" = C G D A E B F♯, corresponding to "angels with trumpets,"

CHART 26

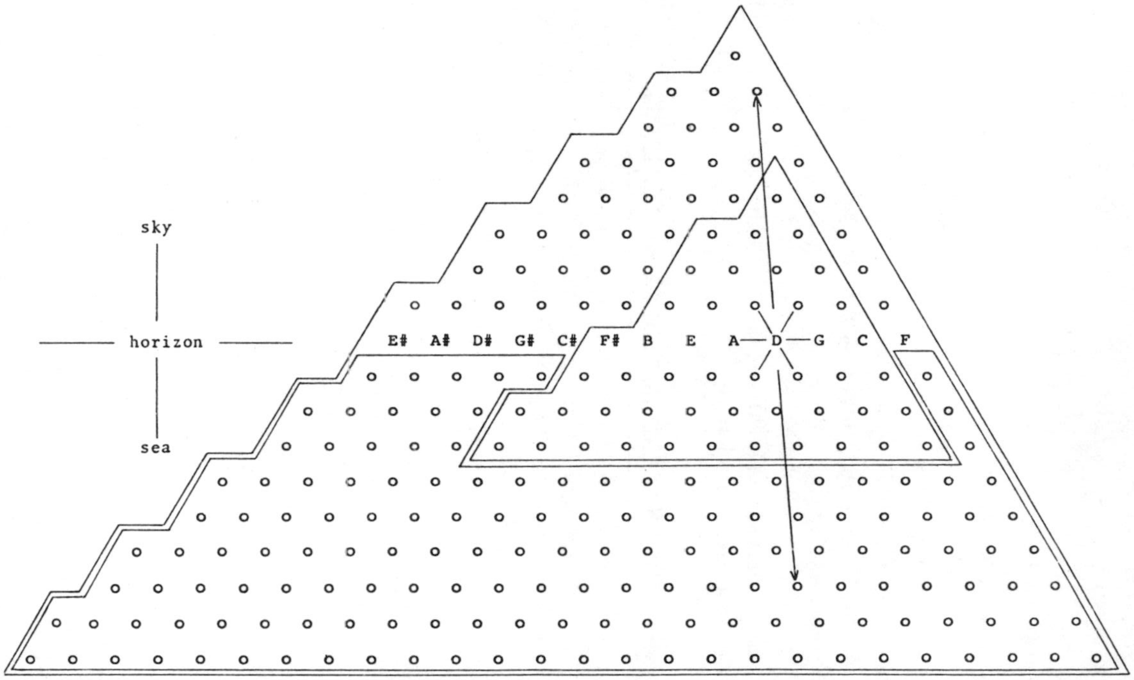

"New Jerusalem" as $12{,}000^3 = 1{,}728{,}000{,}000{,}000$

The "male choir" of 144,000 is shown inside the "city" limits. Vertical arrows point to the position of the dragon Vṛtra and his celestial opposite in the Kalpa-Brahma yantras of Chart 15 (closest approximations to $\sqrt{2}$ = A♭ = G♯). The central axis contains the "leader" and twelve "angels" or "disciples." Double lines enclose 153 "fish." (Commentary in text.)

thus face him from *within* the yantra of the 144,000 "redeemed from the earth" at the *first* resurrection (Rev. 20:5–6).

> Jesus said to them, "Children, have you any fish?" They answered him, "No." He said to them, "Cast your net on the right side of the boat, and you will find some." So they cast it, and now they were not able to haul it in, for the quantity of fish.
>
> *(John 21:5–6)*

Simon Peter sprang into the sea when he "heard it was the Lord," while the other disciples, "not far from land," dragged the net which later proved to contain "large fish, a hundred and fifty-three of them" (21:7–11). There are exactly 153 elements in the Vedic sea of our yantra for $12{,}000^3$, enclosed by double lines in Chart 26, which do not share in the *first* resurrection.

The thirteen elements in the central axis correspond to the thirteen tones in Pythagorean tuning in the maṇḍala of Chart 19b, with the "Pythagorean comma" of ratio 531441:524288 now falling between F and E#. (*i.e.*, The middle element in this thirteen is B, corresponding to the D of Chart 19b.) If we aim at a twelve-tone tuning then we must gloss over this comma as Aristoxenus and Ptolemy do; not until the irrational was made a friend and accepted as *number*, as Plato, Theaetetus, and Eudoxus accepted it, could musicians find a rationale (in equal-temperament) for improving on Pythagorean tuning as an approximation to a *cyclic* tuning. Unfortunately, the nascent Christian culture inherited, via Nicomachus, only the *earlier* Pythagorean attitudes. It is the twelfth "follower" = 3^{12} which "betrays" the leader with a "kiss," a near-miss of about 24 cents. If he is expelled from the set then we are left with a "false" musical fifth between A# and F rising and a "false" fourth between A# and F falling so that the "leader = 3^0 = 1 = F" must absorb this musical "sin" on himself. It is not surprising that during the theological controversies of the first few centuries the Church felt compelled to impose a creed which insisted upon the absolute unity of a tripartite deity, Father Son, and Holy Ghost; our mathematical notation $3^0 = 1$ conveys this meaning with no offense to common sense and no appeal to mysticism.

Before the seven angels in the first group (C G D A E B F#) sound their trumpets, seven "seals" must be opened by the "Lamb"; when the third seal (*i.e.*, at D) is opened, "behold, a black horse, and its rider had a balance in his hand" (6:5). This corresponds to the "linch-pin" D in Vedic imagery, on which reciprocal yantras rotate. When the fifth seal (*i.e.*, at E) is opened, the author can see "under the altar the souls of those who had been slain for the word of God" (6:9). Notice in Chart 25 that only from the first and fifth tones, C and E, is there a path *downward* to the reciprocal (+) "under the altar" via the "superparticular" ratios (in this case 4:5

and 5:6 respectively) to which *musical generation* was restricted. When the sixth seal (at B) is opened, "behold, there was a great earthquake . . . and every mountain and island was removed from its place." Now the sixth tone (B) among our seven angels is the symmetric center of the set of thirteen elements in its row; from its perspective, the leader on F and his "betrayer" on E♯ are *reciprocal* meanings of 3^6. This is a dramatically different perspective on the elements we are observing. Furthermore, the only path *downward* to "Satan" = Vṛtra is along the diagonal (↘) beginning on B (*i.e.*, from *within* the yantra for 144,000, in Chart 26, assuming that we want to traverse a straight exponential path). "When the Lamb opened the seventh seal [*i.e.*, at F♯], there was silence in heaven for about half an hour" (8:1). That seems an appropriate amount of time to contemplate the "new song" which emerges as a result of F♯ replacing F in the historically normative Vedic and Greek sets.

Now come seven purifying tribulations for the world as the seven angels each in turn blow their trumpets. Curiously, after the first angel blew, "a third of the earth was burnt up," after the second, "a third of the living creatures of the sea died," after the third, "a third of the waters became wormwood," after the fourth, "a third of the sun was struck, and a third of the moon, and a third of the stars," and after the sixth, "a third of mankind was killed" (8:7–9:15). The author is emphasizing diminution by one third. On a monochord string sounding F, diminution each time by one third would produce the C G D A E B F♯ associated here with the seven angels (*i.e.*, a succession of musical fifths of ratio 3:2).

When the fifth angel (E) blew his trumpet, "I saw a star fallen from heaven to earth, and he was given the key of the shaft of the bottomless pit" (9:2). Notice in Chart 25 that the path downward from E leads to the reciprocal (+) lying outside the yantra, as mentioned earlier when "seals" were discussed.

When the seventh angel (F♯) blew his trumpet, "then God's temple in heaven was opened, and the ark of his covenant was seen within his temple; and there were flashes of lightning, loud noises, peals of thunder, an earthquake, and heavy hail" (11:19), appropriate acoustical and lighting effects for a "modulation" of the importance of this one. The diagonal upwards from F♯ (↗) leads to the angel who will defeat Satan.

THAT ANCIENT SERPENT, WHO IS CALLED THE DEVIL AND SATAN

"A great red dragon, with seven heads and ten horns," engages in a war in heaven against "Michael and his angels" (12:7). "And the great dragon was thrown down, that ancient serpent, who is called the Devil and Satan, the deceiver of the whole world" (12:9). Later the author saw a "beast rising out of the sea, with ten horns and seven heads," "allowed to make war on the saints and to conquer them" for forty-two months (*i.e.*, the number of elements in the 144,000 yantra which require purging, 13:1–7). "Then I saw another beast which rose out of the earth; it had two horns like a lamb and it spoke like a dragon. It exercises all the authority of the first beast in its presence, . . . It works great signs, even making fire come down from heaven" (13:11–13). "Let him who has understanding reckon the number of the beast, for it is a human number, its number is six hundred and sixty six" (13:18).

Drawing on our study of Vṛtra and his reciprocal in the Kalpa-Brahmā yantras of Chart 15, we note that in this tone-field there is one pair of elements which approximates very closely the equal-tempered A♭ = G♯ = $\sqrt{2}$, indicated by the vertical arrows in Chart 26. In the Kalpa yantra of Chart 15, Vṛtra (below) actually had the numerical value of $3^6 = 729 \times 2^{11}$, but the cyclic identity of $1 = 2^n$ includes $2^9 = 512$ so that in effect 729 means 729:512, a so-called "tritone," equivalent to three consecutive wholetones of 9:8. This is the *diabolus in musica* of the medieval music theorist, to be shunned wherever possible in a melodic progression. Now this tritone arises on the "land" between any pair of tones in the horizontal axis which are six places removed from each other. For instance, as noted earlier, the F and E♯ are both removed from the central B by the ratio 729:512; the Pythagorean comma is generated by 729^2. The "Devil" in our yantra of Chart 26 has 3^6 as a factor in his genetic make-up while his heavenly protagonist has no powers of 3 at all. (His angel opposite *within* the tone-set bounded by $12{,}000^3$ is 5^{16}, sixteen places above the generating unit in the lower-right-hand corner.) We have identified *diabolus in musica* as 3^6, and we have identified Satan (who is a more accurately tuned tritone from an equal-temperament point of view) as having the same genetic element. Is it too much to suggest that 666, the number of the beast "for those who know how to reckon" is simply 3^6? Western theology has not even begun to ponder the riddles it inherited from the slow accumulation of adequate mathematical symbols. Again and again ancient cosmologists resorted to very thinly disguised rational meanings which have become totally meaningless as we have progressively forgotten earlier modes of thinking.

If Satan, the dragon, the ancient serpent, is 3^6 in its various contexts, then "seven heads" seems an appropriate reference to the seven tones embraced by the chromatic tritone or the seven traversed by consecutive fifths or fourths. As for his ten horns, the Devil *below* can only show his power when multiplied ($2^{23} \times 3^6$) into a ten-digit number. (See Chapter seven.) A "land" dragon requires far smaller numerosity.

An angel "coming down from heaven" bound Satan and threw him into a pit for 1,000 years. "After that he must be loosed for a little while"

(20:1–3). The 144,000 male virgins who sing the new song likewise enjoy resurrection 1,000 years earlier than anyone else. Notice that multiplication of 144,000 by 1,000 would produce 144,000,000, the *area* (*i.e.*, square) of New Jerusalem; its yantra would extend only six rows below the axis (one row for each factor of 10), hence Satan, seven rows below the axis, would still be "bound." Multiplication now by 12,000 into the city's cube would free Satan but expose him to the purging plagues of the mythology.

In Book IX of the *Republic* Plato "measures" the "beastly" nature of a tyrant by the number $9^3 = 729$ ($= 3^6$) so that the number and the metaphor were linked in Greek long before John wrote Revelation (*Republic* 587–588).

THE DIVINE MOTHER

> And a great portent appeared in heaven, a woman clothed with the sun, with the moon under her feet, and on her head a crown of twelve stars; she was with child and she cried out in her pangs of birth, in anguish for delivery. And another portent appeared in heaven; behold a great red dragon . . . And the dragon stood before the woman who was about to bear a child when she brought it forth; she brought forth a male child, one who is to rule all the nations with a rod of iron, but her child was caught up to God and to his throne, and the woman fled into the wilderness, where she has a place prepared by God, in which to be nourished for *one thousand two hundred and sixty* days.
>
> *(Rev. 12:1–6)*

The number 1,260 is so important to the author of Revelation that he mentions it twice and alludes to it three more times. At 11:3 a voice from heaven grants "witnesses power to prophesy for one thousand two hundred and sixty days." At 11:2 the nations "trample over the holy city for forty-two months," or $42 \times 30 = 1{,}260$ days. At 13:5 the beast "was allowed to exercise authority for forty-two months," or 1,260 days. At 12:14 the Divine Mother is given the "wings of the great eagle that she might fly from the serpent into the wilderness, to the place where she is to be nourished for a time, and times, and half a time." (*i.e.*, A "time" = a year of 360 days, plus "times" meaning 2×360, plus "half a time" of 180, a total of 1,260 days.) So great an emphasis on 1,260 prompts the question: For what demonstration in mathematical harmonics does a limit of 1,260 ensure that it is presented in *smallest possible integers*? Now $1{,}260 = 2^2 \times 3^2 \times 5 \times 7$ has four prime divisors and a complicated set of possibilities, which will be shown later. The question as to why it is so important can be answered, I believe, rather simply: The octave 630:1260 is the *smallest module* within which the "lunar" *diesis* of 125:128 (Chart 19a) can be related to the "Jubilee" comma of ratio 49:50 (Chart 19c). The *diesis* is generated by 5^3 (*i.e.*, by the discrepancy between three pure thirds and the octave); the "jubilee" comma is generated by the reciprocal meanings of 7:5. Both intervals enclose the square root of 2 which would "open the womb" exactly in the middle of the octave, and the imagery of a woman "in

CHART 27

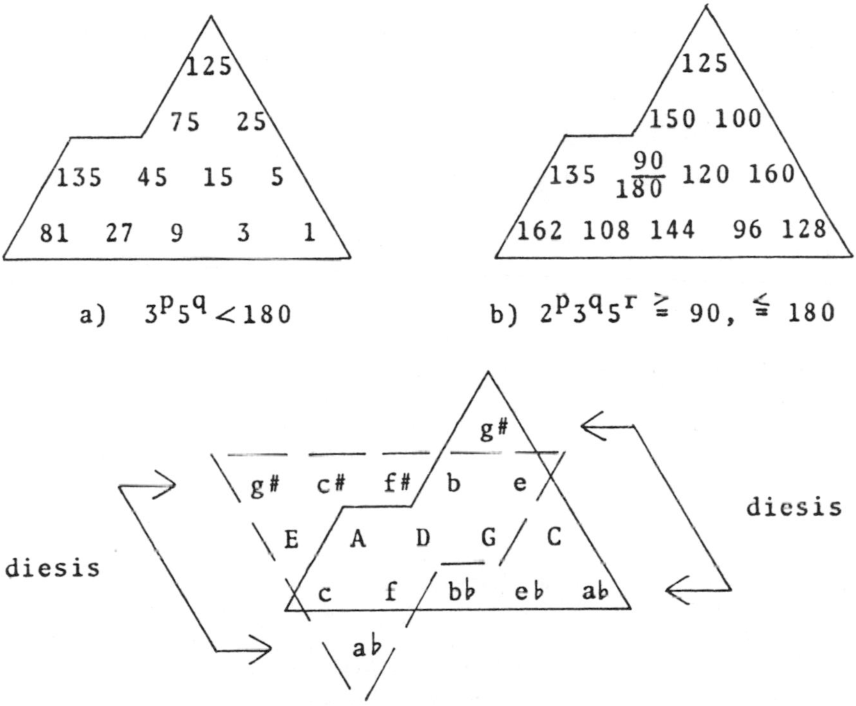

a) $3^p5^q < 180$ b) $2^p3^q5^r \geq 90, \leq 180$

c) "Wings of the Great Eagle"

Analysis of the Gestation Number 1260 = $2^2 \times 3^2 \times 5 \times 7$

Argument: Since products generated by 7 are of interest only in relation to those generated previously by 2, 3, and 5, the first step is to divide the limiting number (least common denominator), 1260/7 = 180, to find the limit generated by smaller primes. Twelve odd "male" products of 3 and 5 less than 180 in yantra a) are projected into one octave by appropriate multiplication by 2^n in yantra b), and they correlate with the reciprocal tonal yantras of c). Only within 90:180 does the diesis lie in the middle of the octave in smallest integers, 125:128, where it lies in the "calendrical octave" 360:720, symbolizing the lunar shortage with the solar cycle. Thus no limit smaller than 7 × 180 = 1260 permits the "jubilee comma" of ratio 49:50 which arises from reciprocals of ratio 7:5 to be correlated directly with the diesis arising from progression through three pure musical thirds of ratio 4:5.

anguish for delivery" focuses attention once again on that problematic area where the "Savior" must be born for as long as we persist in using *rational* numbers to *approximate* more precise values requiring the irrational expressions among *real* numbers. Factors of $2^2 \times 3^2 \times 5 = 180$ ensure that we are working with a subset of the calendrical set, 360:720 in Chart 8. For greater simplicity the table in Chart 28 below contains only the subset limited by 180 plus *one pair* of elements generated by 7:5 reciprocally from the reference tone, an operation which requires multiplication by 7 (*i.e.*, $7 \times 180 = 1260$). Notice especially the relations which emerge

CHART 28

Alternate basic sets		3 x 60 = 180 720/4 = 180	x 7 = 1260	falling scale	rising scale	
72	60	180	1260	D	D	
80	54	162	1134	c	e	
(81)		160	1120	C	E	
	(50)	150	1050	b	f	
90	48	144	1008	b♭	f#	
96	45	135	945	A	G	
			900			← (x 5/7)
		128	896	a♭	g#	
	(42)	(126)	882			← (x 7/5)
		125	875	g#	a♭	
108	40	120	840	G	A	
120	36	108	756	f	b	
		100	700	e	c	
135	32	96	672	e♭	c#	
144	30	90	630	D	D	

"Disjunction" (45–40); diesis (128–125); 49:50 "Jubilee" (900–882); "Passover" = diesis (896–875)

Gestation of the Savior

The only module within which the diesis of 125:128 shows itself *in smallest integers* in the middle of the octave (as it arises in the "calendrical" module 360:720) is that of 90:180. Multiplication by 7 is required to compare its approximations to the square root of 2 with those reached symmetrically by 7:5, the "jubilee comma" of 49:50.

Interpretation is necessarily speculative, but the demonstration proves that multiplication by 7—which would force "gigantism" on number theory—does not improve on approximations to the square root 2 available to musicians from the very beginning. (See $7/5 \times 30 = 42$ in the smallest set $= 1.4$ and the even better $180/128 = 45/32 = 1.40625$ in the third column.) The victory then belongs to $128 = 896$ in the sets shown here, and to $128 \times 4 = 512$ in the calendrical set. But 128 and 512 are powers of 2, hence merely octave replications of 1, the unit which generates all the others. Thus God = Unity has metaphorically taken the "sins of the world" on himself. (Further discussion in text.) When the diesis is multiplied by 7 it shows the Passover period divided into 14 and 7 by "God's own son," the prime number 7 in the ratio 7:5, the holiest of all ancient numbers. (Appearing as 42, 126, and 882 in the various sets above.)

within the so-called "interval of disjunction" between A and G (*i.e.*, the disjunction between two similar tetrachords in standard heptatonic scales).

The demonstration develops from the basic scale, projected into the 90:180 octave to let the diesis of 125:128 (= 500:512 in the calendrical double of Chart 8) show itself *in smallest integers*. Further multiplication by 7 is essential to showing *in smallest integers* how those approximations to the square root of 2 compare with the "jubilee" comma of ratio 49:50 generated by the sacred number 7. And what do we learn? That reciprocal ratios of 7:5 do produce a better approximation *on one side* (compare 882/630 with 875/630) but a *worse* one on the other (compare 896/630 = 45/32 with 900/630 = 10/7). The better approximation (multiplication by 7/5) can be reached from any number divisible by 5; the worse one (multiplication by 10/7) forces a useless "gigantism" on a cosmology wedded to "Ten-ness" and to reciprocity, for we must multiply the basic sets by 7 merely to get an integer product which proves useless. I suggest that this demonstration must have been known to the people who invented the Babylonian sexagesimal system in the third or fourth millenium B.C. when they developed a system in which only the primes 2, 3, and 5 generate "regular" numbers. The absence of 7 as a prime factor—while remaining the most sacred number—in Hindu cosmological periods suggests that the poets of the *Ṛg Veda* were not unfamiliar with this lesson. The three-unit interval in the diesis of 125:128 becomes a twenty-one-unit interval in this cabala, and our poets sing of "*thrice-seven* mystic things contained *within*" Agni, Savior, "Knowing the Law, the *seven* strong floods from heaven" (R.V. 1.72.6–9). Among the Hebrews, the seven-day "Passover" is preceded by fourteen days of preparation (Exodus 12:18 and Leviticus 23:5–8); the holy number 7, in the ratio 7:5, subdivides the inflated diesis into periods of 14 and 7. It is interesting that the number 128/90 = 896/630 = 512/360 = 45/32 = a♭ in our calendrical maṇḍala and again in our precessional maṇḍala (Chart 22) represents the unit, 1 (times some relevant power of 2), from which all of our calendrical tunings are generated. Thus it correlates with the *beginning* of the Hebrew year and symbolizes the *beginning* of all new counting cycles where "one" takes "all the sins of the world" on himself so that astronomers, musicians, and calculators of all kinds gain a fresh beginning with the intractable data of experience.

Further meanings in this "gestation" cabala will no doubt emerge as Old Testament numbers are studied within the intentionality of their time. The author of Revelation notes that the Divine Child "was caught up to God and to his throne" (12:5), and in the context of his time 7 was referred to as a "virgin" which "does not generate," so that it seems reasonable to speculate that attention is directed to 7/5 × 630 = 882 as a "celibate son." (The sin of approximation extends from 875 to 896.) In the basic, irreducible number set, $7/5 \times 30 = 42$ ($= 882/21$), and in the geneology of Matthew, Christ is forty-second in descent from Abraham.

> So all the generations from Abraham to David were fourteen generations, and from David to the deportation to Babylon fourteen generations, and from the deportation to Babylon to the Christ fourteen generations.
>
> *(1:17)*

Christ as 42 means $42/30 = 7/5$ when bluntly reduced to the "intentionality" of the ancient world, "savior" from the abominable difficulties of wrestling with the square root of 2. (Chapter 10 will amplify this interpretation.)

CONCLUSION

Justification for a musical interpretation of otherwise baffling Revelation imagery rests wholly upon the ability to produce enough circumstantial evidence—correlations with then current musical and mathematical methodology—to seem credible. Here we need claim no more than that musical methods seem promising. Without our Ṛgvedic insights, little progress would have been possible. The Gospel of John opens with a thought which could have come right out of the *Ṛg Veda*: "In the beginning was the Word." The Apocalypse of the same writer may prove, in a way nothing else can, the unity of East and West. If the cabala for 1,260 were not present in Revelation we should have had to invent something similar to show how the prime number 7 generates musically with the other primes smaller than 10, for the *Ṛg Veda* presupposes a rigorous methodology in using numbers, which function by analogy as archetypes of more general truth. In the language of modern mathematics, this cabala, which shows how nearly the products of 2, 3, 5, and 7 converge, is a lesson in "Diophantine analysis," that is, in "simultaneous Diophantine approximation of the generators." It is a lesson which had to be learned, I suggest, *before* cosmology could be founded on a mathematical base, at least before the Hindu and Babylonian cosmology we know was formulated. It is a lesson which no Hindu poet, so I believe from other examples, would ever have made public. The John of Revelation, however, assumed that TIME was about to end.

In the Tantric Buddhism which emerged from the same Hindu roots as Revelation, there is a myth of Kuṇḍalinī, translated "Serpent Power" and meaning "coiled," which may preserve the same cabala for 1,260. Kuṇḍalinī "normally lies asleep in the form of a serpent in three and half coils surrounding a penis in a mythical center or circle (*cakra*) or nerve plexus at the base of the spinal column."[9,10] There is precedent for supposing that a "coil" may represent the unit of a year of 360 "days," in which case $3\frac{1}{2}$ would allude secretly to 1,260.

There is a stronger link to world mythology, however, in Revelation's reference to the destruction of Babylon, possibly the direct source of Jewish numerology. "The sound of harpers and minstrels, of flute players and trumpeters, shall be heard in thee no more; . . . and the sound of the millstone shall be heard in thee no more" (18:22). So said "a mighty angel" who "took up a stone like a great millstone and threw it into the sea" (18:21). The myth of the millstone thrown into the sea has been tracked all over the globe by de Santillana and von Dechend in *Hamlet's Mill.* At the lower-right-hand corner of the yantra for $12{,}000^3$ is the unit, 1, from which all other numbers are generated as multiples, in the octave cycles whose rotations correlate with the "whirling" of Vṛtra. According to Revelation, at $12{,}000^3$ that dynamism stops: New Jerusalem "has no need of sun or moon . . . for the glory of God is its light" (21:23). The "millstone" must turn, like a Buddhist prayer wheel, until it reaches our goal, that is, until it arrives at numbers which solve all problems by least common denominators. The wheel turns in our maṇḍala-yantras, I suggest, until the "transcevering axis" reaches the limit of interest, and the New Jerusalem axis stops at 3^{12} where musicians learn all that higher powers of the divine number 3 can teach them. (After that *convergence* at the Pythagorean comma, *divergence* begins, by an additional comma for each subsequent cycle.) Having reached the necessary limit—a limit defining the essential materials of musical mathematics in a unique way, setting Christian numerology apart from that of other religions—the author casts his "Babylonian millstone" in the sea and purges, mythically, all the "corruption" which occurred in the process of generating "angels" systematically in a context which included man.

I do not want to invent a new myth, or to abuse the musical truth of Revelation with a careless imagination. Some splendor we have never quite understood seems encoded there, and I must hope that others will review that book anew, illumined by its possible musicality. The author certainly never intended his Gospel to be read as a fishing yarn, nor his Revelation as a music lesson. He was illustrating an inspired vision according to the most conventional method of his time—by musical analogy. His numbers encode only a small part of his meaning, and his *rationality* is partly at the mercy of our skill in recovering his *intentionality* in the use of numbers. That he was a mystic is evident. That he was at all deficient in the pure, cold light of reason is unproven. That he inspired some of the sorriest unreason in history was a development which owed at least as much to the musical and mathematical ignorance of later readers as to their theological fervor.

POSTSCRIPT ON THE CREATION OF THE WORLD

After my manuscript was finished, I learned of a Chassidic interpretation of *Genesis* 1:2 which allows the creation myth to be tied musically to the numerology of Revelation. Such an interpretation would have served as a foundation both for this chapter and for the following one. The Chassidic tradition is suffused with "Pythagorean" feeling, evident for example in the esoteric *Tanya* written by Rabbi Schneur Zalman of Liadi between 1776 and 1796.[11] In his essay "Mystical Concepts in Chassidism," accompanying the new English translation of the *Tanya*, Rabbi Jacob Immanuel Schochet expresses what may prove to be one of the most priceless clues to Old Testament numerology. The clue is apparently traceable to the sixteenth century cabalist Isaac Luria, and to commentaries by Rabbi Chayim Vital, 1543–1620.

It must be remembered throughout the following interpretation that Biblical cabalists in general were somewhat at odds with the mainstream of Biblical interpretation, both Jewish and Christian. The cabalists took Genesis to be a pure allegory that encoded a hidden doctrine, one of the highest spirituality and deepest philosophical understanding. The fragment of the *Tanya* I use here is taken from a context that is philosophical and allegorical. But a separate musical treatise on the *Tanya* would be required to make clear why I believe its numerology has a musical basis. It is with apologies both to the Chassidim and to my readers that the following bare outline is inserted here.

Rabbi Schochet's number is hidden in the second sentence of Genesis in the phrase translated in the Revised Standard Version as follows: "and the Spirit of God was moving over the face of the waters." The word for "moving"—or "hovering" as the Hebrew translators prefer to render it—is מרחפת.[12] Rabbi Schochet separates the first and last letters (prefix and suffix) from the root רחפ, which in Hebrew alphabetical notation gives the number 288 (*i.e.*, ר is 200, פ is 80, and ח is 8).[13] Now 288 and 120 are alternate "indices" for the double-octave form of our basic diatonic scale (see Charts 1 and 28, where the single octaves have an index of 144 or 60), and the double-octave was standard in the Greek world during the centuries when the Bible was being edited into its present form. According to Rabbi Schochet, the "Divine Light"—"the spirit of G-d"—divides into "288 sparks" at this moment of creation. The 288 sparks are the "first egression towards substantiality" into *Atzilut*, "the World of Emanation," which stands closest to the Divine Unity itself.[14] A further argument for the derivation of 288 from the Hebrew word for "hovered" is that this most unusual word occurs only twice in the Bible, the second time being linked to the eagle, whom we have already identified with the same scale in Revelation (Chart 27c).[15]

As an eagle that stirreth up her nest,
Hovereth over her young,
Spreadeth abroad her wings, taketh them,
Beareth them on her pinions

The Lord alone did lead him [Israel]
And there was no strange god with Him.

(Deuteronomy 32: 11–12)

Now in David's temple the number of Levites

who were trained in singing to the Lord, all who were skilful, was two hundred and eighty-eight. And they cast lots for their duties, small and great, teacher and pupil alike"

(I Chronicles, 25: 7–8).

In Solomon's temple there were 120 "priests who were trumpeters" (2 Chron. 5:12). Here are the reciprocal arithmetic forms of our basic double-octave scale with their alternate terminal indices of 288 and 120.

reciprocal tones		length/frequency reciprocals	
D	D	30	288
e	c	32	270
f♯	b♭	36	240
G	A	40	216
A	G	45	192
b	f	48	180
c♯	e♭	54	160
D	D	60	144
e	c	64	135
f♯	b♭	72	120
G	A	80	108
A	G	90	96
b	f	96	90
c♯	e♭	108	80
D	D	120	72

The Greek world founded its musical system on a two-octave "Pythagorean" diatonic scale; we have formed its Hebrew correlative in a Just tuning which integrates the "human male number 5" with the "divine male number 3" and the "female number 2."

From this beginning it is easy to sympathize with Philo's rigorously Pythagorean interpretation of the six "days" of creation (Genesis 1:3–31).[16] Our scale is generated by the ratios of the first six numbers; God rests on the seventh, which "does not generate" here. The *material* is identical with that in the Babylonian sexagesimal system to be studied in Chapter 10, but the Hebrews are wedded to a decimal mode of thought. Philo directs attention to the "perfection" of 4, to the appropriateness of the sun and moon being formed on the fourth "day"; we have already seen that "solar" models are generated by the ratios 2:3 and 3:4. Birds of the air and fish of the sea are generated on the fifth "day"; 5 generates all that is above or below the central transevering axis of our yantras. The world is completed on the sixth day, 6 being a *perfect* number in the sense that it is the sum of all of its divisors (1 + 2 + 3 = 6); our musical meanings are far richer, for all of the ratios generated from the first six integers are employed in the "great and small" sense of multiple and submultiple hinted at in the quotation from I Chronicles and insisted on by Plato.

Genesis 2 offers a contrasting account to Genesis 1 of the generation of man and the derivation of woman. Instead of man and woman being generated with the other animals on the sixth day as in Genesis 1, Adam in Genesis 2 is generated later (as a hermaphrodite, as some commentators point out), and Eve is generated still later from him. Now the Hebrew letters for Adam are ADM, corresponding to the numbers 1–4–40. If we read these cabalistically as 1,440 we have a correlation with our 288 "sparks" and "singers" and our 120 "trumpeters."[17] The two-octave scale whose alternate indices are 288 and 120 has a chromatic index of 1,440, that is, when the *reciprocal* diatonic scales shown above are coalesced, both the string-length index and the frequency index are 1,440, double the number 720 which served the same function for a *single* octave in Chart 8. Genesis then would seem to be built on the materials discussed in Chapters 1 through 5, with the Hebrews, however, using a double octave, like the Greeks. (See Chart 28a, opposite.)

The interpretation just outlined should help us penetrate further into the numerological meanings hidden in the Old Testament. The interpretation of Adam, for example, both as "earth" and "primordial man" and the monochord number 1,440 leads to the very beautiful musical notion of Adam as containing the "seeds" of all future generations. We read in the *Zohar*:

> When God showed Adam all future generations, he saw them in the Garden of Eden in the form which they were destined to assume in this world.[18]

Is this an extravagance of mystical imagination or an interpretation of the mathematical allegory suggested above? The literature of Chabad Chassidism possesses very possibly many clues to the original Biblical meanings, clues which can be properly utilized only by those expert in both Hebrew and Greek as well as in the materials of mathematical harmonics.

CHART 28a
Monochord Harmonization of Bible and Kabbala

Adam = ADM = 1,440
(smallest "index" for a two-octave chromatic system)

diatonic origin			chromatic length	super-set frequency
30	72	360	D	D
32		384	c#	eb
	80	400	c	e
36		432	b	f
	90	450	bb	f#
40	96	480	A	G
45	108	540	G	A
48		576	f#	bb
	120	600	f	b
54		648	e	c
	135	675	eb	c#
60	144	720	D′	D′
64		768	c#′	eb′
	160	800	c′	e′
72		864	b′	f′
	180	900	bb′	f#′
80	192	960	A′	G′
90	216	1,080	G′	A′
96		1,152	f#′	bb′
	240	1,200	f′	b′
108		1,296	e′	c′
	270	1,350	eb′	c#′
120	288	1,440	D″	D″

120 "priests with trumpets" = 288 "sparks" or "professional musicians" = 1,440 (ADM = Adam).

FOOTNOTES

1. *Peake's Commentary on the Bible* (London: Thomas Nelson and Sons, Ltd., 1962), Mathew Black, gen. ed. This standard commentary is based on the Revised Standard Version of the Bible. The chapter on Revelation by N. Turner draws heavily on the work of other scholars and aims to present as balanced a view as modern scholarship is able to provide. See paragraph 921a on page 1051.
2. *Ibid.*, par. 920a, 921b, 921f, and 925h.
3. *Ibid.*, par. 913e.
4. *Ibid.*, par. 913f.

5. Bernard R. Goldstein, "The Arabic Version of Ptolemy's Planetary Hypotheses," *Transactions of the American Philosophical Society* (Philadelphia: The American Philosophical Society, 1967), p. 11.
6. Joseph Campbell, *The Masks of God: Oriental Mythology* (New York: Viking Press, 1962), pp. 290–296.
7. *Peake's Commentary on the Bible*, par. 922b.
8. George Sarton believes that *abacus*, derived from the Greek *abax*, may have a more remote Semitic origin, from *abaq*, meaning *dust* in Hebrew (*A History of Science*, Vol. 1: New York: W. W. Norton & Co. Inc., 1970, page 209). Sarton points out that the use of pebbles is much older than that of the abacus (first mentioned by Aristotle), and that "the abacus is a machine devised for a better utilization of the pebbles (or their equivalent)." (*Ibid.*, p. 206). While Herodotus describes the Greeks as "moving the hand from left to right" both when writing and calculating, not much more is known about its use in antiquity.
9. W. Norman Brown, "Mythology of India," *Mythologies of the Ancient World*, Samuel Noah Kramer, ed., (New York: Anchor Books, 1961), p. 313.
10. Arthur Avalon, *The Serpent Power*, (New York: Dover Publications, Inc., 1974; republication of first edition, London: Luzac & Co., 1919), p. 118.
11. Schneur Zalman, *Likutei Amarim-Tanya*, (London: The Soncino Press, 1973), Bi-lingual Edition.
12. *Pentateuch and Haftorahs*, J. H. Hertz, ed., (London: The Soncino Press, 5735–1975), 2nd ed., p. 2.
13. *Tanya*, pp. 868 and 870. I am indebted to Siegmund Levarie for his additional explanations of the Hebrew.
14. *Ibid.*, pp. 853–854.
15. *Pentateuch and Haftorahs*, pp. 2 and 898.
16. Nahum N. Glatzer, *The Essential Philo* (New York: Schocken Books, Inc., 1971), pp. 1–41.
17. Leo Schaya, *The Universal Meaning of the Kabbalah*, trans. by Nancy Pearson (London: George Allen & Unwin, Ltd, 1971), pp. 107–110 and 127, discusses the name Adam = ADM. Carlos Suares, in *The Cipher of Genesis* (New York: Bantam Books, 1970), expounds at length on these letter-numbers.
18. *Zohar*, Harry Sperling and Maurice Simon, trans., Vol. I, (London: Soncino Press, 1933), p. 300.

10

BABYLON AND SUMER

We have traced New Testament numerology to India; now let us look for Hindu links to the Old Testament. The search will take us through Babylon and Sumer and into the fourth millenium B.C. Only in the last century, with the discovery and decipherment of several long-forgotten languages, have we begun to understand that Sumerian cosmology, theology, ethics, and system of education,

> permeated to a greater or lesser extent the thoughts and writings of all the peoples of the ancient Near East. . . . And the Hebrews of Palestine, the land where the books of the Bible were composed, redacted, and edited, were no exception.[1]

The home of the Sumerian Gods in the fabled land of Dilmun—a paradise to the East, where the sun rose—has been tentatively identified by Samuel Noah Kramer as the Harappan culture of pre-Vedic India.[2] I am concerned here with those common mathematical elements in Sumerian, Hebrew, and Hindu mythology which support Kramer's hypothesis, fully aware that only a small part of the Sumerian record has yet been translated, and that only part of this has been understood. Since virtually none of the arithmetical elements in any of these three mythologies makes any sense today, we have something to gain and nothing at all to lose by searching for rational meanings common to Hebrew, Sumerian, and Hindu mythology.

The Sumerians were of unknown origin, with a language reminiscent of Ural-Altaic languages, but among them the original Semitic stock of southern Mesopotamia were "probably predominant." The Sumerians ruled that land from about 3500 B.C. to 2000 B.C. when hegemony then passed to the Semitic Babylonians who took over their culture "lock, stock, and barrel."[3] That culture included cuneiform writing, a sexagesimal system of mathematics, a pantheon of deities, a considerable literature, and a fund of musical instruments important enough to be classed among the divine principles. It is startling to learn from Otto Neugebauer that the art of calculation in third millenium Babylon—before the time of Abraham—was already comparable in many aspects with the mathematics "of the early Renaissance," thirty-odd centuries later.[4] Computation was made easy by the possession of tables (of which we have many copies) of "reciprocals, multiplications, squares and square roots, cubes and cube roots, the sums of squares and cubes, . . . exponential functions, coefficients giving numbers for practical computation, . . . and numerous metrological calculations giving areas of rectangles, circles," etc.[5] The Pythagorean theorem was known in Babylon "more than a thousand years before Pythagoras."[6] The foundations were laid for the discovery of the irrationality of $\sqrt{2}$ "exactly in the same arithmetical form in which it was obviously re-discovered so much later by the Greeks."[7] Traditional stories of discoveries made by Thales or Pythagoras must be discarded as "totally unhistorical"; much of what we have thought was Pythagorean must now be credited to Babylon.[8]

It is not yet clear how much of the Greek theory of music was also Babylonian. Scholars are still in the process of reconstructing the Babylonian tonal system, with similarities to that of Greece.[9] The advanced state of both stringed and wind instruments in Babylon, Sumer, and ancient Egypt convinces organologists that Pythagorean string-length ratios were "recognized by both Mesopotamia and Egypt at least two millenia before the dawn of Greek civilization."[10] Babylonian mathematicians treated the ratio of two numbers—like the length ratio of two harp strings— as an entity, "a very important step in the development of algebra."[11] They were completely at home with reciprocals in the whole field of rational numbers, and their logarithmic tables "exhibit a knowledge of the basic laws of operating with exponents," essential to our musical yantras.[12] Just how much the Babylonians owed to the preceding Sumerians may never be known. What is certain is that by the beginning of the second millenium B.C. Semitic mathematicians were such virtuosi in computation that all of the mathematics in this present study would have been child's play for them. The Hebrew Bible is thus the product of a Semitic culture which had mastered the fundamentals of music and mathematics a thousand years and more before its oldest pages were written. The stage was set for mathematical allegory on a grander scale than the relatively late Christian civilization has ever realized. Western misconceptions concerning the ultimate origins of many of its most cherished beliefs could not have been more mistaken, as has been proven since about 1890 when the tide of translation began to flow in full strength, bringing Biblical parallels to light all over the ancient world. Not until the 1930's, however, did the full strength of Babylonian computation begin to be appreciated, and historians of mathematics are still pondering its influence on the Greeks. Let us examine first the sexagesimal system itself, probably the most convenient language for acoustical arithmetic the world ever knew until the system of logarithmic cents was introduced late in the nineteenth century. The first sixty integers counted as deities in their own right. It is the numerical values associated with the greatest gods which permit the mythology to be examined mathematically. And it is the Babylonian development of "the greatest system of musical ritual in any ancient religion" which makes it imperative that we not neglect possible associations between her mathematics, her music, and her religion.[13]

SEXAGESIMAL ARITHMETIC

The most significant feature of our modern Hindu-Arabic decimal system is that it allows ten digits (0 to 9) an infinite number of interpretations according to their *positions* to the right or left of the "decimal point." The Babylonian-Sumerian sexagesimal system possessed this "place value" positional characteristic for the digits from 1 to 60. No "place marker" like our zero was employed, hence the operator had to remember mentally or determine from the context whether a number meant simple units or was to be interpreted as multiplied by $60^{\pm j}$. Reciprocals were studied assiduously; the standard multiplication tables, of which many copies exist, concern thirty pairs of reciprocals, shown in Chart 29 together with their tonal implications and their associated deities.[14] Each multiplication table normally contains twenty-three items, multiples from 1 to 20, and then by tens through 30, 40, and 50. The so-called "regular numbers" (Neugebauer's term) have the form $2^p3^q5^r$, hence their reciprocals can always be represented by finite sexagesimal fractions. The standard tables employ three "places," meaning that $60^3 = 216{,}000$ would be the equivalent decimal common denominator, but auxiliary tables employ six and seven places freely even in "Old Babylonian" times (c. 1800 B.C.), and many more places in later times. Notice the musical advantages: tones in the 30:60 octave constitute reciprocal diatonic scales and will retain the same numerical *appearances* under all conditions so long as sexagesimal notation is strictly adhered to. Derivative tones, or "transpositions," will require successively larger numbers of "places" (commas are introduced in modern transcriptions to avoid ambiguity), but their

CHART 29

Tonal Interpretation of the Sexagesimal System

The standard multiplication tables of the Babylonian sexagesimal system were generated from these thirty pairs of reciprocals whose products are 1 = 60. (Commas indicate "places, each "place" having a base of 60.)

Gods	*Sexagesimal reciprocals*		*Tonal reciprocals*		
	2	30	c♯	e♭	(string length versus
	3	20	f♯	b♭	frequency as viewed from
	4	15	c♯	e♭	the perspective of
	5	12	A	G	60 = 1 = D)
	6	10	f♯	b♭	
	8	7,30	c♯	e♭	
	9	6,40	b	f	
Adad	10	6	A	G	
	12	5	f♯	b♭	
Ishtar	15	4	D	D	
	16	3,45	c♯	e♭	
	18	3,20	b	f	
Shamash	20	3	A	G	
	24	2,30	f♯	b♭	
[Marduk]	25	2,24	f	b	
	27	2,13,20	e	c	
Sin	30	2	D	D	⎤
	32	1,52,30	c♯	e♭	⎥
	36	1,40	b	f	⎥ diatonic and
Ea-Enki	40	1,30	A	G	⎥ chromatic octave
	45	1,20	G	A	⎥
	48	1,15	f♯	b♭	⎥
Enlil	50	1,12	(f	b)	⎥
	54	1,6,40	e	c	⎥
Anu-An	1	1	D	D	⎦

- -

(not deified)	1,4	56,15	c♯	e♭	(=64/60 × 3375/3600)
	1,12	50	b	f	(=72/60 × 3000/3600)
	1,15	48	b♭′	f♯′	(=75/60 × 2880/3600)
	1,20	45	A	G	(=80/60 × 2700/3600)
	1,21	44,26,40	a	g	(=81/60 × 160,000/216,000)

(Fractions are intended to suggest simplest decimal equivalents.)

"numerosity" need never change. The entire system seems perfectly engineered to fit the specific needs of mathematical harmonics. In the basic 30:60 octave the invariant tones are 6:8::9:12, appearing as 30:40::45:60, while the other numbers define "moveable sounds," summarizing the material in Charts 6 and 7.

The only tonal redundancy in the 30:60 octave is that associated with the number 50 (*i.e.*, f and b, which duplicates the *earlier* meanings of 36 as b and f). This number is "free," then, in a sense. Later we shall study the reasons why it may have been assigned to the Babylonian Bel, the earlier Sumerian Enlil. Notice immediately, however, that from our later perspective, apprised as we are that "every number is the product of primes in *one way only*" (the "basic theorem" of modern arithmetic), we can see that all of the "tone-values" in the multiplication table are the products of three primes, 2, 3, and 5. Looking again at the three greatest Babylonian-Sumerian gods, Ea-Enki = 40, Bel-Enlil = 50, and Anu-An = 60, in the ratios 4:5:6, and remembering our acoustical arithmetic from Chapters 2 through 5, we can see that these three "greatest Gods" actually generate the whole tonal universe. The "Divine Patron of Music," Ea-Enki = 40, *means* 40/60 = 2/3, hence he *embodies* the power of the "divine prime number 3" thousands of years *before* the Greeks defined prime numbers.[15] Bel-Enlil = 50 *means* 50/60 = 5/6, hence he *embodies* the power of the "human prime number 5," and the transformation of this God = 50 into an "adult, male Hebrew" worth fifty shekels is one of the main subjects of this chapter. The greatest god of all, Anu-An = 60 = 1, turns out to be our familiar "transformation point" in the field of rational numbers, equivalent to Mitra-Varuna in Vedic metaphor, father of all, in a sense, but remote from the affairs of man.

Before we leave the multiplication table, however, several more matters are worth studying. First, look at the last pair of reciprocals, 1,21 and 44,26,40, comparable in decimal arithmetic to $3^4 = 81$ and its reciprocal. How do we "prove" that such a pair is reciprocal? Let us make a straightforward interpretation within decimal arithmetic: 1,21 means $1 \times 60 + 21 = 81$, and 44,26,40 means $44 \times 60^2 + (26 \times 60) + 40 = 160{,}000$.

$$\frac{81}{60} \times \frac{160{,}000}{216{,}000} = \frac{12{,}960{,}000}{12{,}960{,}000} = 1$$

Now the number $60^4 = 12{,}960{,}000$ is the number which the Socrates of the ***Republic*** declares to be "sovereign of better and worse begettings" in a universe generated by the numbers 3, 4, and 5.[16] This is the number from which Plato generates the mathematical model of "Atlantis," and its "sovereign" role here in the *standard* table of reciprocals raises the suspicion that Pythagoras may have brought such a table home from Babylon along with the ratio 6:8::9:12 which became the foundation for Greek musicology and the Greek "theory of means." Chapter 11 will develop the Atlantis arithmetic.

A second curious correlation with this table of reciprocals, from which the multiplication tables were generated, concerns its single tonal omission: there are eleven tones in "Just tuning," a first approximation to "equal-temperament," but there is no tone at all in the middle of the octave to correspond with A♭ = G♯ = $\sqrt{2}$. There is a remarkable Babylonian solution.

The Babylonian approximation to the square root of 2 reads 1,24,51,10 in Neugebauer's modern transcription and is correct to five decimal places in our own modern system. The interpretation is as follows:

$$1 + \frac{24}{60} + \frac{51}{60^2} + \frac{10}{60^3} = \frac{305{,}470}{216{,}000} = 1.41421^+$$

(Neugebauer theorizes that the solution was arrived at by taking alternate arithmetic and harmonic means within successively smaller modules.) Now there is one Old-Babylonian tablet catalogued as YBC 7289 which applies this value to the computation of the diagonal of a square whose side is thirty units. It is shown below in Chart 30 in Neugebauer's transcription.[17] Across the diagonal of the drawing is the Babylonian value for the square root of 2, and beneath is the computation for 30 times that value, reading 42,25,35, and with the following meaning:

$$42 + \frac{25}{60} + \frac{35}{60^2} = \frac{152{,}735}{3600} = 42.42638^+$$

Here, then, is the missing Babylonian value for the twelfth tone in our standard table of reciprocals, computed for us on YBC 7289. Now historians of mathematics, although aware that the sexagesimal system has a decimal component, assume that the "place-value" character of decimal arithmetic was not established until thousands of years later. Yet this particular example, when translated into decimal form, shows the solution 42.42^+ with *decimal* numbers playing a "great and small" role on each side of the decimal point, analogous to the roles of sexagesimal numbers, in this case 100/42 versus 42/100. Mere coincidence? Yes, if we believe our historians. Looking back at Chart 28 we see the important role 42 played in the Christ numerology as 7/5 times 30; the new "corrected" value of 42.42^+ is very close to the accurate value of $\sqrt{2}$. From a purely musical point of view, any further arithmetical development beyond 60 is mainly for the purpose of improving on the other numbers available in the 30:60 module as approximations to equal-temperament. The last number in the standard table is suspiciously musical as a limit: 1,21 = 81

CHART 30

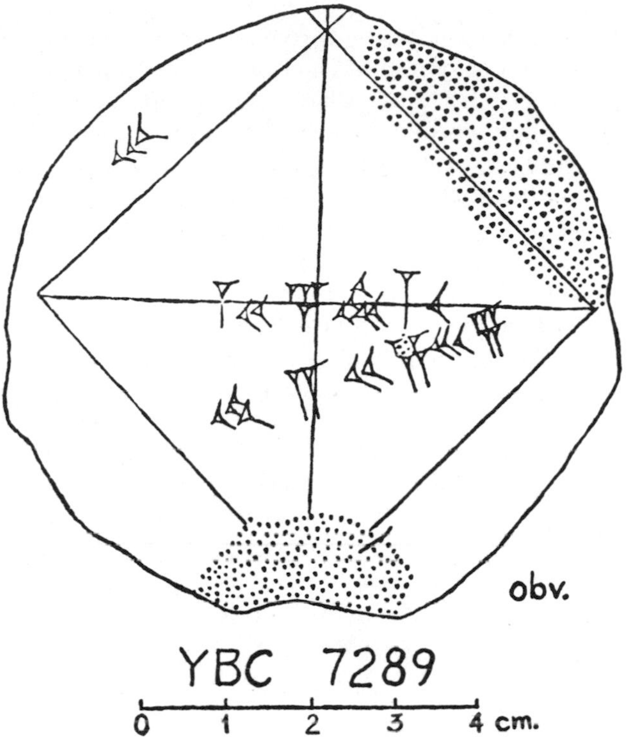

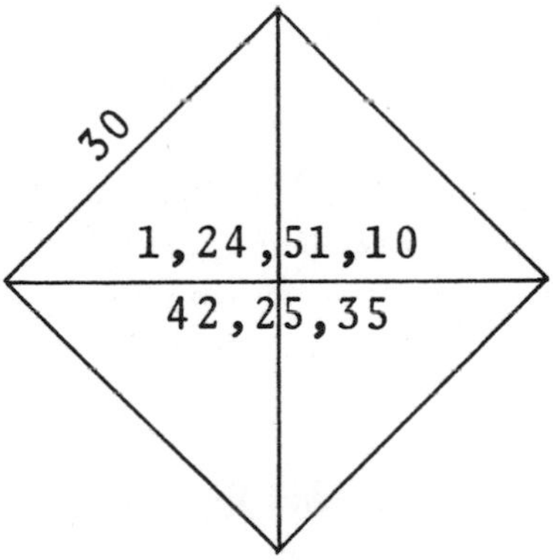

The Babylonian Solution to $\sqrt{2}$

The Old-Babylonian (c. 1800 B.C.) computation of the diagonal of a square with a side of 30 units, as interpreted by Otto Neugebauer. The diagonal value of 1,24,51,10 is correct to five decimal places (1.41421) and its multiplication by 30 (to 42,25,35 = 42.42638 +) supplies the only value missing from Chart 29 in approximating twelve-tone equal-temperament.

is essential to showing the "syntonic comma" of ratio 80:81 which arises in Just tuning (between pure fifths and pure thirds), present in the basic calendrical octave 360:720 (see Chart 8 at C-c and E-e). Since nobody knows how or why the sexagesimal system was ever invented in the first place, musicians should feel free to imagine that it may have been invented by musicians for essentially musical purposes, under a certain lunar-solar influence in favor of a twelve-tone scale, reducible to a diatonic "double perspective," and confronted from the very beginning with that plague of number theory, the "tritone" $\sqrt{2}$.

The correlation between the tones of the scale, the Babylonian-Sumerian deities, and the basic geometry of square and circle are shown below in Chart 31. Notice that 60 is the "unit" radius and also the "side" of an inscribed hexagon. The Biblical *pi* value of 3 makes the circumference 3 × 120 (the diameter) = 360, later interpreted as "degrees," but possibly first thought of as the hexagonal (6 × 60) approximation to the circumference. (Neugebauer found a better Babylonian value to *pi* in 3 1/8.[18])

The basic sexagesimal diameter = 2 × 60 = 120, later used by Ptolemy for his monochord scales, is indigenous to the Babylonian-Sumerian system and controlled both astronomy and mythology in ways we do not yet understand. Neugebauer reports an Old-Babylonian text which reads:

> 19 from the Moon to the Pleiades; 17 from the Pleiades to Orion; 14 from Orion to Sirius", and so on for eight stars or constellations, ending with the statement that the total (of what?) is 120 "miles" and the question "how much is one god (*i.e.*, star) beyond the other god"?[19]

On Tablet X of the Gilgamesh epic, Urshanabi, the boatman, instructs the hero to cut for himself 120 "punting poles," each 60 cubits long, to punt their boat across "the waters of death," each pole to be used for just one thrust.[20] In the Bible, 120 was the age of Moses when he died, short of being allowed to cross over the Jordan into the Promised Land,[21] and it is the number of Solomon's priests who were trumpeters,[22] and the number of disciples who gathered in an "upper room" in Jerusalem soon after the ascension of Jesus[23] (*i.e.*, disciples at the first Pentecost). In the Book of Genesis (6:3) the "days of man's life" are decreed as 120 years, but this figure did not apply to the ten generations from Adam to Noah.[24] According to Berossus, the last priest of the Babylonian religion of Marduk, writing in the third century B.C., the ten antediluvian Babylonian monarchs reigned for a total of 432,000 years, but since each of their reigns is divisible by 60^2 = 3,600 we may properly suspect that they really totalled 120 according to some arcane calculation still lost to us, and their numbers

CHART 31

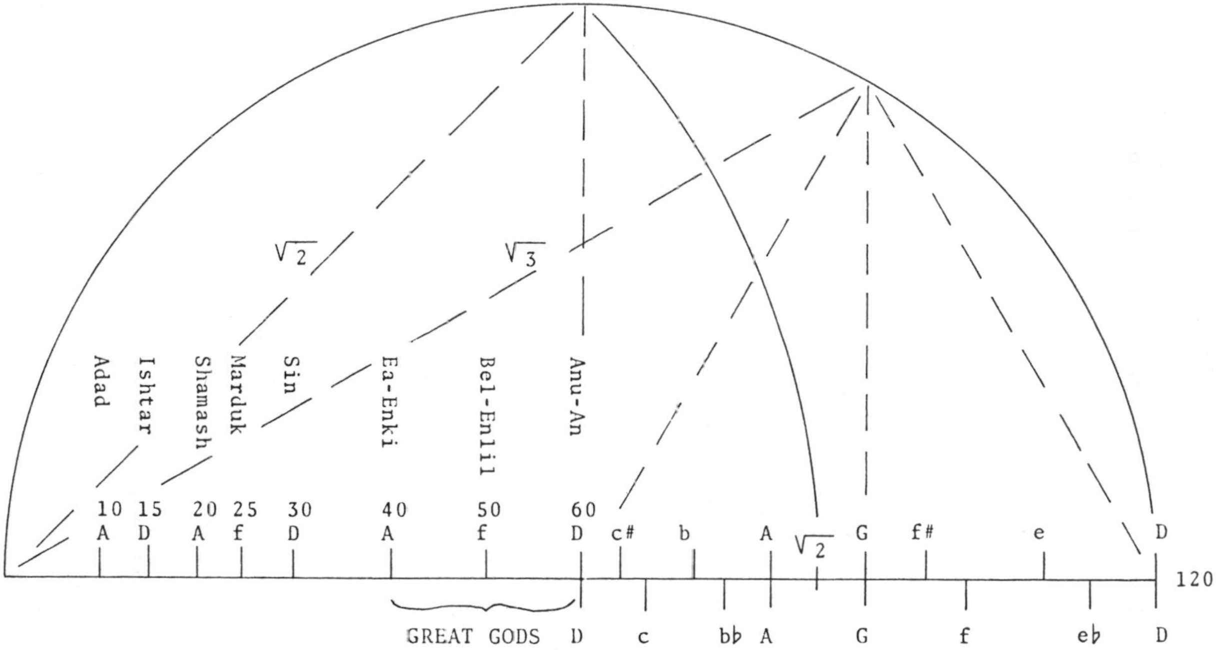

The Babylonian Pantheon and the Calendrical Scales on Ptolemy's Monochord

The sexagesimal system and its reciprocal diatonic scales can be thought of as generated by the first six integers (1:2:3:4:5:6 = "days of creation"), or by the "Great Gods" 40:50:60 = 4:5:6, or by the prime numbers 2, 3, and 5. Since 60 = "1," unit radius of the circle, the diameter = 2 = 120. Sexagesimal fractions of "minutes" and "seconds" are equivalent in decimal arithmetic to a multiplication $120 \times 60^2 = 432{,}000$, least common denominator if fractions are avoided.

CHART 32

King	Reign	Division by $60^2 = 3600$
Aloros	36,000	10
Alaparos	10,800	3
Amelon	46,800	13
Ammenon	43,200	12
Megalaros	64,800	18
Daonos	36,000	10
Euedoraches	64,800	18
Amempsinos	36,000	10
Opartes	28,800	8
Xisuthros	64,800	18
Total	432,000	120

Monochord Reduction of the Babylonian King List

Berossus' ten antediluvian kings in the Marduk mythology, reduced to linear measures on a monochord-diameter of 120 units. Numbers larger than 432,000 belong to the metaphorical "flood."

have been multiplied by 60 "minutes" and 60 "seconds," in Ptolemy's manner, and so allude to another monochord-diameter demonstration.[25]

One of the most impressive of the Old-Babylonian tablets, catalogued as "Plimpton 322," is a text concerning Pythagorean right triangles whose sides are integers arranged in a sequence in which angles vary approximately linearly from 45° to 31°. In Chart 33 I have translated Neugebauer's sexagesimal notation into its decimal equivalent, via appropriate common denominators, and have substituted *secant* values (ratio of the hypotenuse to the longer side) for the ratios of the square of the hypotenuse to the square of the longer side which the tablet gives.[26]

In Chart 34 I have graphed schematically the triangles of Plimpton 322 on Ptolemy's monochord-diameter, adding the perpendiculars which show how such triangles relate directly to tones on the monochord. This set of fifteen triangles subdivides the musical fifth between 60 and 90; taken in reverse order along the string, they would differentiate the octave between 30 and 60. Two thousand years later Ptolemy worked out the trigonometric ratios applying to the whole circle, at half-degree intervals, computing ratios from the lengths of chords. His dramatic increase in the power of mathematical reasoning was coupled with a continuing use of the ancient arithmetical foundation, 60 remaining the unit radius, 120 the diameter, and subdivision into minutes and seconds preserving the limiting character of our Kali Yuga number, $120 \times 60 \times 60 = 432{,}000$,

CHART 33

Line	L	B	D	Secant	Degrees
3	120	119	169	1.408	45°
4	3456	3367	4825	1.396	
5	4800	4601	6649	1.385	43°
6	13500	12709	18541	1.373	
7	72	65	97	1.347	41°
8	360	319	481	1.336	
9	2700	2291	3541	1.311	39°
10	960	799	1249	1.301	
11	600	481	769	1.281	37°
12	6480	4961	8161	1.259	
13	60	45	75	1.25	35°
14	2400	1679	2929	1.220	
15	240	161	289	1.204	33°
16	2700	1771	3229	1.195	
17	90	56	106	1.177	31°

Translation and Interpretation of Plimpton 322

Fifteen Pythagorean right triangles, whose numerical dimensions at first glance appear chaotic, prove to be arranged according to an approximately one degree variation in angle. L = longer side, B = shorter side, D = hypotenuse (always the diameter of the circle in Chart 34). The secant ratio D/L is substituted here for D^2/L^2 in the original. (The basic formula is simply $L^2 + B^2 = D^2$, but the complexity of development here suggests that the Babylonians knew the formula for producing all such Pythagorean triples.) Only in line 13, where 3:4:5 appears as 45:60:75, and in line 17 is the principle of "smallest integers" violated.

the duration of the antediluvian kings. Babylonian astronomers seem to have concentrated on "horizon" phenomena; this set of triangles would have been of interest in studying transits across a perpendicular (*i.e.*, on a primitive astrolabe) from the pole star.

Viewed against the background of the powerful Babylonian methods of computation, the construction of our tonal yantras appears a very simple task indeed. Once the principle of octave identity is grasped, and when tonal symmetry is understood as arithmetical reciprocity, the procedure unfolds quite systematically under the principle of "smallest integers for a given context." The only difficulty is that of finding appropriate *least common denominators* for a given set of ratios. If any people were demonstrably capable of inventing the acoustical theory expounded in this study it was the Babylonians c. 1800 B.C., yet the evidence points beyond them a thousand years and more to a Sumerian foundation. That evidence is primarily mythological; it concerns the "holy mountain."

CHART 34

Comparative Cosmology: The Pythagorean Triangles of Plimpton 322 ("Old Babylonian," 1900–1600 B.C.) on Ptolemy's Monochord

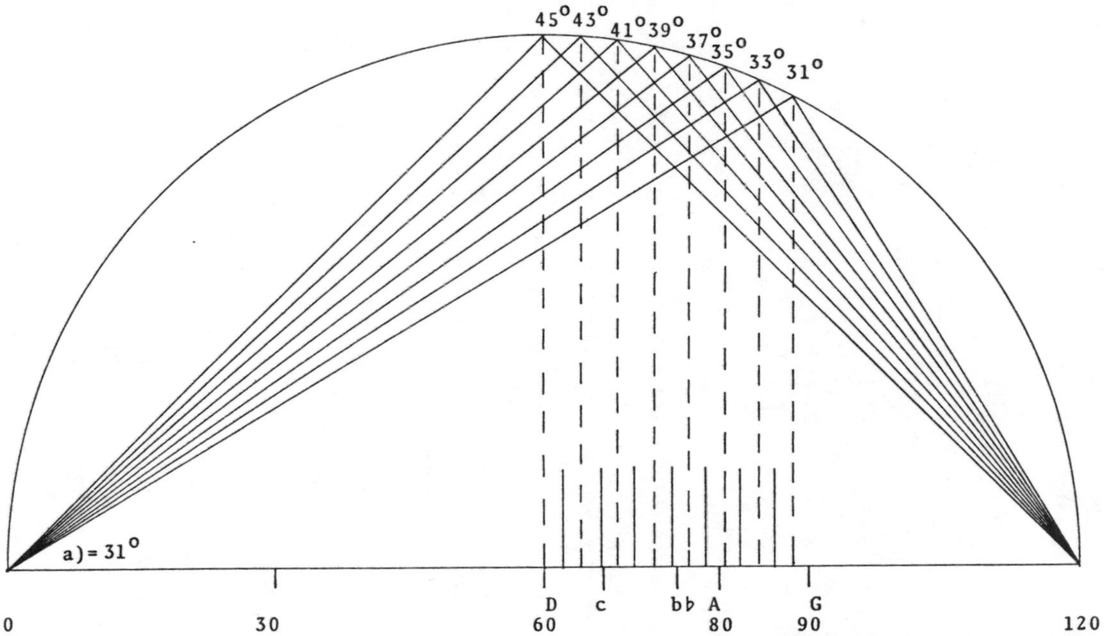

An interpretation of pp. 39–41 of *Mathematical Cuneiform Texts* by Otto Neugebauer. The tablet provides integer approximations for fifteen triangles whose angles a) vary by about 1° in the range between 30° and 45°. Perpendiculars to the monochord fall within the perfect fifth 60:90, or taken oppositely, within the octave 30:60. For visual clarity, intermediate triangles have been omitted.

From here on we shall be studying twin-peaked Mt. Mashu of the Sumerians and its transformations through Babylonian, Greek, and Hebrew forms into a "Pascal" triangle India knew as Mt. Meru in the second century B.C. We are studying the transition from polytheism to monotheism as mathematicians discover stronger and more abstract methods.

GOD ON THE MOUNTAIN

The story of "God on the Mountain" or the "Mountain of God" can be read best while looking at the "cartoon" yantras for numbers $3^p5^q < 60$, the diatonic scale, and for $3^p5^q < 720$, the chromatic scale. Remember that reciprocals can be shown either as paired or as interlocked triangles or, as Nicomachus does, stipulated as applying to integers interpreted as both multiples and submultiples, *i.e.*, so that one triangle does double duty. The three "Great Gods" of the pantheon, Anu-An = 60, Ea-Enki = 40, and Bel-Enlil = 50, inhabit the "peak" of the yantra for the diatonic scale. Enlil (50), at the very peak, is "father of the Gods," "the king of heaven and earth," and "the great mountain" without whom "no cities would be built."[27] He deifies the prime number 5, responsible for the *vertical* dimensions of our yantras. It is he who copulates with the "great mountains" to bring forth creation:

> Enlil, who sits broadly on the white dais, the lofty dais, . . .
> He does not tolerate . . . evil in the city,
> The great net, . . .
> Heaven—he is its princely one; earth—he is its great one.[28]

According to Kramer, Enlil is a "friendly, fatherly deity who watches over the safety and well being of all humans, particularly the inhabitants

CHART 35

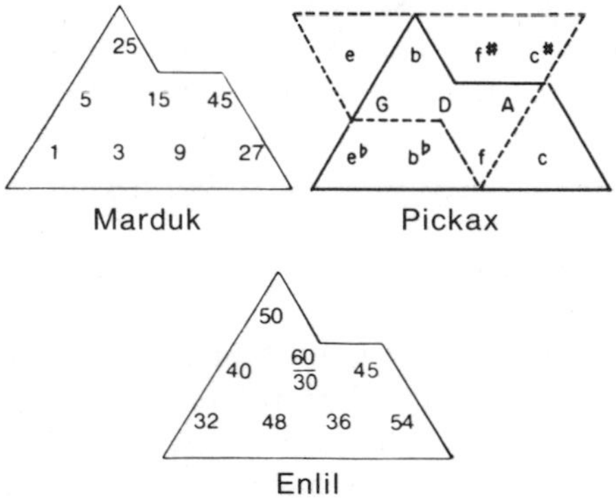

God on the Mountain

of Sumer."[29] It is Enlil (deified 5) who differentiates heaven and earth, and his most important gift to man is a curious one: Enlil is the creator of the "pickax," much-exalted in Sumer, the pickax "whose *tooth* is a one-horned ox ascending a large wall."[30] (*Tooth* is problematical for the translator.) Notice the position of 50 in the yantra, a tooth indeed, or a pickax, or a male triangle (phallus), and notice its reciprocal tonal meanings.

In the later Babylonian religion, Bel-Enlil is replaced by Marduk = 25 under fascinating acoustical conditions. Apsu, the primeval "begettor" of the gods, is disturbed by the *noise* of his celestial children (note the confusion of *irregular* arithmetic progressions in the 30:60 "Enlil" yantra) and decrees their death:

> By day I cannot rest, by night I cannot sleep;
> I will destroy (them) and put an end to their way,
> That silence be established, and then let us sleep![31]

The gods quickly organize themselves under the leadership of Marduk (notice the orderly arithmetic in his yantra), who vanquishes Tiamat, serpent and holy mother, and gains for himself "double equality." His fifty names are recited at the important New Year's temple service, when the central activity is the mounting of a new bull's hide on the ceremonial drum. Notice Ishtar = 15 in the center of Marduk's yantra. Since 15 means 15/60, it is a deification of the power of the even, female number 4, the number which creates the octave matrices 15:30 and 30:60, numbers reaching "marriage eligibility" in the first, and achieving full adulthood in the second. With a Babylonian captivity behind them, it is no accident that the authors and editors of the Old Testament, anxious to differentiate the Hebrews from their Semitic cousins, decreed that the "valuation of a male from twenty years old up to sixty years old shall be fifty (*sic*) shekels of silver, according to the shekel of the sanctuary" (Leviticus 27:3), thus making any male Hebrew worth the greatest Babylonian god. With similar appropriateness the new religion adds: "If the person is a female, your valuation shall be thirty shekels," 30 being the number of the moon-god Sin, but meaning 30/60 and hence showing the *power* of the female prime number 2. Monotheism took as its God not the Great God 60 (actually written in Babylonian-Sumerian as a large ONE), but the irreducible unity itself, that is, the unity whose multiplicity creates all the diversity of number, that unity which alone can subdivide prime numbers, the active agents of all creation. The prime numbers 3 and 5 are the values of Hebrew children; in Plato's metaphor they are children who have reached the age where they can "walk alone," *i.e.*, as integers.

The Sumerian Enki, Babylonian Ea = 40, deifies the prime number 3, for 40 means 40/60 = 2/3, showing us 3 in action, and his responsibilities are commensurate with the importance of 3 in Vedic, Platonic, and Christian numerology. It is Enki who "organizes the earth," that is, he is responsible for the *lateral* extension of our yantras. Appropriate to the prime number 3, he is the "first born son" of the great Anu-An = 60, *i.e.*, the first odd, hence male integer.[32] According to Kramer, the Sumerians had relatively superficial notions about nature and its mysteries; they were content with the notion that "Enki did it."[33] Thus a deified 3 played a role in Sumerian times which the prime number 3 played in later Pythagorean and Platonic mythology. Enki, god of the sweetwaters, is the Sumerian counterpart to the Greek Poseidon, Kramer suggests, and we shall examine Poseidon's children in the myth of Atlantis. It is Enki's role in creating our yantras which makes sense out of the following line from a Sumerian tablet:

> The great prince put the "net" upon the pickax, then
> directed the mold.[34]

It is Enki who creates the "brick-god" Kulla, among endless other activities; the standard Babylonian measure for building bricks is the *Sar* of 720, the number of digits required for our chromatic scale. Here is the yantra for 720 in its reciprocal tonal forms, its "confused" Sumerian chromatic octave form, and its "orderly" Babylonian reduction to smallest integers.

Notice the shape of this yantra, an expanded version of that in Chart 11a. To celebrate Marduk's victory over the designs of his angry progenitor, the gods promise him a temple worthy of his greatness, a place where

CHART 36

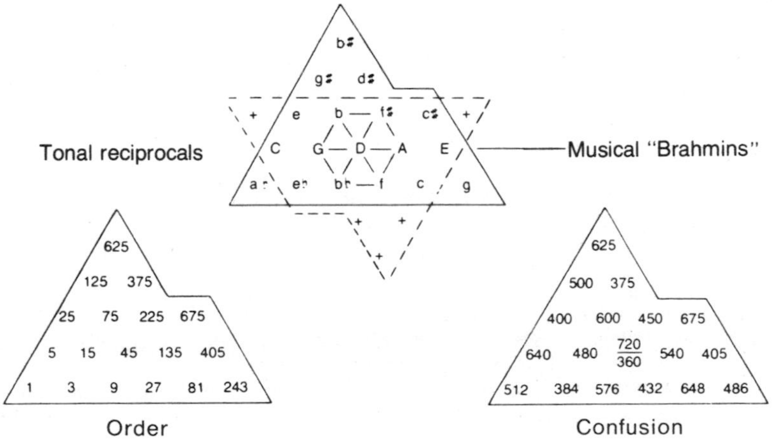

The "calendrical" Yantras from Chart 11

gods and men may meet:

> Come, let us make (something) whose name shall be called "Sanctuary."
> It shall be a dwelling for our rest at night; come, let us repose therein!
> There let us erect a throne dais, a seat with a back support. . . .
> When Marduk heard this, His countenance shone exceedingly.[35]

The yantras can be viewed, I suggest, as a schematic temple tower, like the Esagila ziggurat, that is, like a "throne dais . . . with a back support." It required two years to build the Marduk temple ($2 \times 360 = 720$); the first year was spent solely in making bricks.[36] Nonsense? Or mathematical allegory? Marduk is a spring equinox sun-god, and creator of the calendar.[37]

The imagery appropriate to our yantras suggests an arithmetical solution to the problem of twin-peaked Mt. Mashu, the Babylonian-Sumerian holy mountain. Each morning the sun-god Utu rises between those peaks, and the Sumerian cartoons have survived on small "cylinder seals," untouched by time for four or five thousand years. The original symbol for mountain was three bricks, , although more are shown for Mt. Mashu.[38] (The symbol for woman, appropriately, was .) The reciprocal meanings of Babylonian-Sumerian integers (as multiples and submultiples of 60) justify, I suggest, the following yantra as a legitimate substitute for those shown previously. For convenience, I limit numerosity to that of the "Marduk" yantra:

CHART 37

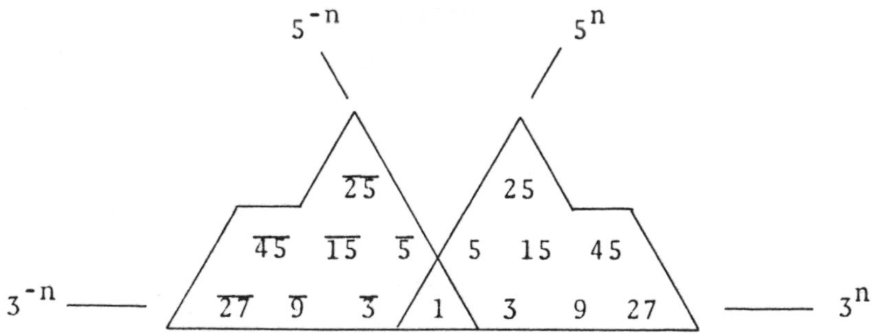

An Interpretation of Mt. Mashu as Reciprocal Yantras

One triangle contains integers, the other reciprocals, and Utu, the Sun, can be imagined as "rising" between them. Alternatively, reciprocal powers of 3 and 5 can be thought of as the "four world rivers," or perhaps the four eyes and ears of Marduk. The distinctive feature of Mashu is "twin peaks." One tablet suggests that the same "twin" mountain watches over both the rising and the setting of the sun.[39] The distinctive feature of Mt. Ararat, on which the Hebrew ark came to rest, is also "twin peaks."

CHART 38

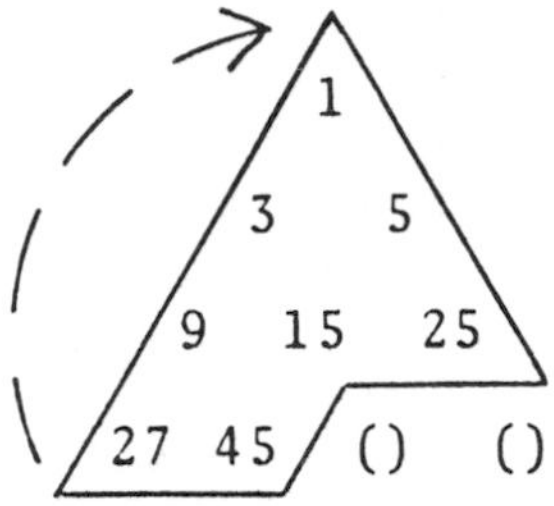

Hebrew Monotheism

$$(1)$$
$$A \quad B$$
$$A^2 \quad AB \quad B^2$$
$$A^3 \quad A^2B \quad AB^2 \quad B^3$$

Greek Rationalism

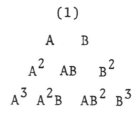

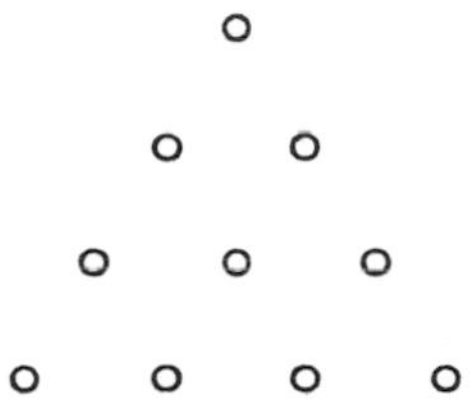

Pythagorean Holy Tetractys

The Evolution of Monotheism

The evolution of monotheism and rationalism from Sumerian-Babylonian polytheism. The "reductionism" pictured here can be thought of as a victory of "spirit" over "matter," for in the end it is only *pattern* which counts, thus not even number belongs to the exclusively spiritual realm, at least for Plato. The Pythagorean pebble pattern is a "holy mountain" in the most perfectly abstract, spiritual sense.

There is a total cohesiveness between twin-peaked Mt. Mashu, Enlil's "disorderly" brothers, Marduk's "orderly" realignment of them, the later Hebrew reduction to monotheism, and the still later Greek transformation to an abstract algebra. In the above yantras I have first "rotated" the Sumerian-Babylonian yantras to bring the unit, 1, to the top of the mountain, and then translated the numbers into the abstract algebraic information they encode, using van der Waerden's notation.

BABYLONIAN AND HEBREW FLOODS

The extensive correlations between Hebrew and Babylonian mythology have been pursued by many scholars, including Joseph Campbell, Alexander Heidel, S. H. Hooke, and Samuel Noah Kramer, on whose work I draw freely.[40] Some of the most interesting correspondences—and differences—concern the legendary flood and the dimensions of the arks which preserve a remnant of mankind to start life anew. There is an older, Sumerian flood myth, but the tablets which record important arithmetical detail are badly damaged, hence it is impossible to know how much of its numerological content was identical with that of the Babylonian mythology. The flood itself, I am inclined to believe, is an allegory for the flood of numbers it is necessary to generate to find out how close the powers of 3 and the powers of 5 can coincide, especially near the elusive locus of the square root of 2. The Vedic solution, in smallest integers, was reconstructed in the yantras of Chart 15, involving numbers of ten digits. The saving arks, so I assume from the correspondences being developed here, are the minimal yantras various cultures found useful in preserving the essential data, *after* it was known that the very largest ones were not going to pin down the arithmetical locus of a number we now know to be irrational. In Chart 39 I have graphed the Babylonian and Hebrew arks, using their "cubic dimension" as the bounding number of a yantra for numbers 3^p5^q. The Babylonian "flood" presumably concerns numbers larger than 432,000. The Sumerian ark of $60^3 = 216{,}000$ was shown in the "Prajāpati" yantra of Chart 12b.

The Babylonian ark is a cube, $120^3 = 1{,}728{,}000$, identical with the Hindu Kṛta Yuga in numerosity, but its yantra differs from that in Chart 14 for this reason: the Hindu yuga was interpreted as the first of four periods within an all-embracing Mahā Yuga, while the Babylonian ark is a number "out of context." While most of the Babylonian tablets still remain untranslated, crumbling in our museums faster than scholars are able to study them, it seems unwise to try to harmonize the Vedic and Babylonian numbers any further. Notice, however, that along the axis of the Babylonian ark are nine tones in Pythagorean tuning (perfect fifths) to correlate with the nine compartments on each floor of the ark, and along the base are fourteen elements to correlate with the fourteen human beings Enlil created after the flood to speed the repopulation of the earth. (I should make clear that the yantra does not answer all questions concerning numerosity. The ark is also described as having "six decks *below*," seven in all, hence presumably $7 \times 9 = 63$ compartments, versus the seventy elements shown here, and it is "two-thirds submerged.")

The Hebrew ark appears to be a very clever variation on the Babylonian one. Notice how the yantra for the chromatic scale and the 720 "days and nights" of the year fits neatly into its apex, and notice that its overall shape or boundary coincides with the "canonic" Vedic-Babylonian yantra for 432,000 (Chart 14). The twelve elements along the base correspond with the twelve tribes—perhaps, because there are further elements in the Biblical story to be accounted for.

Strictly arithmetical procedures may explain why the two arks are so different numerically. The Babylonian system is biased in favor of 60 and its multiples as terminating numbers. Since 120 is written sexagesimally as "2," its cube is "8," and the number 1,728,000 would be written as "8," *meaning* 8×60^3 (the operator remembering that each multiplication corresponds to raising to the next higher power). Now 8 is a cube number in both decimal and sexagesimal systems, and the cube plays a sacred role in many religions, including that of Mecca and Delphi. "Doubling the cubical altar at Delphi" is the classical form in which Greek geometers of the fourth century B.C. were challenged to find the cube root of 2, equivalent to determining an equal-tempered major third. The Hebrews are obviously moving away from sexagesimal arithmetic, away from polytheism and toward monotheism, and away from the rigid mathematical determinism of Sumer and Babylon, and they are laboring under the necessity of differentiating themselves from rival religions while preserving the same core of tonal-calendrical associations. The Hebrew ark shown here is firmly rooted in an ancient tradition, it is properly respectful of numbers essential to scale and calendar, and it boldly affirms a new perspective with a strong aesthetic appeal of its own. (In the sexagesimal system, 450,000 would be written as 2,5, meaning $2 \times 60^3 + (5 \times 60^2)$, perhaps a pun on Marduk = 25.) The cabalistic *Zohar* speaks of 450,000 "beings" in the community or "vineyard" of Israel.

There may be a deeper "harmonical" pun in the Babylonian flood story. In mathematical harmonics we first meet the number 8 in the "musical proportion" 6:8::9:12 which establishes tetrachord frames, multiplied to 30:40::45:60 in the model octave. Hence 8 in the first context corresponds to 40 in the second, 40 being the number of Enki, "god of the sweetwaters," so that the ark number 8,0,0 sexagesimally may have carried with it an overtone of meaning linking the god of the fresh waters ultimately falling from the sky with the ark which preserves a remnant of the mankind he is responsible for.

There are further curious numerical correspondences. Note that the *sum* of the tone-numbers in the 30:60 octave (*i.e.*, 32 + 36 + 40 + 45 + 48 + 50 + 54 + 60) = 365, the number of days in a year (*i.e.*, when the five additional days are added to the schematic 360; the actual calendar, however, was strictly lunar). In the "Marduk" yantra, however (see Chart 35), where these "Sumerian" numbers are reduced to smallest possible integers, the sum of the eight numbers in the yantra (*i.e.*, 1 + 3 + 9 + 27 + 5 + 15 + 45 + 25) = 130, the age when Adam fathered his first son. Furthermore, the sum of the integers in the base of the yantra (1 + 3 + 9 + 27) is 40, the number of days and nights

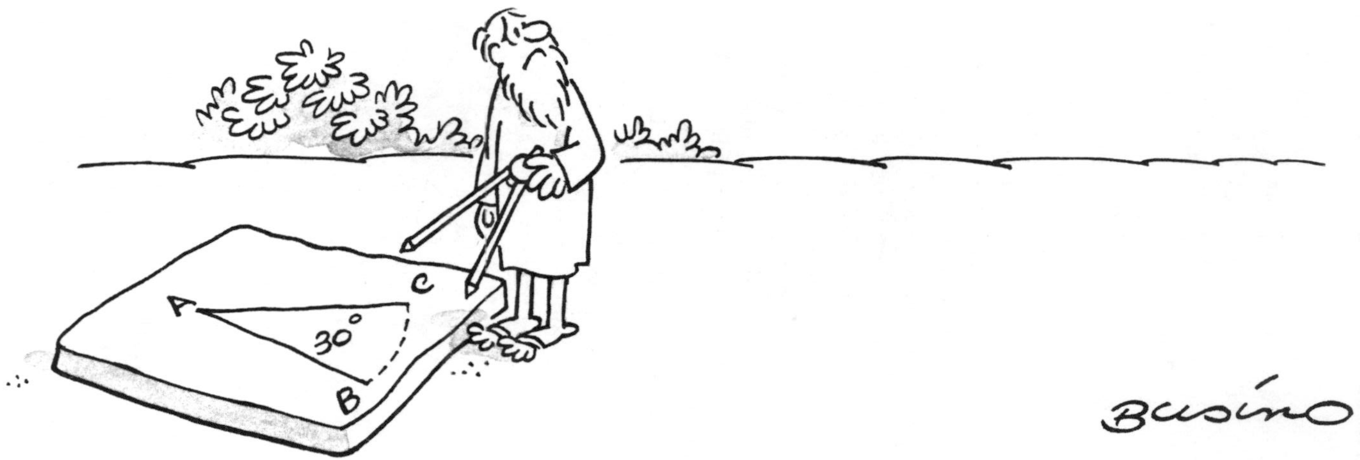

"NO! NO! I SAID BUILD AN *ARK*!"

CHART 39

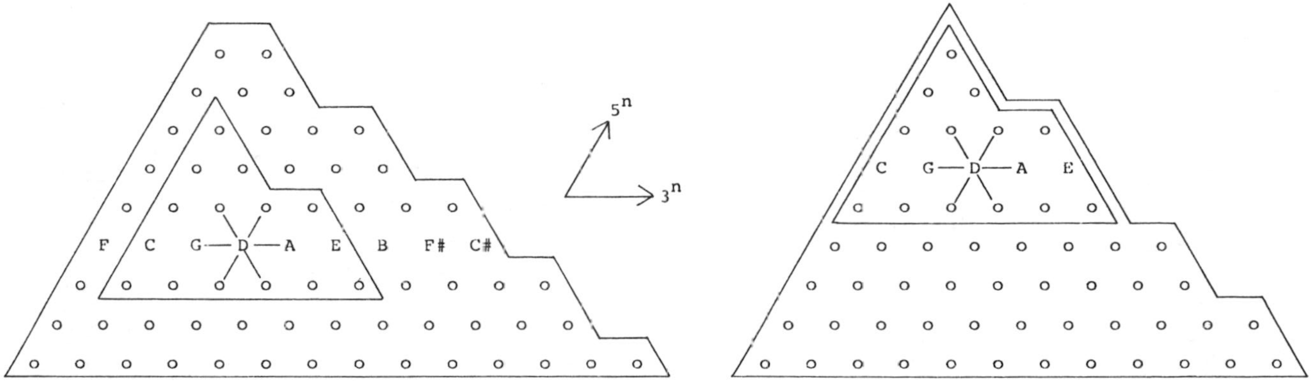

Babylonian Ark

$3^p5^q < 120^3 = 1,728,000$ (Krta Yuga)

Hebrew Ark

$3^p5^q < 300 \times 50 \times 30 = 450,000$

Babylonian and Hebrew Arks

The Babylonian ark has the same "numerosity" as the Hindu Kṛta Yuga ("Golden Age"). The Hebrew ark has the same *boundary* as the Hindu Kali Yuga (432,000). The yantra for the chromatic scale and the calendar—720—is shown inside both arks. The horizontal axis of the Babylonian ark contains nine tones (F C G D A E B F♯ C♯), corresponding with the nine "compartments" on each floor, and the base of the yantra contains fourteen elements, corresponding with the fourteen "human beings" created by Enlil "for the speedy re-population of the earth." The base of the Hebrew yantra contains twelve elements, possibly symbolizing the twelve tribes. This comparison is intended to show how the Hebrew ark may have been conceived as a variation on a Sumerian-Babylonian theme of very great antiquity. The Hebrew ark "grows" naturally out of the calendar yantra. The Sumerian ark of $60^3 = 216,000$ is the Prajāpati yantra of Chart 12b.

Hebrew prophets often spend in meditation; these are the four numbers determining the *moveable* sounds in the tetrachords, determining whether the scale is Greek Dorian or modern major. Kramer has pointed out also a possible correlation between the Biblical Eve, formed from Adam's rib, and the Sumerian goddess Nin-Ti, the "Lady of the Rib."[41] It is tempting to associate such females with the "rib" which divides the monochord in half, displaying the power of the female, matrix number 2, within which all gods, men, and irrational "devils" also are born. The six days of Biblical creation correspond numerically with the main Babylonian gods, Adad = 10, Shamash = 20, Sin = 30, Ea = 40, Bel-Enlil = 50, and Anu = 60, *i.e.*, with the ratios 1:2:3:4:5:6 incorporated into sexagesimal arithmetic and Just tuning to make a total isomorphism of number theory and tuning theory. God's resting on the seventh day obviously corresponds to the omission of 7 as a generator of "regular" numbers. *Ten* commandments deify that number for Hebrews as well as Pythagoreans, and *twelve* tribes are as sacred to Judaism as to music and astronomy. The reciprocity of heaven and hell is as clear in Jewish lore as in Babylonian mathematics.

Joseph Campbell has discovered a correlation between the 432,000 years from the creation to the flood in Babylonian mythology and the 1,656 years from the creation of Adam to the flood in the Hebrew account.[42] Campbell points out that these numbers have a common factor of 72, and that 1656/72 is 23. Now 23 Jewish years of 365 days plus five extra days for leap years equals 8,400 days or 1,200 seven-day weeks; multiplying by 72 to find the number of Jewish seven-day weeks in 1,656 (= 23 × 72) years yields 86,400 (1200 × 72). But the number 86,400 is 432,000/5, *i.e.*, the number of Babylonian five-day weeks to the flood. Thus there is *no necessary contradiction* whatever in these different flood chronologies. Chart 40 is the yantra for numbers $3^p5^q < 86{,}400$, the harmonical link.

There is further numerical detail in the flood mythologies than either Campbell's ingenious analysis or mine can account for. We must hope that our clues may prove useful to others. The Sumerian flood is the fault of Enlil, deified 5, responsible for both the rain from heaven and the flooding of the rivers—and for the height of our yantras. Enlil is furious when he learns that Enki, deified 3, has connived at the salvation of a remnant of mankind. It is obvious that the Babylonian-Sumerian flood concerns numbers larger than 432,000, and that the Hebrew account is coordinated with it in some way. It is a personal hunch that all flood mythologies concern multiplication tables for 3^p5^q larger than 5^{13} and smaller than 5^{15}, that is, for yantras fourteen or fifteen steps high, like the Kalpa-Brahmā yantras of Chart 15. Only at this numerosity can "gods" and "devils" meet face to face as close approximations to $\sqrt{2}$

CHART 40

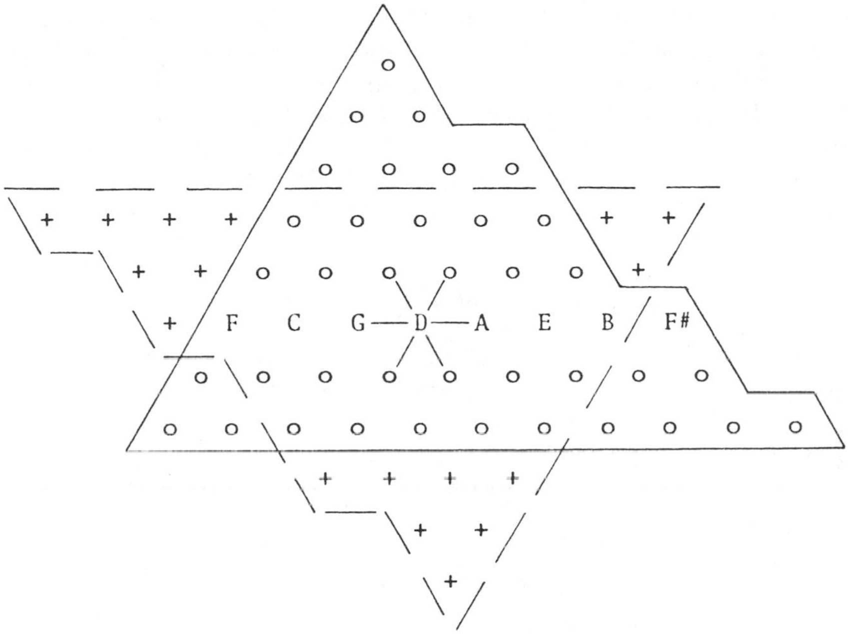

Harmonization of Babylonian-Biblical Flood Chronology

The yantra for numbers $3^p5^q < 86,400$ adds a possible musical interpretation to Joseph Campbell's discovery that Babylonian and Hebrew flood chronologies can be harmonized:

Babylon: $432,000 \div 5 = 86,400$ "five-day weeks"

Bible: $1656 \div 72 = 23$ cycles of 365 days + 5 intercalated days for leap years. $(23 \times 365) + 5 = 8,400$ days or 1200 seven-day weeks. Therefore $72 \times 1200 = 86,400$ seven-day weeks in 1,656 years.

The number 72 is the Hebrew "translation number" (see Chapter 9). The interpretation is wholly speculative; the coincidences may be purely accidental. Note, however, the determinative role of the Hindu digits 864, the invariant reciprocity within the diatonic scale along the central axis, the overall similarity of the design to the interlocked triangles of the "shield of Solomon," and the intermediate role of this yantra between the calendrical yantra for 720 and the flood yantra for 432,000 or the ark yantras in Chart 39. Irrespective of its possible relevance to the floods, this yantra belongs to the orderly expansion of the basic harmonical materials.

via chains of exponents, within "regular numbers" of the form $2^p3^q5^r$. In such a yantra it would be easy to read "the descent of Inanna to the underworld" and watch the goddess being stripped of one garment at each of seven levels (*i.e.*, losing one power of 5 at each step of the descent) so that she arrived "naked" at least of powers of 5. I don't believe it is possible to find a more elegant yantra than the Hindu one, but similar confrontations around $\sqrt{2}$ would occur in yantras of comparable numerosity, and we have seen good evidence that rival religions actively seek their own variants of each others "arithmology." Let us hope that further Babylonian and Sumerian materials are forthcoming.

To illustrate alternative possible computations I present two quite speculative yantras, one derived from the Bible, hence possibly authentically Hebraic, and the other derived from the Mayan calendar arithmetic of the New World.

OLD TESTAMENT ARITHMOLOGY

In the Book of Exodus (30:22–33) there is a cabalistic formula for mixing the "holy oil" for "a people set apart." The mixture calls for 500 shekels of myrrh, 250 shekels of cinnamon, 250 shekels of aromatic cane, 500 shekels of cassia, and 1 hin of olive oil, and this one batch must last for all time, "throughout your generations." Now the product,

$$500 \times 250 \times 250 \times 500 \times 1 = 15{,}625{,}000{,}000$$

is the "limiting index" of a yantra which is fifteen rows high, and which has twenty-two elements (powers of 3) across the base, correlating with the twenty-two letters of the Hebrew alphabet.[43] The yantra has a curious feature in that the "linch-pin" reciprocity on D = 1 = transformation point and geometric mean in the field of rational numbers can be made to coincide with the irreducible "1" at the lower-left-hand corner of the "Marduk" or "Adam" basic octave yantra in Chart 11, *i.e.*, so that the basic yantra from which all else unfolds exactly fits the "top of the mountain." If the Hebrews were actually looking for variations on our ancient arithmetical scheme, here is one which is intrinsically appealing and clever, uniting as it does the hitherto contradictary meanings of "One." The yantra is shown in Chart 41, in a purely exponential notation. The letters D A E B in the thirteenth row represent 5^{12}, $\times$ 3, 3^2 and 3^3; they correspond with e♭ b♭ f c and the numbers 1, 3, 9, and 27 in the "Adamic" yantra.

MAYAN COSMOLOGY

There are many resonances between Mayan mythology and that of the Middle East and Far East. I believe it will be possible someday to show that our Central American and Mexican mythologies are integral parts of the same family of world religions as those we have been studying. Translators have performed prodigious feats in the last few generations in bringing to life the strange glyphs long eroding in crumbling temples,

CHART 41

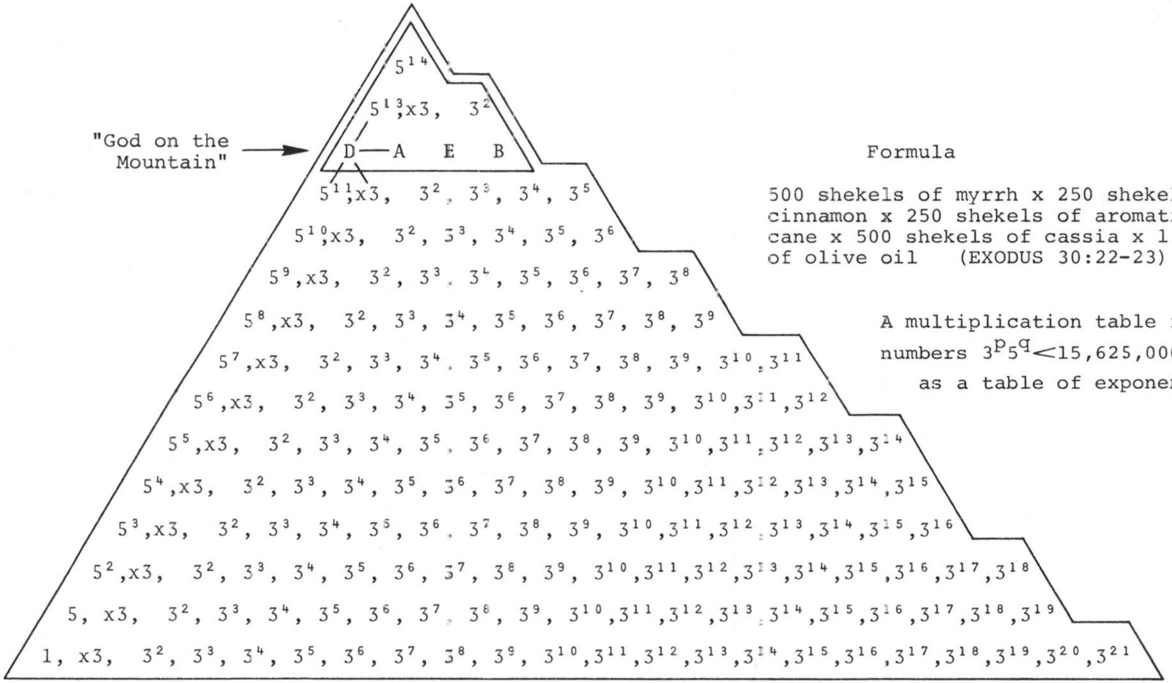

Formula

500 shekels of myrrh x 250 shekels of cinnamon x 250 shekels of aromatic cane x 500 shekels of cassia x 1 hin of olive oil (EXODUS 30:22-23)

A multiplication table for numbers $3^p 5^q < 15{,}625{,}000{,}000$ as a table of exponents

A Speculative Old Testament Yantra:

15,625,000,000 ''measures of holy oil'' for a people ''set apart.'' The ''Adamic'' yantra (whose integers total 130) stands on the ''peak'' of this holy mountain so that the ''linch-pin'' D symbolizing ''1'' as geometric mean in the field of rational number also corresponds to the generative unit ''1'' in the atomic yantra. ''Beginning and end'' thus coincide on D = 1 in its double sense, and allow the whole field of possibilities to emerge as a growth from a single perspective. Reciprocity is *assumed*.

CHART 42

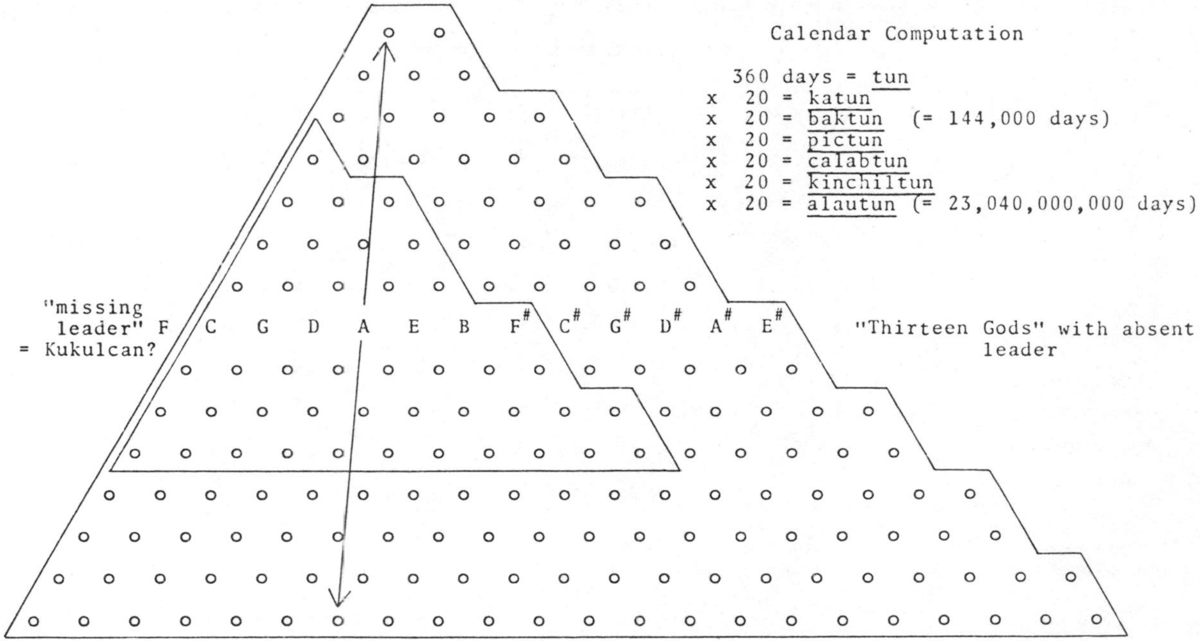

A Speculative Mayan Yantra

"*Alautun*" of 64,000,000 *tuns* × 360 = 23,040,000,000 "days." The small time period of a baktun = 400 × 360 = 144,000 corresponds with the number of "male virgins" in the Revelation yantra of Chart 25. The height and breadth of the yantra corresponds with the Vedic yantra of Chart 15 and the Hebraic yantra of Chart 41. The twelve "gods" along the central axis correlate with the "disciples" of the Revelation yantra if the "absence" of Kukulcan-Quetzalcoatl is considered. Vertical arrows point to Vedic approximations to $\sqrt{2}$ within the octave on A.

and their work continues. The youthful science of archaeology must be granted more time in both East and West to produce the evidence on which any serious synthesis could be built. Here I want to examine only one kind of evidence, that provided by the calendar calculation, projected backward in the Indian manner to cover what once must have seemed the whole of cosmic time. The Mayans deified the first twenty numbers and possessed a fully developed "vigesimal" place system. As in Vedic cosmology and Greek arithmetic, the use of fractions was "against the whole Maya philosophy of numbers."[44] The computation of very long periods of time centered on finding cyclic repetitions; the Mayans were in love with the "majesty and rhythm" of time, and revelled in numbers as large as those of Babylon. The basic year of 360 days was called a *tun*, meaning "precious stone," and became the "unit" for vigesimal expansion. Curiously, the *baktun* of 400 tuns means $400 \times 360 = 144{,}000$ and produces a possible correlation with the 144,000 "male virgins" of the New Testament. And the large period of $20^6 = 64{,}000{,}000$ *tuns*, when multiplied by 360 days, defines a yantra with startling similarities to our Vedic-Hebraic ones. The yantra in Chart 42 is fifteen steps high and has a central horizontal axis containing the twelve tones ("disciples" now interpreted as "gods") of the Revelation yantra *minus* the F symbolizing the "leader." Mayan mythology had thirteen gods; their leader, Kukulcan, dropped out of sight rather early, but Mexican neighbors were anticipating the return of equivalent Quetzalcoatl from the East when Cortés appeared with his Spaniards, confounding everything, being welcomed at first as the missing god. It might be irresponsible to jump to the conclusion that New Testament arithmetic was being acted out in the New World, but there is a considerable body of supporting evidence to be examined someday when we have learned how to reconstruct fractured cosmologies by comparison with those which have remained more nearly intact.[45] My purpose here is to illustrate how the same basic mathematical materials possess a rich enough variety of perspectives to have allowed distinctive cultures their own preferred numerology (or "arithmology") without implying contradiction at the radical level of calendar, scale, and related number theory. If all the various gods on their respective mountains are "thunder-gods," it is, I suspect, because all are Indra's cousins, and we are just beginning to penetrate their disguises.

MT. MERU

Buddhist mythology has an "hour-glass" shaped holy mountain, Mt. Meru, or Sumeru, reminiscent of our "drum of Śiva" in Chart 10 or, more loosely, our reciprocal yantras in Chart 15. By the second century

"Pretty good, but I'll bet you can't hit him again."

• •

Drawing by C. Barsotti; © 1975 The New Yorker Magazine, Inc.

B.C., however, Mt. Meru was clearly identified with a triangle which the West later credited to Pascal. Pingala (c. 200 B.C.) describes explicitly what *Meru* meant to him; his aphorisms are explained by Halāyudha, quoted by A. N. Singh in his essay "On the Use of Series in Hindu Mathematics."[46]

Draw one square at the top; below it draw two squares so that half of each of them lies beyond the former on either side of it. Below them, in the same way, draw three squares; then below them four; and so on up to as many rows as are desired: this is the preliminary representation of the *Meru*. Then putting down 1 in the first square, the figuring should be started. In the next two squares put 1 in each. In the third row put 1 in each of the extreme squares, and in the middle square put the sum of the two numbers in the two squares of the second row. In the fourth row put 1 in each of the two extreme squares: in an intermediate square put the sum of the numbers in the two squares of the previous row which lie just above it. Putting down of numbers in the other rows should be carried on in the same way. Now the numbers in the second row of squares show the monosyllabic forms: there are two forms each consisting of one long and one short syllable. The numbers in the third row give the disyllabic forms: in one form all syllables are long, in two forms one syllable is short (and the other long), and in one all syllables are short. In this row of the squares we get the number of variations of the even verse. The numbers in the fourth row of squares represent trisyllabic forms. There one form has all syllables long, three have one syllable short, three have two short syllables, and one has all syllables short. And so on in the fifth and succeeding rows; the figure in the first square gives the number of forms with all syllables long, that in the last all syllables short, and the figures in the successive intermediate squares represent the number of forms with one, two, etc. short syllables."

Thus according to the above, the number of variations of a metre containing n syllables will be obtained from the representation of the *Meru* as follows:

CHART 43

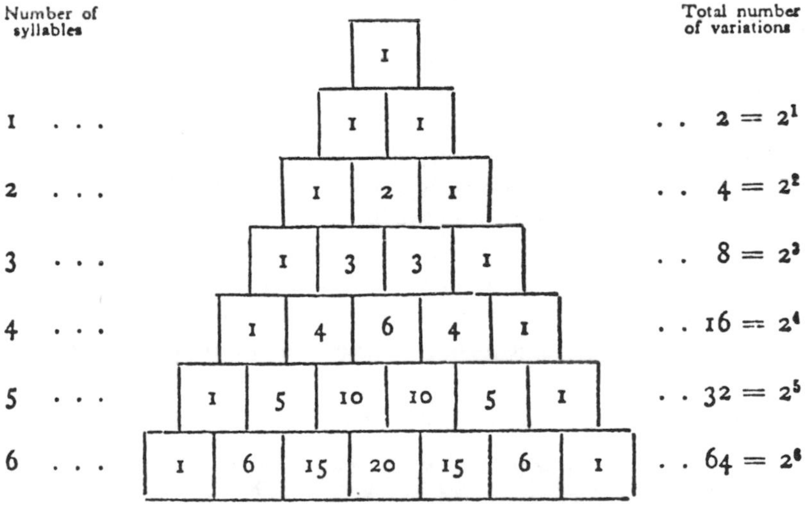

(Meru prastāra)

Mt. Meru, the "Holy Mountain," c. 200 B.C.

Piṅgala's Mt. Meru, or "Pascal" triangle, is related intimately to our tables of ratios, and in a way certainly known to the Babylonians who were experts with quadratic equations. Our yantras are charts of continuing ratios of the form A:B::B:C, etc., that is, of logarithmic progressions held rigidly to the integers available in particular sets. Piṅgala's numbers are "coefficients of binomial expansions," *i.e.*, $(A + B)^n$. For instance, $(A + B)^2 = 1A^2 + 2AB + 1B^2$, while $(A + B)^3$ is $1A^3 + 3A^2B + 3AB^2 + 1B^3$, as shown in the third and fourth rows from the top of Chart 42, corresponding to the variations in meter of two and three syllables respectively. We see in this how perfectly the Hindus wedded music, mathematics, and poetry. Note the further happy fact that the *sums* of these coefficents (see Piṅgala's "total number of variations") in each row always numbers some power of 2, hence our familiar female prime number *continues* to play its "mother" matrix role.

Neugebauer has shown the Babylonians solving "quadratic equations" with routine ease and working with unknowns to the sixth and eighth degrees; hence it is not surprising that nearly two millenia later Piṅgala knew a table of coefficients.[47] The question of *origins*, however, remains as baffling as ever. While it is easy to admire the Babylonians, they were conscious of their own debts to Sumer, while the Sumerians in turn looked for enlightenment from the East.

In this chapter we have rambled over vast areas of time and space without reaching the limit of what we can learn from the multiplication table we started with. We are searching for the roots of number theory, of musical theory, and of religious conviction, for the radical assumptions on which culture is grounded. In India, as in no other land, we can watch the birth of the gods in the minds of musical poets and discover that continuity of tradition which maintains a perfect unity between music, mathematics, and metaphysics. What happened to this intensive unity, whose beginnings are shrouded in the mystery of the moon and the seductive voices of pipes and strings, that the tradition was lost in the West? Where was the line of transmission sundered? In the next chapter, in Plato's myth of "Lost Atlantis," we shall explore the "poetic lie" in which he tried to bequeath this Eastern tradition to the West.

FOOTNOTES

1. Samuel Noah Kramer, *The Sumerians* (Chicago: The University of Chicago Press, 1963), p. 291.
2. *Ibid.*, pp. 147 and 281.
3. *Ibid.*, pp. 42 and 288. I quote this cliché to make clear that the emphasis on Babylonian debts to Sumer is Kramer's.

FOOTNOTES

4. Otto Neugebauer, *The Exact Sciences in Antiquity* (New York: Dover Publications, Inc., 1969), p. 48.
5. Kramer, *op. cit.*, p. 93.
6. Neugebauer, *op. cit.*, p. 36.
7. *Ibid.*, p. 48.
8. *Ibid.*, p. 148.
9. David Wulstan, "The Earliest Musical Notation," *Music and Letters*, Vol. 52, 1971, pp. 365–382.
10. Henry George Farmer, "The Music of Ancient Egypt," *New Oxford History of Music* (London: Oxford University Press, 1957), Vol. 1, p. 275.
11. Neugebauer, *op. cit.*, p. 51.
12. *Mathematical Cuneiform Texts*, Otto Neugebauer and A. Sachs, eds., (New Haven: American Oriental Society, 1945), p. 36.
13. Henry George Farmer, "The Music of Ancient Mesopotamia," *New Oxford History of Music*, Vol. 1, p. 236.
14. Neugebauer, *The Exact Sciences in Antiquity*, p. 32. Numerical values of the deities are given by E. A. Wallis Budge in *Amulets and Talismans* (New Hyde Park, N.Y.: University Books, 1968), p. 427.
15. *New Oxford History of Music*, Vol. 1, p. 230.
16. *The Republic of Plato*, Allan Bloom, trans. (New York: Basic Books, 1968), p. 546c.
17. *Mathematical Cuneiform Texts*, pp. 42–43.
18. Neugebauer, *The Exact Sciences in Antiquity*, p. 52.
19. *Ibid.*, p. 99.
20. Alexander Heidel, *The Gilgamesh Epic and Old Testament Parallels* (Chicago: The University of Chicago Press, 1946 and 1963), pp. 76–77.
21. *The Holy Bible*, Revised Standard Version (New York: Thomas Nelson and Sons, 1952), Deuteronomy 34:7.
22. *Ibid.*, II Chronicles 5:12.
23. *Ibid.*, Acts 1:15.
24. *Ibid.*, Genesis 6:3.
25. Joseph Campbell, *The Masks of God: Oriental Mythology* (New York: The Viking Press, 1970), p. 119.
26. *Mathematical Cuneiform Texts*, pp. 37–41.
27. Samuel Noah Kramer, *History Begins at Sumer* (Garden City: Doubleday & Company Inc., 1959), p. 171.
28. *The Sumerians*, pp. 120–121.
29. *History Begins at Sumer*, p. 91.
30. Samuel Noah Kramer, *Sumerian Mythology* (Philadelphia: University of Pennsylvania Press, revised edition 1972), p. 52.
31. Alexander Heidel, *The Babylonian Genesis* (Chicago: The University of Chicago Press, 1963), lines 38 to 40 of Tablet I of *Enuma Elish*, p. 19.

32. *History Begins at Sumer*, p. 91.
33. *Ibid.*
34. *The Sumerians*, p. 181.
35. Heidel, *op. cit.*, Tablet VI of *Enuma Elish*, p. 48.
36. *Ibid.*, lines 58–62, p. 48.
37. J. Norman Lockyer, *The Dawn of Astronomy* (Cambridge: The M.I.T. Press, 1964; first edition, 1894), pp. 375–376.
38. Kramer, *The Sumerians*, p. 304.
39. Heidel, *The Gilgamesh Epic*, p. 65.
40. Among the valuable writings of S. H. Hooke are *Middle Eastern Mythology* (Harmondsworth: Penguin Books, 1963) and *Babylonian and Assyrian Religion* (Norman: University of Oklahoma Press, 1963).
41. Kramer, *The Sumerians*, p. 149.
42. Campbell, *op. cit.*, p. 129. In regard to sexagesimal arithmetic, Campbell states explicitly his belief that "the Book of Genesis may carry her secretly throughout, in the mathematics of the destiny of its People of God." I share that belief; some subtlety in calendar arithmetic, however, remains elusive.
43. The systematic unfolding of a multiplication table for numbers 3^p5^q is abruptly interfered with by the limiting numbers in our yantras, thus producing the jagged "lightning" side of what otherwise would be perfect triangular arrays. Ernst Levy suggests that these arbitrary and changeable limiting numbers be called the "index" of the yantra. They function as least common denominators for some restricted viewpoint.
44. J. Eric S. Thompson, *Maya Hieroglyphic Writing* (Norman: University of Oklahoma Press, 1960, 1971), p. 155.
45. In 1890 Daniel G. Brinton titled his anthology of pre-Colombian hymns *Rig-Veda Americanus* in clear recognition of their many parallels to our Hindu hymns. The extensive debts of the Mayan calendar to India are developed in detail by Hugh A. Moran and David H. Kelley in *The Alphabet and the Ancient Calendar Signs*, 2nd ed. (Palo Alto, CA: Daily Press, 1969). There are very many parallels in the arithmetic elements in the mythologies, but I hesitate to try to develop them without the assistance of an expert in Mesoamerican languages and literature.
46. A.N. Singh, "On the Use of Series in Hindu Mathematics," *Osiris*, Vol. 1, (January, 1936), pp. 623–624.
47. Neugebauer, *The Exact Sciences in Antiquity*, pp. 41 and 48.

11

LOST ATLANTIS

PLATO'S MUSICAL CITIES

In Plato's Greece the harmonical wisdom of India and Babylon was transformed into political theory. Men now acted out the roles once assigned to gods. Plato's four model cities—Callipolis, Ancient Athens, Atlantis, and Magnesia—were each associated with a specific musical-mathematical model, with individual algebraic yantras and related tone-maṇḍalas.[1] These four models were generated from the first ten integers, Socrates' "children up to ten," and are reducible to a study of four primes, 2, 3, 5, and 7. Plato's last city, Magnesia, developed in detail in *Laws*, not quite finished at his death in 347 B.C., is complicated by the presence of all four primes and will not be presented here. Callipolis and Ancient Athens, however, simple "Drum of Śiva" subsets of a star-hexagon Atlantis tuning, are intimately related to Hindu constructions we already know.

"Lost Atlantis" was invented to illustrate the political theory of the *Republic*. Its acoustical model is established in Socrates' famous "marriage allegory" or "Muses' jest" of the *Republic*, Book VIII. I propose to summarize Plato's allegorical arithmetic, coupling a logical analysis of his *Republic* mathematics with a subjective interpretation of his *Critias* metaphor to show how Atlantis dramatizes the meaning of the *Republic*. Finally, I shall suggest how Plato's Atlantis material—in many respects identical with the musical mythology of India, Mesopotamia, and Palestine—may have come to him straight out of Egypt, exactly as he claimed.

Atlantis was the worst possible city Plato could conceive. And for one reason: it lacked a *principle of limitation*. "Self-limitation" is the most important Socratic principle, applicable to individuals as well as to states. Its absence can lead only to strife, within the soul of the individual as within the community of nations. Atlantis, an island paradise created by the descendants of Poseidon, was so ignorant of any method of "birth control" that it reached a population of 12,960,000 in just four generations; this led to such an uncontrollable inflation of its needs that "it insolently advanced against all Europe and Asia" and Atlanteans finally had to be chastised by Zeus himself to "bring them back to tune."[2]

We can thank Glaucon for inspiring the tale. When Socrates waxes eloquent describing an ideal city "created by our needs" and strictly limited to what man finds *necessary*, he stipulates a health-fad diet of "salt, olives, cheese, . . . onions and greens, . . . figs, pulse, and beans, . . . myrtleberries and acorns." At the mention of berries and acorns, Plato's older brother, a lover of luxury, rudely interrupts:

> If you were providing for a city of sows, Socrates, on what else would you fatten them than this?

Glaucon's sarcasm startles Socrates only for a moment, and in that moment there is born the idea of a second city, to serve as a foil for the "best" one:

> All right. I understand. We are, as it seems, considering not only how a city, but also a luxurious city comes into being. Perhaps that's not bad either. For in considering such a city too, we could probably see in what way justice and injustice naturally grow in cities. Now the true city is in my opinion the one we just described—a healthy city, as it were. But, if you want to, let's look at a feverish city too. Nothing stands in the way.[3]

The second city is not actually named Atlantis until the story is continued in the *Timaeus* dialogue, and the city is not fully developed until the second half of *Critias* where Plato overloads its description with so much arithmetical and geometrical detail that it seems evident that Atlantis concerns mathematics and nothing else. It is a city rich in the luxuries Socrates knew would appeal to Glaucon's tastes:

> perfume, incense, courtesans, and cakes . . . painting and embroidery . . . rhapsodes, actors, choral dancers, . . . wet nurses, governesses, beauticians, barbers, . . . relish makers and cooks.[4]

Such a city would need an ever-larger army, Socrates points out, to support its encroachment on "neighbor's land, if we are going to have sufficient for pasture and tillage," and a still larger one "which will go out and do battle with invaders for all the wealth and all the things we were just now talking about." If Glaucon insists on inflating the *necessary* into the *luxurious*, tribulation is bound to follow, and a younger brother's pen revels in the obtuseness of an elder as it spins this moral lesson through the trilogy of *Republic*, *Timaeus*, and *Critias*.

GILBERT RYLE'S HYPOTHESIS

Before I begin an interpretation of Plato's myth of Atlantis as a kind of Pythagorean Grand Opera complete with an all-star cast, a water show, dazzling scenery, and a tragic finale, let us pause a moment to consider Plato's first audience. In *Plato's Progress* Gilbert Ryle tried to establish a plausible chronology for Plato's dialogues.[5] Parts of the *Republic*, which lays the mathematical foundations for Atlantis, and the unfinished *Critias*, which elaborates the mathematics into a colorful island empire, were written in the spring of 367 B.C., Ryle believes, in preparation for Plato's second visit with the Pythagorean community in Sicily. I like Ryle's hypothesis because it explains why so many mathematical jests would have been understood perfectly by Plato's first audience while passing completely over the heads of uninitiated later readers who could enjoy only the play of surface imagery. Mathematical humor is strictly for mathematicians, or for those who can multiply and divide well enough not to be intimidated by experts. Whoever has understood my earlier chapters would have been more than qualified to attend that feast in Syracuse where Plato possibly first read *Critias* to the local Pythagoreans gathered at the home of his host, Archedemus, chief disciple of their current leader, Archytas. That audience, presumably, had already listened to essential parts of the *Republic*, and it belonged to the tradition devoted to keeping alive in the Greek world the mathematical models inherited from the ancients via the long travels of Pythagoras in Egypt and Babylon.

Any Pythagorean audience would have recognized immediately—as did Ernst Levy, a modern Pythagorean—that the formula "4:3 mated with the 5," which Socrates asserted governed all children in all "musical" cities for all time, contained a genetic flaw which Socrates knew and intended to be fatal.[6] Ernst Levy pointed out that the ratio 4:3 produces tones linked by perfect fourths and fifths, that "mating" with 5 produces pure musical thirds, and that the "unmusical children" Socrates predicted from his formula must therefore be those plagued by the notorious commas which make "Just tuning" impractical and motivate the eventual adoption of some form of "temperament." It was Robert Brumbaugh, however, in his *Plato's Mathematical Imagination*, who actually articulated the significance of an octave matrix, of the principle of smallest integers, of the functions of geometrical metaphor, and the utility of graphical methods in studying Plato.[7] The Levy-Brumbaugh insights lead to a musical analysis of Socrates "Muses' jest."

THE MUSES' JEST

In the "Muses' jest"[8] Socrates develops his formula for "mating" 4:3 with 5 to the limit of $60^4 = 12{,}960{,}000$, a number he declares to be "sovereign of better and worse begettings." He introduces his formula for generating "musical" cities by a statement that emphasizes *cycles*: "bearing and barrenness of soul and bodies come . . . when revolutions complete for each the bearing round of circles." All elements in his formula "make like and unlike, and . . . wax and wane"; they generate *reciprocals* arithmetically, and rising-falling (waxing-waning) scales tonally. Everything must be "conversable and rational"; fractions are banned and results are expressed according to least common denominators. With these stipulations, Socrates then proceeds with the formula for a number "sovereign of better and worse begettings," meaning, I believe, that no larger number was of any interest to an aulos-playing philosopher like himself. The formula is to the uninitiated marvelous gibberish; but to the initiated it condenses a textbook on tuning theory into three sentences.

> The root 4:3 mated with the 5, thrice increased, produces two harmonies. One of them is equal an equal number of times, taken one hundred times over. The other is of equal length in one way but is an oblong; on one side, of one hundred rational diameters of the five, lacking one for each; or, if of irrational diameters, lacking two for each; on the other side, of one hundred cubes of the three. This whole geometrical number is sovereign of better and worse begettings.

My musical interpretation is based on James Adam's definitive arithmetical analysis, published in 1902.[9] Adam reasoned that "4:3 mated with the 5" meant the multiplication $3 \times 4 \times 5 = 60$ in order that by establishing a least common denominator for a set of ratios a *starting point* be given. "Three increases" for the "geometrical number" of 60 means *geometrical progression* through the sequence 60, 60^2, and 60^3 to 60^4 ($= 12{,}960{,}000$). Then taking Socrates' words literally, Adam factored this number into certain mathematical components out of which a musical analysis would follow but which he never thought of trying. Adam's two numerical components are Socrates' "two harmonies," and each contains significant musical "indexes."

1) $12{,}960{,}000 = 3600^2 = (36 \times 100)(36 \times 100)$
2) $12{,}960{,}000 = 4800 \times 2700 = (48 \times 100)(27 \times 100)$

In the first equation or harmony each side contains the factor 3,600; hence sides are "equal an equal number of times," that is, twice, "taken one hundred times over," referring to 36×100. The second harmony is an "oblong," 4800×2700. The number 48 is 1 less than 49 and 2 less than 50. The square root of 49 is the *rational* approximation to the length of the diagonal (Socrates' "diameter") of a square with sides of 5 units (note the allusion to the "Jubilee comma" of 49:50). "One hundred cubes of the three" then comes out as $100 \times 3^3 = 2700$.

Consider now what these factors mean as Levy "musical indexes," that is, as arbitrary limits of a potentially infinite arithmetical-tonal expansion. The number 60 is the foundation of *diatonic reciprocity*, as shown in Chart 3. The numbers 36, 48, and 60 are the terminal numbers for the *pentatonic* subsets in Chart 7, "Indra as Dancer and Lord of the Five Tribes." The number 27 is the terminal number in the "Drum of Śiva" in Chart 10b, that is, for a diatonic scale in "Pythagorean tuning," assuming reciprocity and octave equivalence. The "Jubilee comma" of 49:50 results from the reciprocal meanings of 7/5 and 5/7 (see Charts 19c, 20, and 28). Each of Adam's factors is a Levy tonal index except for the musically gratuitous factor of 100 which playfully brings the tone-numbers into harmony, as it playfully expands Atlantean dimensions to outrageous sizes. We have already exhausted the musical meanings of 36, 48, 49, 50, and 60, and also of $60^2 = 3{,}600$, limit of the Sumerian "universe" (see the Bṛhaspati yantra in Chart 12a), and of $60^3 = 216{,}000$ (see the Prajapāti yantra in Chart 12b). The only new element in Plato's construction is the *new context* provided by Socrates' all-embracing index of $60^4 = 12{,}960{,}000$. In Chart 44 I have graphed the reciprocal tonal meanings of numbers 3^p5^q in successive powers of 60 up to the new limit Socrates proclaims sovereign. Looking at this nest of yantras, we now begin that exercise in imagination which transforms a prosaic multiplication table into the majestic "plain of Atlantis," and its related tone-maṇḍalas into the concentric islands of its capital city.

THE PLAIN OF ATLANTIS

When the gods divided the whole earth into lots, some larger, some smaller, Poseidon received as his lot the isle of Atlantis, where lived a mortal woman, Clito, "just husband-high when her mother and father both died."[10] She was just fifteen, Ishtar's number, I suppose, when Poseidon "had to do with her," for when he had fortified her abode with three concentric rings of sea and land, she bore him "five twin births of male offspring" who developed an empire from the ratios of the first six numbers, linking everything in Atlantis to sexagesimal arithmetic. The five "twin births" are the five pairs of tones graphed in the inner yantra of Chart 44 as the reciprocal meanings of *male* numbers $3^p5^q < 60$, the same ten tone-children on which our whole study has been based, and the larger yantras define the integer limits of successive generations via the same ratios. Atlas and Gadirus, the first-born twins, actually correspond with the

CHART 44

The Tone-Field Bounded by the Successive Powers of 60 Interpreted Dialectically

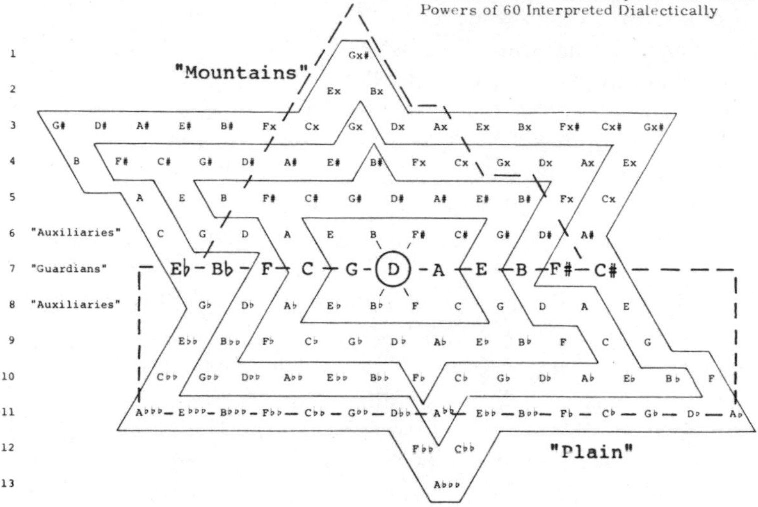

The "Plain of Atlantis" Derived from Reciprocal Tonal Meanings of the Yantras for Numbers $3^p5^q < 60, 60^2, 60^3$, and 60^4

Two tonal "harvests" from the same set of integers makes one-half of the table redundant *arithmetically*. If either upper or lower half is eliminated, then the circular capital city(D) stands at the side of a vast plain, whose "naturally quadrangular" borders are easily "straightened." The plain is traversed by two sets of "canals," a rectangular grid (perfect fourths of 3:4 left to right, and chromatic semitones of 24:25 vertically), on which is superimposed a grid of major thirds of 4:5 along the one axis, /, and minor thirds of 5:6 along the other \. EVERY ELEMENT HAS "REFLECTIVE" SYMMETRY THROUGH THE REFERENCE D. My tonal labels preserve the sense of Plato's algebra (*i.e.*, as sequences of logarithmic or equal-interval progressions), but since each row is displaced from the next by a syntonic comma of ratio 80:81, tone names must not be associated with those in modern equal-temperament.

tones I label A and G, but that is merely a happy coincidence in the history of modern notation. They are the double meanings of "3," or *arithmetic* and *harmonic means* in the octave within D = Poseidon and D′ = Clito. The other twins are derivative via the ratios 5:4 and 5:6. The tone-numbers for any five of them automatically produce the other five as reciprocals. (Consult Chart 29 if this is not intuitively clear.) The house of Atlas, equivalent to A and to both ground-tone and *Mese* in the Greek two-octave scale system, "retained the throne for many generations, the eldest being always king," eldest twins (= "guardians" and "best" children) being graphed along the central horizontal axis of the nest of yantras. Plato, however, forces us to view the construction in a new way.

Notice that the upper and lower halves of my nest of yantras in Chart 44 have "rotational symmetry" around the central axis so that the reciprocal tonal meanings of one set of integers (in either half) are sufficient to produce the total tonal material. My *tonal* yantras are thus *arithmetically redundant* and hence an offense to Platonic model building; we must banish one-half and *assume* dialectical reciprocity to achieve the lofty viewpoint of a Socrates. The dashed lines in Chart 44 suggest, I believe, what Plato intended by his "Plain of Atlantis." The "mountains" which enclose it are still larger numbers. The circular islands of the capital city (the small circle around D) are set in the side of a vast plain, "naturally quadrangular, oblong, and nearly rectangular." "Departures from that shape had been corrected" by Atlantean engineers who not only dug a huge canal around the border but also constructed two canal systems on the plain itself. On a basic rectangular grid (my horizontal arrays of fifths and fourths, ratios 2:3 and 3:4, and vertical arrays of chromatic semitones, ratio 24:25) they superimposed a radial system abstracted from my arrays of major thirds of 4:5 along one axis, /, and minor thirds of 5:6 along the other, \. EVERY ELEMENT IN THE TABLE IS REFLECTED THROUGH D TO ITS OPPOSITE, hence Plato's *radial* system directs our attention to a level of reflective symmetry more subtle than the simple rotational symmetry to which it is allied. His canal network can thus be read as the logarithmic (equal interval) progressions through a yantra from which arithmetical redundancy has been eliminated. But if we agree to banish one-half of the yantra, how is the total tonal sense of Chart 44 to be preserved? Easily, by the "two harvests" Atlantis enjoys each year, one directly from the winter rains, the other by the release of flood-waters through the canals in summer.

Atlantean canals are prodigious. The main one around the borders is 100 feet deep and 600 wide, the others being only 100 feet wide. In the temple of Poseidon, on the sacred acropolis, built from the ratios 3:4:5:6, there are golden statues of one hundred "Nereids round him riding on dolphins." Socrates needed dolphins in the *Republic*. "We too must swim and try to save ourselves from the argument," he said, when his own argument about the differences between men and women got into deep water, "hoping that some dolphin might take us on his back or for some other unusual rescue."[11] In his "Muses' jest" 100 is the extramusical, "playful" factor which harmonizes the tone-numbers, and there is no accident in its recurrence here as the playful factor in Atlantean dimensions, or in the coincidence of dolphins in both the *Republic* and *Critias*. These dialogues, according to Ryle, were never "published" (*i.e.*, copied for others) until after Plato's death, so that he had twenty years to tinker with such internal coincidences. Atlantean bridges are also 100 feet wide, and we study them next in the tone-maṇḍalas which constitute, I believe, the "Islands of Atlantis."

CHART 45

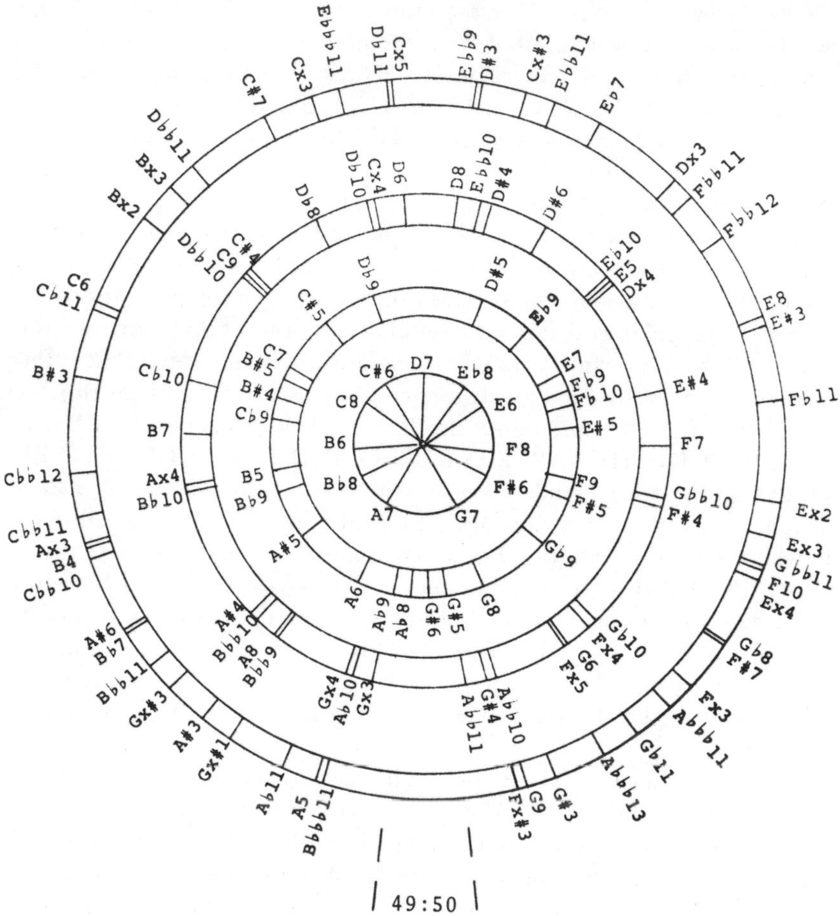

The Islands of Atlantis as Concentric Maṇḍalas for numbers $2^p3^q5^r \leqq 60, 60^2, 60^3$, and $60^4 = 12{,}960{,}000$

For visual clarity only the tones established by new integer ratios in each set are graphed in the outer circles; the largest circle, symbolizing the Atlantean "Sea-Wall" with its closely set houses and clamorous confusion, should also contain all the "cuts" of the inner circles. Numbers refer to rows in the yantras of Chart 44; "best" children or "guardians" are in row 7 (approximating equal-temperament best), "auxiliaries" are in rows 6 and 8, and "children of worse births" are in rows 1–5 and 9–13. The "jubilee comma" alluded to in the "marriage allegory"—ratio 49:50—is superimposed. Because of the restricted space on a page this schematic representation makes no effort to preserve Plato's specifed diameters for the rings of sea and land.

THE ISLANDS OF ATLANTIS

I am assuming that the musical octaves bounded by the successive powers of 60 in Chart 45 constitute the concentric islands of Atlantis, and that the "numerical spaces" between those octaves constitute the intervening rings of water. For visual clarity only the new "tone-children" in the expanding number sets are graphed; radial cuts must be imagined as continuing from the inner island to the outer "sea-wall."

OCTAVES

Poseidon and his ten sons	30:60	= Central island
60 to 1800		= 1st ring of water
Children of the first generation	1800:3600	= 1st ring of land
3,600 to 216,000		= 2nd ring of water
Children of the second generation	180,000:216,000	= 2nd ring of land
216,000 to 6,480,000		= 3rd ring of water
Children of the third generation	6,480,000:12,960,000	= 3rd ring of land

Plato's three "rings of water" have the width ratios 1:2:3, corresponding to the exponents of the sexagesimal expansion. The three rings of land are pierced by "canals," which can be seen, I suggest, at the bottom of the maṇḍalas where someday the equal-tempered A♭ = G♯ = $\sqrt{2}$ will narrow them to a point. The canal to his inner harbor (the *diaschisma* between a♭8 and g♯6) is only wide enough for a "single trireme"; the canal to his outer harbor, however, "would admit the largest of vessels," being 300 feet wide and 100 deep. Bridges to the inner island are 100 feet wide. All canals are "covered over," meaning, I believe, that the octaves representing "land" are in each case a *continuum*, broken by commas or "canals" under some perspectives, but completely "bridged over" under other perspectives.

There are 121 radial cuts in the Atlantean sea-wall. Plato describes it:

> This wall was completely filled by a multitude of closely set houses, and the large harbor and canal were constantly crowded by merchant vessels and their passengers arriving from all quarters, whose vast numbers occasioned incessant shouting, clamor, and general uproar, day and night.[12]

No human ear could make musical sense out of 121 tones in an octave: "incessant shouting, clamor," etc. is an aural disaster. In just four generations we have arrived at an acoustical abomination. Children of "best" births—the musical fourths and fifths along the central axis of the yantras in Chart 44—and of "better" births—those differing by only one syntonic comma in rows 6 and 8—are swamped by "worse births" differing by two or three commas. Poseidon has done no better than the Babylonian Apsu or the Hebrew Jehovah in creating an *orderly* universe. It is the human number 5 (*i.e.*, pure musical thirds) which causes the trouble; every one of the original "guardians and their auxiliaries" is surrounded now by a pair of discordant "great grandchildren" (three rows away in the yantra, along the diagonals ///, etc.) at the ratio of the diesis, 125:128. The diatonic limitation within which "Just tuning" works acceptably has been violated. It cannot be extended into a practicable chromatic transposition system. Socrates was not joking when he warned, in his "Muses' jest," that "4:3 mated with the 5" would produce children who "will become more unmusical." Nor was Plato joking at the end of *Critias* when, seeing the Atlantean's "human temper to predominate" over "the god's part," (*i.e.*, 5^n predominating over 3^n), he has Zeus intervene:

> Zeus, the god of gods, who governs his kingdom by law, having the eye by which such things are seen, beheld their goodly house in its grievous plight and was minded to lay a judgment on them, THAT THE DISCIPLINE MIGHT BRING THEM BACK TO TUNE. So he gathered all the gods in his most honorable residence, even that that stands at the world's center and overlooks all that has part in becoming, and when he had gathered them, he said . . .

What Zeus said the reader must imagine for himself, for there the dialogue ends, in the middle of a sentence.

Someday—if musicians and mathematicians can learn to philosophize together again—perhaps there can be a new symposium where, when the wine has flowed freely and cold reason takes flight in poetic fancy, many other numerical cues in the Atlantis story can be developed musically. The "two springs" on the Atlantean acropolis, I suggest, may be two "Nicomachean triangles," one for the prime numbers 2 and 3, the other for 3 and 5. And the ten kings who assemble there "at alternate intervals of five and six years, thus showing equal respect for even number and odd," may be maintaining the ratios 5:4 and 6:5 which generate their descendants. Some of this fun should be left to others.

But Socrates claimed that his number $60^4 = 12{,}960{,}000$ was sovereign of *both* "better and worse begettings." We have watched Atlantis disintegrate; how could it have been saved? Callipolis and Ancient Athens show us how.

CALLIPOLIS AND ANCIENT ATHENS

The eleven tones along the central horizontal axis of the yantras in Chart 44 belong to "Pythagorean tuning," and they are the *maximum* number which can display the symmetry beloved in the ancient world without coming to grief with the Pythagorean comma at A♭ ≠ G♯. By themselves, such tones need only the numbers 2^p3^q, and in Callipolis, Plato's "absolutely best" city—his "celestial city," the *diatonic* scale sung by the Sirens in his planetary model—seven numbers required for the diatonic scale produce all eleven tones.

	384	432	486	512	576	648	729	768
rising	D	E	F♯	G	A	B	C♯	D
falling	D	C	B♭	A	G	F	E♭	D

Such a city, Socrates declared, would be "truly biggest, even if it should be made up of only one thousand defenders."[13] (The largest genetic element is $3^6 = 729$, and in scale order the octave is bounded by 768.)

In the Atlantis model, there are actually ten tone-numbers for the eleven tones. (Note that E♭ lies outside the basic yantra, indicated by the dashed lines of the "mountain," hence is present only as the reciprocal meaning of the same number as C♯.) Ten such tones, defining nine consecutive perfect fifths or fourths, require as genetic components ten powers of 3 from $3^0 = 1$ to $3^9 = 19{,}683$. In *scale* order and *smallest integers*, the octave for these ten is bounded by the number 20,736. Hence when Plato is describing Ancient Athens, the much smaller but far superior protagonist of Atlantis, he can make a very canny arithmetic jest concerning its army:

> The number of both sexes already qualified and still qualified to bear arms they were careful to keep, as nearly as possible, always the same, roughly some twenty thousand.

The two relevant indexes for the ten "best" children are $3^9 = 19{,}683$ and the octave 10,368:20,736, and the *smallest error* any Pythagorean could make in the calculation involves a factor of 2 or of 3, thus "roughly some twenty thousand" is a more than adequate cue to anyone familiar with Plato's musical methods. My next two charts summarize this arithmetic in ways which can be studied at leisure.

In Chart 46 I have tabulated the arithmetic of Callipolis, Ancient Athens, the "best" guardians in Atlantis, and the Ṛgvedic gods in Kalpa. For those who understand acoustical theory, only the first column—numbers from 3^0 to 3^9—is *essential*; all other numerosity is mere "*appearances*." The principle involved is that of smallest integers for a given

CHART 46

		x	Callipolis	x	Athens	x	Atlantis	x	Ṛgvedic Gods in Kalpa
$3^0 =$	1	2^9	= 512 (A or G)	2^5	= 16384	5^4	= 10,240,000 (F♯ or B♭)	$5^3 2$	= 2,560,000,000 (F or B)
$3^1 =$	3	2^7	= 384 (D or D′)	2^5	= 12288	5^4	= 7,680,000 (B or F)	$5^3 2^2$	= 3,840,000,000 (C or E)
$3^2 =$	9	2^6	= 576 (G or A)	2^5	= 18432	5^4	= 11,520,000 (E or C)	$5^3 2$	= 2,880,000,000 (G or A)
$3^3 =$	27	2^4	= 432 (C or E)	2^5	= 13824	5^4	= 8,640,000 (A or G)	$5^3 2^2$	= 4,320,000,000 (D or D′)
$3^4 =$	81	2^3	= 648 (F or B)	2^5	= 20736	5^4	= 12,960,000 (D or D′)	$5^3 2$	= 3,240,000,000 (A or C)
$3^5 =$	243	2	= 486 (B♭ or F♯)	2^5	= 15552	5^4	= 9,720,000 (G or A)	$5^3 2$	= 2,430,000,000 (E or C)
$3^6 =$	729		= 729 (E♭ or C♯)	2^4	= 11664	5^4	= 7,290,000 (C or E)	$5^3 2^2$	= 3,645,000,000 (B or F)
$3^7 =$	2187		= --- (A♭ or G♯)	2^3	= 17496	5^4	= 10,935,000 (F or B)	$5^3 2$	= 2,733,750,000 (F♯ or B♭)
$3^8 =$	6561		= --- (D♭ or D♯)	2	= 13122	5^4	= 8,201,250 (B♭ or F♯)	$5^3 2^2$	= 4,100,625,000 (C♯ or E♭)
$3^9 =$	19683		= --- (G♭ or A♯)		19683	5^4	= 12,301,875 (E♭ or C♯)	$5^3 2$	= 3,075,468,750 (G♯ or A♭)

Hindu-Greek Modular Equivalents

Powers of 3 are the numerical genetic determinant in Pythagorean tuning, powers of 2 being employed to project them into the preferred octave. Powers of 5 are useful only for relations with pure thirds; they occur in these sets only because of the symmetric expansion of the algebra which makes Just tuning the parent of Pythagorean, or the "superset of all subsets." The diatonic scale for Callipolis requires the octave double 384:768; this contains the material for Plato's planetary model and is the "best" or "celestial" city of the Republic. All the larger number sets belong to ancient history, not to Plato's Greece. In all sets the terminal number is assigned to D to facilitate direct comparisons.

context. In Chart 47 this material is presented as a triangular pattern of pebbles, ten to a side, and as a Nicomachean table for perfect fifths of ratio 2:3. It should be stressed that it is Plato himself, and not I, who identifies the arithmetic numbers of *Timaeus* with "citizens of Ancient Athens." That city was founded from the divine incest of Hephaestus and Athena, children of Zeus. They symbolize, I believe, the male and female

CHART 47

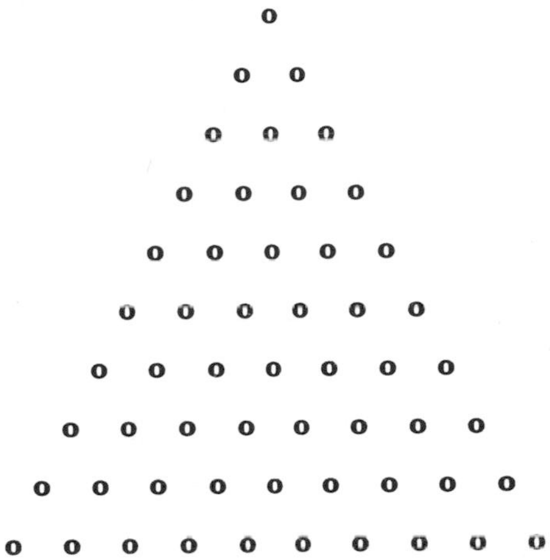

											(freq)		(length)
1	2	4	8	16	32	64	128	256	512	=	F♯	or	B♭
	3	6	12	24	48	96	192	384	768	=	B	or	F
		9	18	36	72	144	288	576	1152	=	E	or	C
			27	54	108	216	432	864	1728	=	A	or	G
				81	162	324	648	1296	2592	=	D	or	D′
					243	486	972	1944	3888	=	G	or	A
						729	1458	2916	5832	=	C	or	E
							2187	4374	8748	=	F	or	B
								6561	13122	=	B♭	or	F♯
									19683	=	E♭	or	C♯

Nicomachean Table for Numbers 2^p3^q, the "Army of Ancient Athens"

Tone names could be chosen from any sequence of perfect fifths; the names in Chart 46 correspond to string-length or wave-length ratios here. The octave ratios 1:2 are set across the "breadth" of the table, powers of 3 which define musical twelfths are set along the "diagonal," and the smallest integers for one or more perfect fifths can be found in the vertical columns. Since this table functions as the example *in smallest integers* for all possible tables of continuing ratios, it can just as well be symbolized by the abstract pebble pattern.

prime numbers 3 and 2 respectively, derivable only from "the One itself." We are cued musically by the very first words of *Timaeus*: "One, two, three. . . . " The Nicomachean triangle for numbers 2^p3^q, I suggest, is the "single spring" on the Acropolis of Ancient Athens.[14]

We have not exhausted the musical implications of Plato's Atlantis, and have barely touched on the extensive musical ramifications of his *Republic*, but we have gone far enough, I hope, to justify Socrates' boast that his "marriage" arithmetic is "sovereign" in "musical" politics. The reader will have noticed how little of Plato's material is really new. But Plato's compression is extreme; we are watching the Greek mind reworking the ancient, inherited material. There are those who do their Plato research in scuba gear, groping in the mud—off Greece, or Spain, or South America—looking for the "Lost" Atlantis which they believe lies buried, and for the golden statues of Poseidon and his ten sons, and a hundred Nereids riding dolphins. But we who study the *Republic*, with or even without its long-ignored musical implications, know that it contains an incomparably greater treasure for the spirit.

EGYPTIAN DERIVATION

When Aristotle was asked what happened to Atlantis, he supposedly replied: "Its inventor caused it to disappear."[15] Through the ages Platonists have treated the story of Atlantis as a kind of invention, like a fairy tale, neither taking Plato literally nor suspecting the musical meaning of the story. Plato attributed the story to a priest of Saïs, in Egypt, and about 320 B.C., Crantor, author of the first full commentary on *Timaeus*, supposedly sent a delegation to Saïs to check on the story. According to Proclus (fifth c. A.D.) the delegation reported that the Atlantis story was engraved on stone, exactly as Plato said. For many years I attributed this report to the credulity in the Academy. Crantor, however, is very important historically; it is from him (via Plutarch and others) that we know the Academy was familiar with 384 as a "multiplier" for the Pythagorean scale, and with a "lambda" arrangement of Plato's "cube of 3," which was itself the lower half of a "Drum of Śiva."[16]

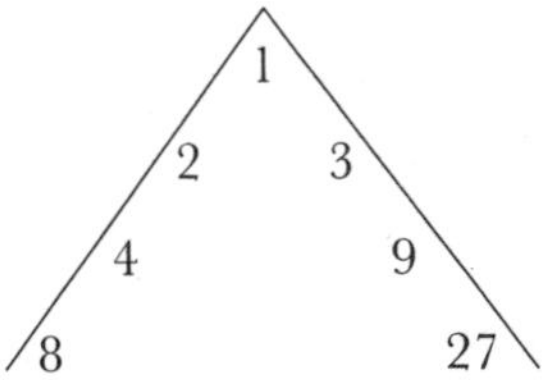

Crantor obviously merits respect; he is a crucial link to the past. Why did he fall for the story from Egypt?

We have inherited a considerable literature from Egypt, and in the last century much of it has become available in translation. More recently the translation of mathematical texts has added another dimension to what we know about the period c. 1800 B.C. It is something of a puzzle to current scholars that the Greeks, who inherited the Babylonian mathematics, as can be demonstrated, nevertheless always credited the Egyptians, whose own mathematics was far inferior, with having been their teachers. So it is with the musical materials of Atlantis; we could, with no difficulty at all, suppose them to have been inherited from Babylon. But Plato said his source was Egypt, and the Crantor anecdote ostensibly confirms him. I propose now to survey quickly elements in Egyptian mythology and mathematics which help to confirm that claim.

EGYPTIAN MUSIC

At the end of the fourth millenium B.C., when Egypt was unified and her dynasties founded, Egyptian musical instruments were identical with those of Sumer.[17] Of Egyptian music itself nothing survives but the instruments and a substantial body of hymns and a wealth of paintings and literary commentary which teach us that "in the wider use of these instruments, Egypt surpassed Mesopotamia a hundredfold."[18] Prominent among typically Sumerian instruments recovered from Egyptian tombs are the harps and pipes which must have taught their makers something about length ratios on strings and pipes. The Egyptian attitude toward tone was purely Vedic, regarding it as the key to the mystery of the universe. In the Egyptian temple,

> the human voice is the instrument par excellence of the priest and enchanter. It is the voice that seeks afar the Invisibles summoned, and makes the necessary objects into reality. . . . But as every one (of the notes) has its peculiar force, great care must be taken not to change their order or substitute one for the other.[19]

EGYPTIAN MATHEMATICS

Historians of science refer to Egyptian computation contemptuously as "elementary household arithmetic which no mathematician would call mathematics."[20] Mathematical papyri from the period 1800 B.C. to about 1600 B.C. show the Egyptians substantially below the level of the Babylonians of the same period and are of interest mainly as "a relatively primitive level . . . which is no longer available in so simple a form, except in the Egyptian documents."[21] My whole study is an effort to recover the earliest methods of mathematical harmonics, thus Egyptian methods are of the very greatest interest. "Elementary household arithmetic" is the kind most convenient on the monochord where experience is rooted in the halving and doubling that produce octave identities. Egyptian methods were adequate for musical theorists until the monochord was supplanted in our own century by the oscilloscope and electronic counter. Whoever has studied the monochord, as Pythagoras reputedly recommended on his deathbed, will recognize Egyptian habits as his own, but with variations most of us are unaware of.

The Egyptians calculated the higher multiple of any number as the *sum* of numbers arising from consecutive doublings, taking advantage of the principle that *every integer can be expressed as the sum of numbers* 2^p.[22] For instance, to multiply 25 by 18, make a table of consecutive doublings of 25; then since 18 can be expressed as the sum of 2^1 and 2^4, the product of 25 by 18 can be found by checking the appropriate elements in the table and adding, as shown below.

	1	25
/	2	50
	4	100
	8	200
/	16	400
	total	450

All steps of the process were exhibited. To divide 450 by 25 required the construction of the same table, hence multiplication and division were actually reduced to addition from a sequence of "octave-doubles." By this ingenious device the "female number 2" was made to "give birth" to all larger numbers. This Egyptian method of calculation maintained itself unchanged into the Hellenistic period and later, "duplatio" being taught as an independent operation even during the Middle Ages.[23]

Where fractions were required, the Egyptians had recourse to "unit fractions" of the form 1/n (*e.g.*, 1/2, 1/3, 1/4, 1/5, etc.), with which they were virtuosi. There was a special sign for 2/3, but a number like 2/5 had to be expressed as 1/3 + 1/15. The "superparticular" ratios of the musical theorist are disguised Egyptian unit fractions: the ratio 2:3, for instance, means 2 + 1/2 or 3 − 1/3 in practice. All tones in all the scales we have been studying can be reached by a unit fraction from the tone above or below, or by a *leimma* "left-over" from an earlier operation with unit fractions (see Chart 1).

Where it was desired to avoid fractions, the Egyptians simply transformed the expressions in terms of a least common denominator and changed to red ink to call attention to a change in procedure. These numbers in red ink are called "auxiliary numbers" by modern scholars and are defined as "the numerators of fractions which have been reduced to a common denominator."[24] Our musical "tone-numbers"—limited to integers—are

Egyptian "auxiliary numbers"; they became somewhat obsolete in Greece when Ptolemy expressed all Greek tunings as integers within the 60:120 octave together with *sexagesimal fractions* where necessary, but they continued to be used by men like Proclus and Boethius and their successors on into the sixteenth century and later.

The one superiority of Egyptian calculation over Babylonian is in its better approximation to pi.[25] The Egyptians calculated the area of a

CHART 48

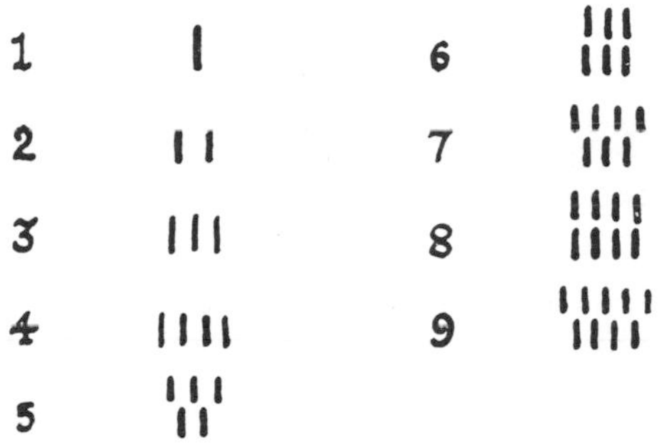

The earliest Egyptian symbols for the numbers 1 to 9.

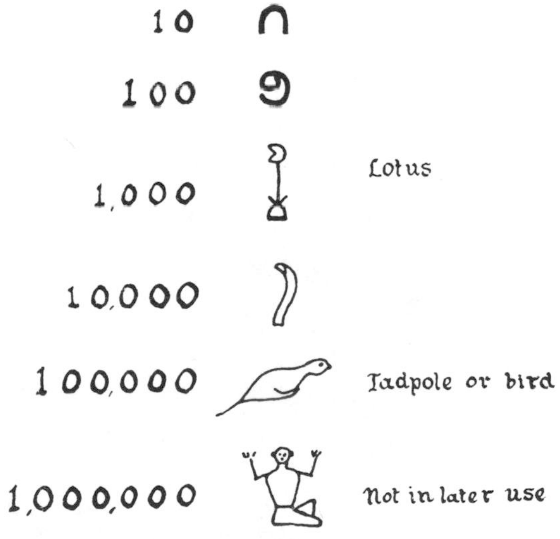

Egyptian symbols for large numbers.

Egyptian Mathematical Notation:

From *Mathematics in the Time of the Pharaohs* by Richard J. Gillings, p. 5.[26]

circle by squaring 8/9ths of its diameter, equivalent to the following formula:

$$pi \sim 4(8/9)^2 = 3.1605$$

Even this has a musical twist: taking the diameter as the ground tone, ascend a wholetone of 8:9 (*i.e.*, subtract 1/9) and square the remainder. (Neugebauer has recently located this value also in Babylon.)

Acoustical theory requires either very small fractions or very large whole numbers, and the earliest Egyptians possessed both a fascination with large numbers and an appropriate notation for them. There were symbols for units, tens, hundreds, etc., up to millions, each symbol being repeated up to nine times where necessary.[26]

The climax of Egyptian arithmetic is in the so-called "aha-calculations," similar to our linear equations in one unknown.

> They bear witness to the purely theoretical interests of the Egyptian computers. They have obviously been set up by people who enjoyed pure calculations and who wanted to drill their pupils on really hard problems.[27]

Egyptian geometry, like that of Babylon, was not a science in the Greek sense of the word, "but merely *applied arithmetic*."[28] The primary fascination was with number itself.

Of special interest are the "Horus eye" fractions used in computing measures of grain (specifically, fractions of a *hekat*, a half-peck dry measure for barley, wheat, corn, and grain generally). Each line in the eye of Horus, the hawk, son of Osiris and right eye of the Sun, represents one of the reciprocal powers of 2 from 1/2, 1/4, 1/8, 1/16, 1/32, to 1/64. Hence the "female number 2" not only produces all larger numbers but also all smaller quantities of the grain on which man feeds.

CHART 49

Eye of Horus — Interpretation[29]

We have Plutarch to thank for the information that the Egyptians considered 2 to be "female," but we owe deeper thanks to the heroic efforts of modern scholars who by deciphering the ancient mathematical papyri help us understand in how many ways 2 is the matrix number in all Egyptian calculation.

Primitive as it seems to others, Egyptian mathematics is in many ways the mathematics of the monochord student and instrument-maker, of the ancient harp-maker and later organ-builder, of the musical theorist and the carpenter alike down through the ages which lacked *a finely graduated and fixed metric scale* and the conveniences of slide rule and logarithmic tables. It exploits doubling and halving to the limit. Nothing in my study was beyond the reach of the Egyptians. I turn now to the evidence that the numerology in Egyptian mythology may have had an essentially musical basis.

EGYPTIAN MYTHOLOGY

Egyptian mythology is at least as colorful as that of India. It exhibits a similar fascination with the generation of the world, with polarities among its pantheon of deities, and with the balance between good and evil both in a man's heart and in the whole universe, with confrontations between the sun in the heavens and the serpent below, and with the exact numbers of everything from the length of a sacred serpent, the eggs of a sacred crocodile, the boats of Osiris (Osiris being the deification of "the Good"), the dimensions of the holy mountain, the offerings of beer and grain, and even with the awesome total of spirit-souls (*Khus*) in the eternal realm of the dead.[30] The numbers and graphic relations used by the Egyptians are often those we already understand from their roles in India, Sumer, and Babylon as having a musical interpretation.

The number 60, "the first of measures for such persons as concern themselves with the heavenly bodies," is the number of eggs of the sacred crocodile, and they hatch in sixty days and live sixty years.[31] The sun rises after a double *hen* period of 120 years (*i.e.*, $2 \times 60 = 120$ is the monochord-diameter) and his daily life of 120 years "is as a single year" (*i.e.*, he traverses the semicircle during the daylight hours).[32] There are thirty rungs in the ladder to heaven,[33] the serpent is a continuum of thirty units,[34] and hundreds of thousands of thirty-year periods (immortality) were promised a king.[35] Typhon, a demonic power represented as an hippopotamus, and an evil deity to whom belongs "all irrational and brutish nature," was born on the third of the five extra days intercalated into Egypt's 360-day schematic year (twelve months of thirty days each);[36] and the manner of his birth—"not in due season or manner, but with a blow he broke through his mother's side and leapt forth"—reads like an allusion to Indra's birth and to $\sqrt{2}$.[37] And Typhon gathers a group of seventy-two conspirators to overthrow Osiris (suspiciously the number of Old-Testament translators from Hebrew into Greek), the number from which the tones of the basic 30:60 octave can be defined in reverse order (see Charts 1 and 28).[38] As in the *Ṛg Veda*, offerings of bread, beer, oil, etc., are in the thousands, and references to millions abound. The sun travels in the "boat of millions of years," or rather in two such boats, like his Sumerian counterpart, changing from his "morning boat" to his "evening boat" at the zenith, *i.e.*, where our yantras and maṇḍalas change from multiplication to division or from rising to falling tonal progressions. Mt. Bakhau, the holy mountain "on which the sky rests," "the Mount of Sunrise," is 300 by 150 rods, *i.e.*, $300 \times 150 = 450{,}000$, exactly the size of the Hebrew ark (Chart 39).[39]

In Egypt the number 7 was deified as implying "completeness."[40] The sun-god Rā possessed seven "souls," the barley grew seven cubits high, the thighs of spirits who lived on the shadows of the dead were seven cubits long, and there were seven Hathors (holy cows), seven undulations in a serpent, seven scorpion-goddesses, seven hands in the royal cubit, and seven zones between the equator and the pole.

We can even find in the mythology of Apis, the sacred bull, a hint that our "Adamic yantra" was known in Egypt, for Apis carried a triangle on his forehead and was sacrificed at the age of twenty-five, the number at the peak of our generating yantra (Charts 11 and 35).[41]

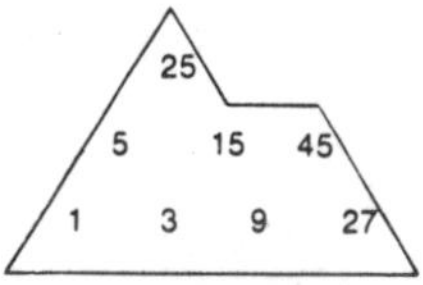

Irreducible integers

I have demonstrated repeatedly the power of a musical "overview" in harmonizing what is an otherwise chaotic mythological numerology. The Egyptian materials, with their powerful resonances with our previous experiences, cry out to be examined in the same way. We should reach for the largest number and grandest vision Egypt knew and then let the fractured pieces of the mythology show themselves to us as parts of a holistic cultural vision.

What I am about to do can be defended only by its results, for the method, I believe, is new and unprecedented. I am reaching for what Plato would have called "the likely story." However, since mine falls short of explaining *all* Egyptian numerology, it must be considered only a first effort. Perhaps it can be refined with the help of Egyptian scholars who possess the requisite philological skills and deeper intimacy with the thought of that ancient land. My primary sources for what follows are the available translations of *The Book of the Dead.*

THE BOOK OF THE DEAD

Inscribed upon the walls of the chambers and passages in the pyramids of kings of the fifth and sixth dynasties (2500–2300 B.C.) at Ṣaḳḳâra are five copies of a series of texts which have come to be known as *The Book of the Dead.*[42] They had been edited earlier by the priests of Heliopolis, "city of the Sun," the biblical On, where a much later priest was to become Joseph's father-in-law. The ancient texts were recopied upon tombs, sarcophagi, coffins, stelae, and papyri, along with rival editions from Thebes and Saïs, until about 200 A.D. This mass of material was organized into chapters by Lepsius in 1842 to facilitate comparisons between the various editions, none of which contains all 186 chapters. The grand vision we are looking for is in chapter 125, the vision of Osiris, "self-created," "Seat-Maker," "lord who makest inquisition in two-fold right and truth," seated on his throne in the Underworld while the heart of a deceased man is weighed on the scales before him against the "feather of the law."[43] The jackal-headed Anubis, "great god of the Underworld," examines the pointer of the Great Balance while Thoth, scribe of the gods, skilled in mathematics, records the judgment. Along the walls of the "Hall of Double Truth" (Maāt) are seated the forty-two gods—twenty-one in each row—who are "the spiritual masters of all Egypt" and "divine assessors at the judgment of the dead."[44] The *Ṛg Veda* gave us a formula for this scene. The Kalpa number—4,320,000,000 was analyzed in Chapter 7 and pictured in the yantra of Chart 15—produces a yantra fourteen steps high and it has twenty-one elements along its base, and a corresponding twenty-one reciprocals opposite.

Now it would be surprising to find the Hindu Kalpa number of 4,320,000,000 as the terminal integer in the Egyptian *Book of the Dead*, for rival cultures have shown us related but idiosyncratic numerologies. And we cannot simply adopt the Hindu number because it appears relevant at first glance, but we must look for a formula within the *Book of the Dead* itself. It is easy enough to understand why a yantra of fourteen steps might have been associated with the fourteen pieces of Osiris' body for he was associated with the moon in an early period, and its waxing and waning periods of fourteen days each.[45] To be fourteen steps high a yantra requires an index larger than $5^{13} = 1{,}220{,}703{,}125$ at its apex, but smaller than $5^{14} = 6{,}103{,}515{,}625$, which would add another row. To have twenty-one elements along its base, and thus twenty-one reciprocals opposite, the yantra index must be larger than $3^{20} = 3{,}486{,}784{,}401$ but less than $3^{21} = 10{,}460{,}353{,}203$. (Consult the multiplication tables of Appendix II if this is not clear.) If we are on the right track, the Egyptian terminal index for the "Hall of Double Truth" must be larger than $3^{20} = 3{,}486{,}784{,}401$ and smaller than $5^{14} = 6{,}103{,}515{,}625$. Furthermore, since the largest known Egyptian hieroglyph is that for millions, the largest possible numeral would be only 9,999,999; the number we need has ten or eleven digits and so would have to be referred to cabalistically as the product of smaller numbers which could be notated.

The number we are looking for can be found, I believe, in Chapter 64 of the *Book of the Dead* where the Sun-god Rā addresses the "Spirit-Souls" directly. "I work for you, O ye Khus," he says, and then numbers them very curiously as "3,300,000 *with* (sic!) 1,200."[46] Early translators were tempted to add these numbers, but there is no excuse for addition to reach a sum which could have been notated easily. The connective "with" is now considered problematical. If we dare to try interpreting it as a command to *multiply*—$3{,}300{,}000 \times 1{,}200 = 3{,}960{,}000{,}000$—we reach a product which falls within the limits necessary for a yantra fourteen steps high and with twenty-one elements along the base, as shown in Chart 50. But there is a problem: we have never yet dealt with a *factor* of 11 in an "index." Let us eliminate it: $3{,}960{,}000{,}000 \div 11 = 360{,}000{,}000$, *i.e.*, the number of days in 1,000,000 years. I have graphed this smaller number within the same yantra as the larger one, and suggest that it may represent the "resurrected" Osiris, for when he had been treacherously murdered and his body cut into fourteen pieces, his beloved Isis scoured the Underworld for the scattered parts of her husband and found only thirteen of them, the phallus having been swallowed by a fish.[47] There are only thirteen steps in the yantra for 360,000,000, hence our double yantra might be considered the "living" and the "dead" or "resurrected" forms of the god.

Now the Egyptian sky was divided into thirty-six "decans" (like the year into thirty-six ten-day weeks), every ten days a new star having the privilege of signaling the Sun's rising by preceding it over the horizon by a few minutes. A huge number whose only digits are thirty-six would seem characteristically Egyptian, especially when the sun travels in a boat of "millions of years," and when 360 are the days in one year and 360,000,000 are the days in a million years, and when $11 \times 360{,}000{,}000 = 3{,}960{,}000{,}000$ is the smallest multiple to produce our "Hall of Double Truth" with its lunar overtones, with the almost requisite ten tones along the horizontal axis, and with its correlation with the Hindu "Chariot of the Gods" (in Chart 17) where the horizontal axis extends "to the east" to 3^7 times our reference D, while the vertical axis extends to $5^{\pm 7}$ from the horizontal axis, an "emblem of completeness." According to Plutarch, thirty-six was the "sacred quaternion" of the Pythagoreans, "given the

CHART 50

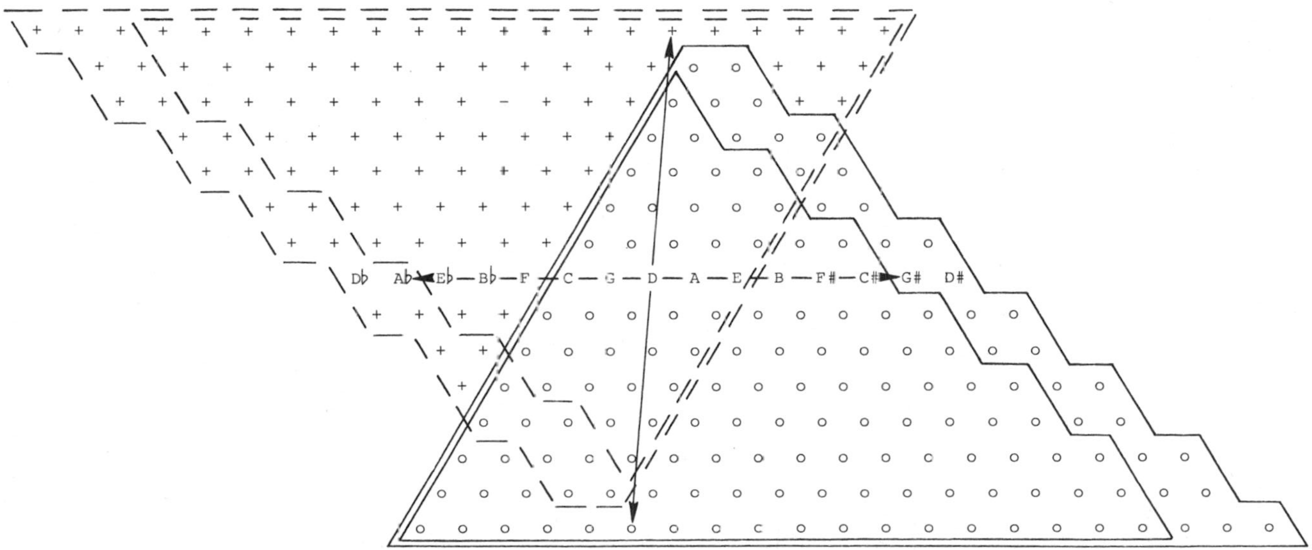

The "Hall of Double Truth" (Maat): Yantra for Numbers 3^p5^q < 360,000,000 and < 3,960,000,000
(Generated as 3,300,000 "with" 1,200)

The fifteen elements of the central axis from D♭ to D♯ can be thought of as "the domain of Osiris," and the five invariances under reciprocation—C G D A E—are the five gods of whom he is chief. The fourteen vertical rows (the fourteen parts of the body of Osiris) wax and wane (like the moon with which he was associated) with multiplications and divisions by 5. The twenty-one elements in the two outer rows correlate with the forty-two judges in the Hall of Double Truth.

name of 'World' since it is made up of the first four even numbers and the first four odd numbers added together."[48]

All this is very pleasant but hardly convincing by itself; in quoting Plutarch we are using a very late source from an epoch in which the hieroglyphs could no longer be read. I return now to the text of the *Book of the Dead* itself for what may be the earliest Egyptian commentary on these yantras.

THE UNDERWORLD

According to Chapters 149 and 150 of the *Book of the Dead*, the domain of Osiris is divided into fifteen numbered parts, like the central axis in our reciprocal yantras which stretches from $D\flat$ to $D\sharp$.[49] Osiris the "Seat-Maker" is head of a company of five gods,[50] a possible allusion to the five invariances—C G D A E—under reciprocation, with Osiris = D = 1 = geometric mean in the field of rational numbers. The hieroglyph for the Underworld—a five-pointed star in a circle, ,[51] can be read as the tone-maṇḍala for these five invariances, the five "musical Brahmins" or "citizens of the highest property class" in the calendrical tone-maṇḍala of Chart 8, as shown again in Chart 51, with the new numerals appropriate to this context. The seventy-two conspirators who helped Typhon dismember Osiris must have known that 72 is the *least common denominator* by which the Osiris pentatonic scale can be expressed in integers *which remain invariant under reciprocation.*[52]

Osiris also possessed thirty-four "boats" which correlate with the thirty-four elements—seventeen pairs of reciprocals above and below the central axis in Chart 50—and in the yearly procession of the god at Denderah he was actually accompanied by thirty-four boats with 365 lamps, as the text prescribes, one for each day in the year.[53] These thirty-four paired elements, together with the five gods in the central axis, are the only ones which enjoy reciprocation around the throne *within* the limit of 360,000,000.

The Egyptian hieroglyph for star is simply a five-pointed star, .[54] Since it is the factors of 5 which differentiate "earth" and "sky" in our yantras, and since 5 was indicated by five single strokes (see Chart 48), it is tempting to suppose that the Egyptians merely rearranged the five strokes into a star, the number 5 generating all symbolic stars.

Thoth, the "heart of Rā" and "left eye" of that Sun-god, is symbolized by an *utchat* reciprocal to the right eye (see Chart 49). But Thoth is also the inventor of music, and he is represented above a set of fourteen steps (*i.e.*, the body of Osiris in Chart 50), symbolizing in this case the full moon.[55]

CHART 51

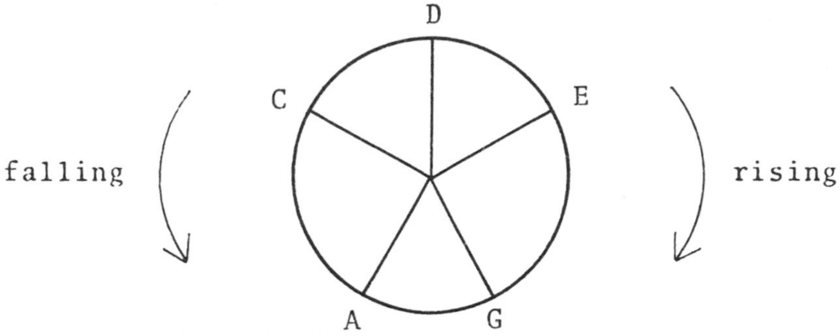

rising scale	D	E	G	A	C	D
falling scale	D	C	A	G	E	D
increasing integers	72	81	96	108	128	144
decreasing integers	144	128	108	96	81	72
ratios	6	:	8	:: 9	:	12
	8 :	9			8 :	9

The Pentatonic Scale as Hieroglyph of the Underworld

The only invariances *within* the "Resurrected Osiris" limit of 360,000,000 are those belonging to five numbers and related tones, the five Gods of whom he is chief. The clue to the pentatonic scale, a subset of "Pythagorean tuning" and of the calendrical tuning in Chart 8, is the number 72, the number of conspirators who dismembered him.

Thoth is "the mind of God," head of the eight gods of Thermopolis (notice C G D A E B F# C# in the axis of the smaller yantra), supposedly the author of forty-two sacred books (like the forty-two judges in Chart 50), and was called by the Greeks Hermes Tristmegistus or "Thrice Greatest Hermes."[56] A special symbol associated with the power to rule is a hieroglyph translated as "flail," 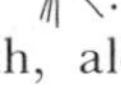. I doubt that we would be making an error in considering Thoth, along with all the other qualities which make him the Egyptian equivalent of Sumerian-Babylonian Ea-Enki, as "deified 3." It is Thoth as "3" who literally organizes our tables "from above."

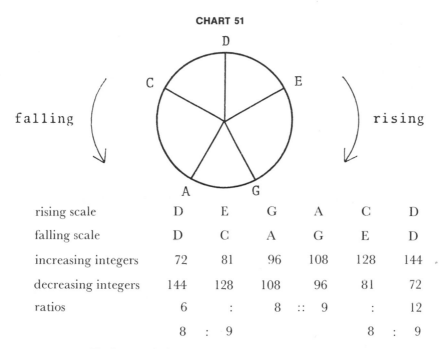

At Memphis there were ten "Great Gods."[57] Note the ten tones in the horizontal axis of the yantra in Chart 50: C G D A E B F# C# G# D#, powers of 3 similar to the 10 in the horizontal axis of our Atlantis yantra in Chart 44 and our Kalpa yantra in Chart 15. It is curious that Osiris killed a hippopotamus with ten darts and the beast was ultimately cut up into eight pieces, 8 and 10 being the two limits of the horizontal axis.[58] Egypt also possessed ten books of hymns, prayers, etc., for temple worship.[59]

The sun-god Rā, "bringer of forms" and "lord of the hidden circles," has a circular hieroglyph: ☉.[60,61] The Sun is also symbolized by Heru, the hawk, oldest god of Egypt, and by Horus, son of Osiris. There are "seven souls of Rā,"[62] perhaps in the sense that the extreme limits of our larger yantra extend to $3^{\pm 7}$ and to $5^{\pm 7}$ from the "seed" or reference mean on D. He can be "bitten by the snake"[63] when he is at the zenith because there he is almost identical with his reciprocal approximation to $\sqrt{2}$. And he can be nursed back to health by Isis, "mother of god," because she deifies the "female number 2" which preserves the continuum of the octave matrix. Isis is the Egyptian incarnation of Pythagorean "Justice," "the female principle of Nature," and "the gentle nurse and the all-receptive."[64]

It was the jackal-headed god Set (=Typhon) who dismembered the body of the dead Osiris into fourteen pieces, and the jackal-headed "embalmer" Anubis who restored the thirteen recovered by Isis.[65] It is tempting to assign this reciprocal pair the deification of the powers of 5 which dismantle our vertical axis by division and restore it by multiplication. Anubis, like Enlil, is "god on a mountain," or "he who is upon his hill."[66] Anubis produces the heart of the deceased when it is weighed on the Great Balance in the Hall of Double Truth, and he reads the pointer on the scale. He is older than Osiris, often fused with Horus, and has been connected with Christ.[67] Plutarch described Anubis as "the horizontal circle which divides visible and invisible realms."[68]

The soul of a man whose heart passes the test on the scales of Double Truth then embarks on a journey to the "abode of the blessed," passing through seven *Ārits* or "mansions" along the way.[69] There are two alternate routes to that Egyptian heaven, like the alternate routes through the octave and its related number sequences, by *land* or by *water*,

> but once having set out on one route, the soul could not change to the other, for the two ways were separated by a river of fire.[70]

The soul of the scribe Ani, whose journey is described in great detail in the papyrus translated by Budge in *The Egyptian Book of the Dead*, passes ten "pylons" or gateways (like the ten elements in our central axis), and the hieroglyphs associated with the third pylon symbolize in a very beautiful way our notion of the "cosmic seed" as D = 1 = geometric mean in the field of rational number. This third pylon

> is guarded by a man-headed deity seated in a shrine, the upper part of which is ornamented with the two utchats and the emblems of the orbit of the sun and of water.[71]

The two utchats are the sun and moon, the "eyes of heaven" (and perhaps $2^{\pm n}$), and the zig-zag lines are the hieroglyph for water (in our yantras they connect tones in the ratio 4:5:6). The disc of the sun above and the cup below complete the symbolism for a genesis from the cosmic waters. Alternative versions of this chapter have the soul passing twenty-one pylons on its journey, like the twenty-one elements in the breadth of our yantra.

During the twelve hours of the night, the boat of the sun must be carried through the dangerous *Tuat*, conceived both as "a long narrow valley, with two equal strips on each side," like our yantras, but also as a *circle*, like our maṇḍalas. The Sun can make that journey successfully only because Thoth (deified "3") has given him the secret names of the demons who guard the pylons or gateways.[72] Each move along the axis of our yantras involves a multiplication or division by 3. Now there is an alternate version of Chapter 64—a chapter thought to date from the first dynasty, at the end of the fourth millenium—containing the cabalistic formula for a still larger yantra, a yantra which correlates with a very ancient conception of Osiris' body as containing sixteen parts of which only fifteen could be recovered by Isis, and this larger yantra has an axis which shows quite clearly the twelve musical intervals (hours of the night?) which make new sense of the Sun's night ride. In this alternate version, the Sun addresses the "Spirit-Souls" (*Khus*) as being "3,300,000 *with* 1,200" and then adds a third dimension (height?) of 12.[73] Multiplying: $3{,}300{,}000 \times 1{,}200 \times 12 = 47{,}520{,}000{,}000$. The yantra for numbers $3^p5^q < 47{,}520{,}000{,}000$ is sixteen steps high, and we can watch Osiris' penis (the peak of the yantra) disappear under reciprocation, as shown in Chart 52. The thirteen elements along the central axis give musical meaning to the notion of a "house of thirteen stars" in the sky,[74] thirteen feathers of Maāt (Justice),[75] thirteen sacred *uraei*,[76] and to twelve *intervals* (musical fifths of ratio 2:3) during the night journey. This Egyptian index is exactly 11 times the Kalpa number, *least multiple* for an axis of thirteen tones. Chart 52 has seven Ṛgvedic invariances along the central axis—F C G D A E B, truly seven "Souls of the Sun"—and its total of thirteen on that axis forms a labyrinth of twelve parts,[77] twelve "halls of punishment,"[78] twelve "cities," or "circles" or "little serpents."[79] The Pythagorean comma of 524288: 531441 between F at the beginning and E♯ at the end helps us understand why in the last hour the boat of Rā must actually pass through the interior of a serpent (representing the continuum to which the comma belongs) before he can be born again in the morning as Khepura, the beetle, the scarab-headed god, the most revered symbol in Egypt.[80]

CHART 52

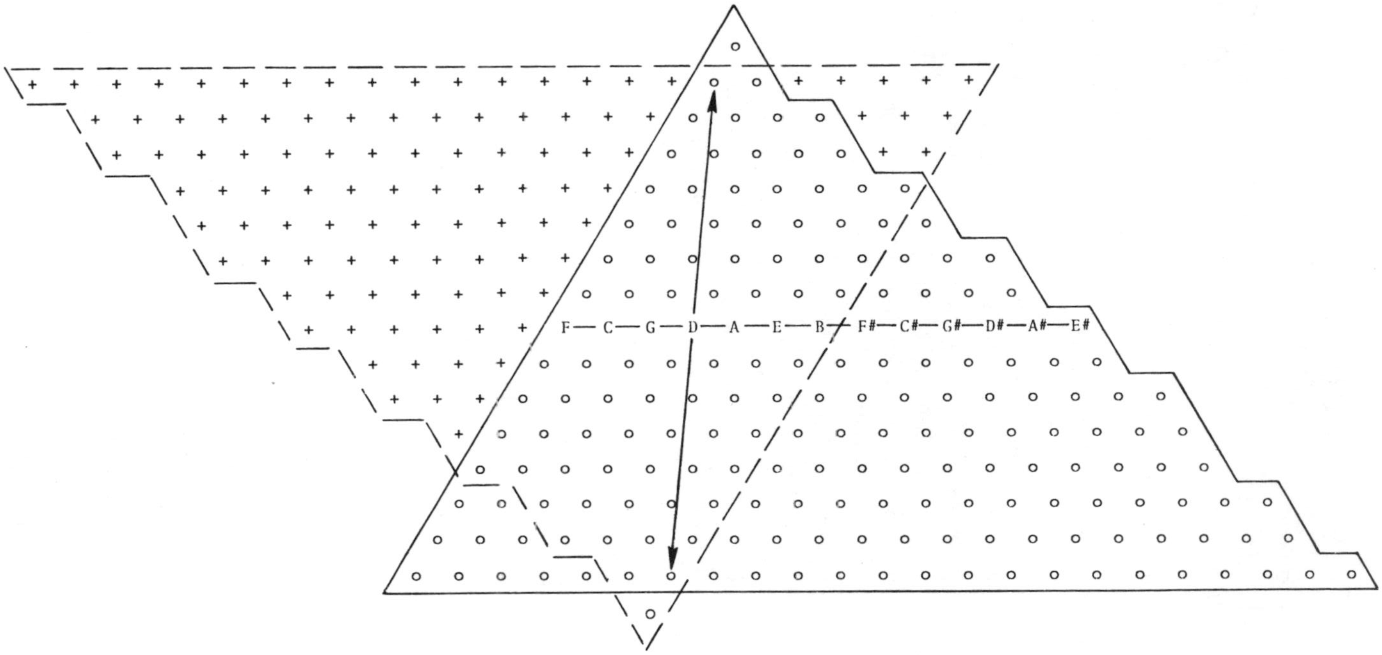

Seven Souls of the Sun and Twelve Hours of the Night: Yantra for $3^p5^q < 47{,}520{,}000{,}000$

The seven invariances on the central axis correlate with the seven souls of the sun and the twelve intervals correlate with the twelve hours of the night. The sixteen levels correlate with an early division of Osiris into that many parts, of which only fifteen could be found in the Underworld. Formula: 3,300,000 × 1,200 × 12 = 47,520,000,000 (Chapter 64 of *The Book of the Dead*).

KHEPURA

Khepura, the scarab beetle and the favorite symbol of the Egyptians, is clearly a deification of a particular concept of the cosmos and of the notion of number—meaning *natural number*, or integer—as a multiplicity of "1's." The beetle was thought to be always male, slight differences between the sexes passing unnoticed in ancient times. He laid his eggs in a mass of dung, and then, standing on his forelegs, he pushed the ball of eggs with his hindlegs into a hole he had dug in the sand, where they were hatched by the sun.[81] He is a symbol of reincarnation, of unity, and his little round ball of eggs is a whole of constituent parts neatly suggesting how logic would divide the universe if it knew how. Khepura is a very old god and one of the most charming in history. He was obviously invented *before* the so-called "crisis of the irrational" spoiled forever the Pythagorean dream that *rational* numbers could explain everything. An Egyptian creation myth has unisexual Khepura, "father of the Gods," giving birth to the universe by masturbation, producing the male-female twins Shu and Tefnut, "daylight" and "rain" respectively, by gestating the seed in his mouth.[82] What the "1" produces by itself, of course, are the prime numbers 2 and 3 which Pythagoreans needed for a start. It is interesting that Khepura means "to become, to turn, to roll."[83] In Chart 53 we see Khepura inside the disc of the sun as the boat of Rā starts its journey through the Tuat.

That the *Book of the Dead* may contain organizing strata of mathematical allegory is suggested by the Egyptians' own way of picturing the scales of justice in the Hall of Double Truth: usually the heart of a man is weighed against the "feather of the law," but here what is being weighed looks suspiciously like a Nicomachean triangle.[84]

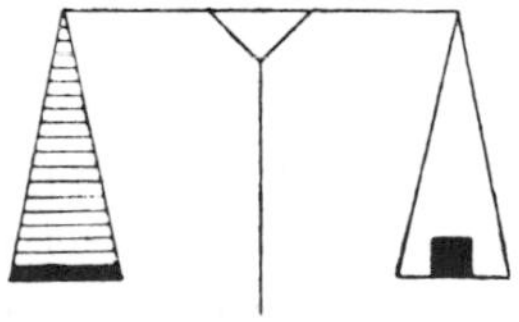

The Scales of Double Truth (Maāt)

There is much more Egyptian numerology to be explored and there is a vast amount of both pictographic and literary evidence to assist in that analysis, but the difficulties are enormous, and I am not an Egyptologist. I hope that I have carried this musical effort far enough to make attractive a renewed effort by scholars properly equipped for the task. My aim here was solely to suggest how Egypt may have possessed the musical-mathe-

CHART 53

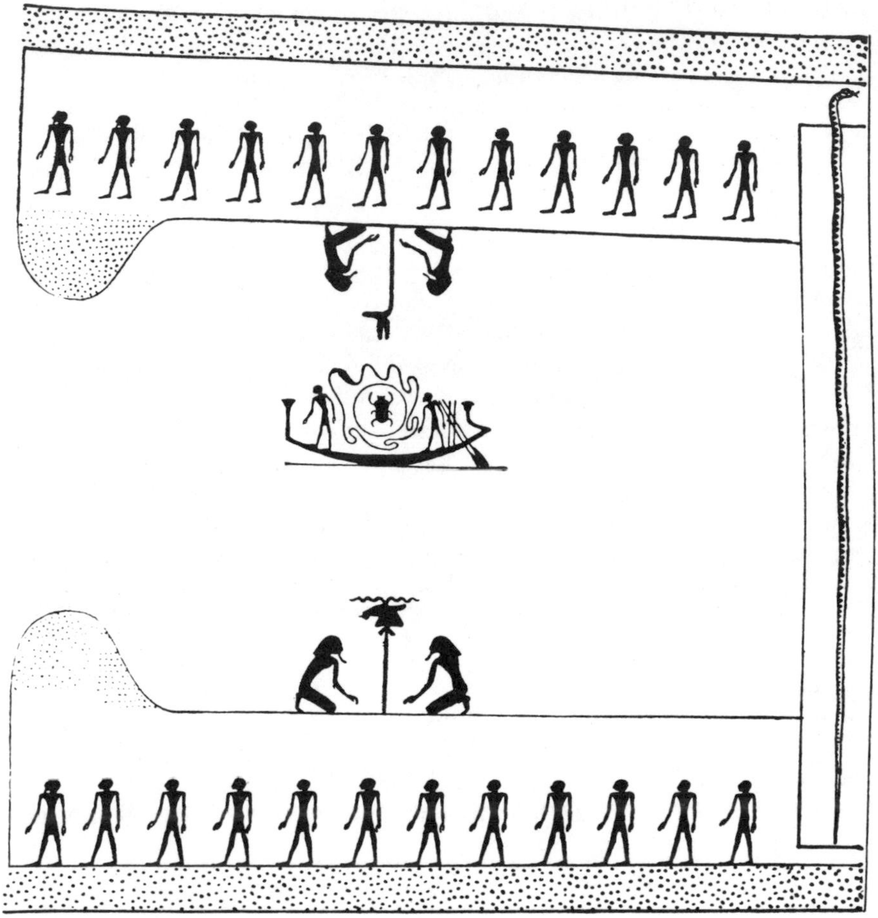

The Boat of Rā in the First Hour of the Night

As the boat of the Sun enters the Tuat through a "hole" on the left (to the west), it passes a jackal-headed standard and a ram-headed one, sacred to the "god of the mountain" and the god of the Tuat. There are twelve gods on each side. In the center the boat of the Sun carries his disc containing a beetle (Khepura), encircled by a huge serpent, which holds its tail in its mouth. Two gods escort the boat which approaches a pylon with closed doors, guarded by a huge serpent which stands on his tail, entrance to the second division or hour. (Reproduced from *The Gods of the Egyptians*, Vol. 1, by E. A. Wallis Budge.) [Boat and pylon are unaccountably reversed–*Ed.*]

matical materials of the Atlantis mythology for thousands of years before Plato invented his story.

FOOTNOTES

1. I am drawing freely on my three published essays, "Plato's Musical Cosmology," "Musical Marriages in Plato's *Republic*," and "A New Look at Plato's *Timaeus*," referred to in footnotes 4, 5 and 6 of Chapter 1.
2. *Critias*, p. 121c.
3. *The Republic of Plato*, Allan Bloom, trans. (New York: Basic Books, 1968), pp. 372c–373a.
4. *Ibid.*, pp. 373b–c.
5. Gilbert Ryle, *Plato's Progress* (Cambridge: Cambridge University Press, 1966), pp. 60–63, 230–244, and 300.
6. Ernst Levy and I were colleagues from 1959 until his retirement in 1966, and he has continued to be a fount of inspiration and good advice on Pythagorean matters. All of my work is simply a continuation of his early studies and an application of his insight into the Pythagorean musical imagination.
7. Robert S. Brumbaugh, *Plato's Mathematical Imagination* (Bloomington; Indiana University Publications, 1954; New York: Kraus Reprint Corporation, 1968), pp. 47–59 and 109–150. Personal correspondence with Brumbaugh has been of considerable further assistance. His work will go down in history, I believe, as a landmark in Platonic studies, although few Platonists today recognize its significance.
8. *Republic*, pp. 545e–547c.
9. *The Republic of Plato*, James Adam, ed. (Cambridge: Cambridge University Press, 1902 and 1969), Vol. 2, pp. 201–210 and 264–306.
10. *Critias* in *The Collected Dialogues of Plato*, A. E. Taylor, trans. (New York: Pantheon Books, 1961), pp. 113–121.
11. *Republic*, p. 453d.
12. *Critias*, p. 117e.
13. *Republic*, p. 423a.
14. *Critias*, p. 112c.
15. Aristotle's comment is quoted in *The Geography of Strabo*, H. L. Jones, trans. (Cambridge: Harvard University Press, 1949) II: 102 and XIII: 598.
16. A. E. Taylor, *A Commentary on Plato's Timaeus* (Oxford: Clarendon Press, 1928), pp. 137–138.
17. Curt Sachs, *The History of Musical Instruments* (New York: W. W. Norton & Company, 1940), p. 86.
18. Henry George Farmer, "The Music of Ancient Egypt," *The New Oxford History of Music* (London: Oxford University Press, 1957), pp. 264 and 274.
19. *Ibid.*, p. 259 (quoting Maspero).
20. Otto Neugebauer, *The Exact Sciences in Antiquity* (New York: Dover Publications, Inc., 1969), p. 71.

21. *Ibid.*, p. 72.
22. *Ibid.*, p. 73.
23. B. L. van der Waerden, *Science Awakening* (New York: John Wiley & Sons, 1963), p. 18.
24. *Ibid.*, p. 26.
25. *Ibid.*, p. 32.
26. Richard J. Gillings, *Mathematics in the Time of the Pharaohs* (Cambridge: The M.I.T. Press, 1972), p. 32.
27. van der Waerden, *op. cit.*, p. 29.
28. *Ibid.*, p. 31.
29. Gillings, *op. cit.*, pp. 210–211.
30. A very beautiful introduction to the endless complexities of Egyptian mythology is the essay by Rudolf Anthes, "Mythology in Ancient Egypt," in *Mythologies of the Ancient World*, Samuel Noah Kramer, ed. (Garden City, New York: Doubleday & Company, 1961), pp. 16–92.
31. Plutarch, "Isis and Osiris," *Moralia* (Cambridge: Harvard University Press, 1936), Vol. 5, p. 381.
32. E. A. Wallis Budge, *The Gods of the Egyptians* (New York: Dover Publications, Inc., 1969; reprint of the London edition of 1904), Vol. 1, pp. 319 and 360.
33. E. A. Wallis Budge, *Osiris & the Egyptian Resurrection* (New York: Dover Publications, Inc., 1973; reprint of the original 1911 edition), Vol. I, p. 124.
34. *Ibid.*, Vol. 2, p. 236.
35. Budge, *The Gods of the Egyptians*, Vol. 1, p. 425.
36. Plutarch, "Isis and Osiris," p. 380.
37. *Ibid.*, p. 355.
38. *Ibid.*, p. 356.
39. Raymond O. Faulkner, *The Book of the Dead* (New York: The Limited Editions Club, 1972), p. 80, spell 108.
40. Budge, *Osiris & the Egyptian Resurrection*, Vol. 2, p. 247.
41. Plutarch, "Isis and Osiris," p. 374.
42. E. A. Wallis Budge, *The Egyptian Book of the Dead* (New York: Dover Publications, Inc., 1967; reprint of the original 1895 edition), p. ix.
43. *Ibid.*, pp. 184–224 and 341–353.
44. Budge, *The Gods of the Egyptians*, Vol. 1, p. 418 and *Osiris & the Egyptian Resurrection*, Vol. 1, p. 342.
45. Plutarch, "Isis and Osiris," p. 368.
46. E. A. Wallis Budge, "The Book of the Dead," Theban Recension, in *Egyptian Literature*, (New York: The Colonial Press, 1901), p. 43. Mr. Thomas Logan, Senior Research Associate at the Metropolitan Museum of Art, very kindly called my attention to an error in Budge's translation of the numbers and to the now problematic connective between 3,300,000 and 1,200, which I have taken the liberty of interpreting in my own way.
47. Plutarch, "Isis and Osiris," p. 358.

48. *Ibid.*, p. 381.
49. Budge, *The Gods of the Egyptians*, Vol. 1, p. 177.
50. Budge, *Osiris & the Egyptian Resurrection*, Vol. 1, p. 28.
51. Gillings, *op. cit.*, p. 487.
52. Plutarch, "Isis and Osiris," p. 356.
53. Budge, *Osiris & the Egyptian Resurrection*, Vol. 2, pp. 26, 28, and 30.
54. Gillings, *op. cit.*, p. 487.
55. Budge, *The Gods of the Egyptians*, Vol. 1, p. 413.
56. *Ibid.*, p. 414.
57. Budge, *Osiris & the Egyptian Resurrection*, Vol. 1, p. 158.
58. J. Norman Lockyer, *The Dawn of Astronomy* (Cambridge: The M.I.T. Press, 1964; reprint of the original edition of 1894), p. 150.
59. *The New Oxford History of Music* (London: Oxford University Press, 1957), Vol. 1, p. 259.
60. Budge, *The Gods of the Egyptians*, Vol. 1, p. 339.
61. Gillings, *op. cit.*, p. 485.
62. Budge, *The Gods of the Egyptians*, Vol. 1, p. 34.
63. *Ibid.*, p. 361.
64. Plutarch, "Isis and Osiris," pp. 352, 372, and 376.
65. *Ibid.*, p. 358.
66. Budge, *The Gods of the Egyptians*, Vol. 2, p. 263.
67. *Ibid.*, pp. 262–266.
68. *Ibid.*, p. 264.
69. Budge, *The Gods of the Egyptians*, Vol. 1, p. 176.
70. Budge, *Osiris & the Egyptian Resurrection*, Vol. 2, p. 156.
71. Budge, *The Egyptian Book of the Dead*, p. 295.
72. Budge, *The Gods of the Egyptians*, Vol. 1, p. 409.
73. See footnote 46. The alternate version is on page 46.
74. Budge, *Osiris & the Egyptian Resurrection*, Vol. 2, p. 361.
75. Budge, *Osiris & the Egyptian Resurrection*, Vol. 1, p. 316.
76. *Ibid.*
77. Budge, *The Gods of the Egyptians*, Vol. 1, p. 96.
78. *Ibid.*, p. 266.
79. Budge, *Osiris & the Egyptian Resurrection*, Vol. 2, p. 233.
80. Budge, *The Gods of the Egyptians*, Vol. 1, p. 257.
81. Plutarch, "Isis and Osiris," p. 381.
82. Budge, *The Gods of the Egyptians*, Vol. 1, p. 298.
83. Budge, *The Egyptian Book of the Dead*, p. 246.
84. Budge, *Osiris & the Egyptian Resurrection*, Vol. 1, p. 316.

12

CONCLUSIONS

Harmonical analysis is a technique for synthesizing the tonal, arithmetical, and geometrical imagery of ancient civilizations. It aims at the reconstruction of the esoteric diagrams which gave the sacred symbols of particular cultures their enduring and magical powers and furnished philosophy with a ground of certainty. The technique is applicable to all cultures which considered tone and number twin keys to the secrets of the universe, and practicable wherever a sufficient mythology and cosmology have survived. I have made explicit the objective elements of that harmonic technique; it is based on the habits of ancients like Plato, Plutarch, Ptolemy, and Nicomachus, and on principles enunciated anew in our time by men like Brumbaugh, de Nicolás, Levarie, and Levy. There is in addition to those elements the personal interpretation which I have proposed in this book: such an interpretation is tested by the intuitions of others and by its fertility in suggesting further interesting integrations. The musical imagination required to employ the technique of harmonical analysis in uncovering ancient meanings encoded in music, number, poetry, and metaphor will not lead to certainty, but used wisely it should lead to a "likely story," one "more likely" than interpretations that have been musically uninformed.

Harmonical analysis exploits the ancient world's fascination with number and with those correlations between tone and number which we call acoustical theory, but which a former age of innocence considered to be cosmology. By studying the most ancient forms of numerology in a tonal context we revive a rationality that was lost. All numbers and all graphic relations in the mythologies of ancient cultures must henceforth be taken as clues to cosmological visions embodying possibly very great mathematical precision and signifying an aesthetic balance between sets of related concerns. The mathematical allegories unveiled here were the products of minds like our own, convinced of the absolute unity of all things visible, tangible, audible, and thinkable, and laying the foundations of a future science by directing attention to what endures.

THE MYTH OF INVARIANCE

What seemed most certain to our ancestors was that physically nothing endured. "From the days of old there is no permanence," Utnapishtim said to comfort Gilgamesh, grieving for the dead Enkidu and suddenly aware of his own mortality.[1] In this sea of restless change man discovered an island he could trust, the octave of ratio 1:2—the "basic miracle of music"—functioning as a matrix for all smaller intervals and providing a metric basis for a tonal algebra. From what we know at the present time it seems likely that the octave invariance was recognized in India, Sumer, Babylon, Egypt, and Palestine well before the variant cycles of sun, moon, and planets—"wanderers" all—were coordinated with even modest accuracy. Calendrical periods of 30, 60, 360, and 720 units and their multiples belong to the essential arithmetic of a systematic mathematical harmonics. Their source was not astronomy though they found a ready application in early astronomy, which knew them to be unsuitable for its own cycles.[2] Within the narrow ranges of voices and instruments, and within the prevailing limits of accuracy in measurement, the invariance of the octave at the ratio 1:2 remained unquestioned until modern times. Today we know that octave invariance is modified in the extreme ranges of pitch where the ear requires ever larger ratios to maintain the illusion of "sameness," and we recognize that the best of tuners fall short of absolute perfection and absolute consistency, and even of absolute agreement on the acoustical ideal. To define musical intervals which enjoy a certain tolerance by the ratios of numbers which enjoy none at all was a systematic mistake that nevertheless had beneficient consequences: it gave man something to "count on" while he developed stronger intellectual tools.

Musical arithmetic—grounded on what Levarie and Levy call "octave equivalence" and Brumbaugh calls a "matrix of doubles"—was primitive in the sense that it fueled a radiant vision of universal harmony while providing both a model and a motive for the development of a rigorously abstract number theory and a related geometrical algebra. That mathematical development led in turn to a musical wisdom which permeates the *Republic*: "tone numbers" are not "laws," but "norms." I use the word "norm" in the sense defined by Levarie and Levy as *principle* or *archetype* admitting the approximation or exception characteristic of organic life, "at the least a reference point, at the best an ideal toward which one strives."[3] The study of number (meaning rational number, the only kind then imaginable) led then inevitably to the insight that number must be dethroned as an absolute and viewed instead as a tool for human rationality to order as best it can the evidence of eye (that a maṇḍala can have twelve spokes equally placed) and ear (that twelve tones can be similarly placed). The wisdom which suffuses the *Republic* was restated more prosaically by Aristotle and Aristoxenus when they affirmed simply that the ear—not number—rules the universe of tone, using enough arithmetical elements in their arguments to prove they had done their Pythagorean homework.[4] Reason advances to wisdom when it understands that what has been worshipped as law deserves to be respected merely as archetype or norm.

For Antonio de Nicolás the great lesson of the *Ṛg Veda* and perhaps of the whole Indian tradition is centered on the *Ṛta*, "Body of Law" (from the root *ṛ*—, to go, meaning that which has already been gone through, that which has already "been formed"), "the *guide* for action of all that can be formed," and a "*norm*."[5]

> The *Ṛta*, as . . . the accumulations of practices, customs, goals, and rules of survival for a community within which individuals are born and foreigners accepted . . . is the *body* of the social group, or the *embodied community*.[6] (Emphasis added.)

Ṛta is the world created by the *sacrifice* of all limiting and partial perspectives, a ceaseless activity whose rationality is protected by *respect for plural norms*. Its fruit is the "Embodied Vision" (*Ṛta dhīḥ*) which Western philosophical rationality cannot dissect successfully. Its radiant "musicality" resonates powerfully in all the great religions of the world. We in the West are capable of feeling these resonances because our souls have finally been emptied of the belief, that for a long time constrained the Western imagination, that one and only one path can lead to truth.

Music can be discussed only in metaphor; reciprocally, music remains one of the richest resources of metaphor for language in general. At the conclusion of my long adventure with musical metaphor, however, methodology requires that the musical perspective achieved here with great labor must also be "sacrificed." We must step outside the frame I have constructed if we are to view it objectively. That is not a step I can take unaided. Furthermore, a study of ancient mathematics must be evaluated by professional mathematicians—not by the musicians who made it—before it can be used confidently by other scholars who lack the essential expertise with both music *and* mathematics. Suppose, for the sake of argument, that some significant portion of my analyses proves acceptable as "a likely story," what, if anything, would that mean to a mathematician? My colleague, Professor Richard Sacksteder, has graciously answered in a way which makes clear his caution where my speculation is involved, and makes no less clear his faith in *how* mathematics serves both man and his gods.

A MATHEMATICAL PERSPECTIVE: RICHARD SACKSTEDER

"Contemporary mathematicians, who usually isolate their professional activities from any tendencies they may have toward mysticism and poetry, will find the poems, myths, and dialogues treated here difficult to handle. The evidence presented in the preceding chapters shows that it is reasonable to begin by regarding them as the thoughts of rational men on important questions, rather than as an arbitrary and impenetrable numerology, but it is still hard to know what a mathematician is to make of them.

"Mathematicians are not likely to find any ancient "lost" wisdom in these works, but they must respect the theoretical accomplishments that lie behind them. To the extent that the concern was with problems of tuning and temperament, the ancients were, in effect, dealing with problems of simultaneous Diophantine approximation, that is the approximation of real numbers by certain combinations of rational ones. Such problems are still difficult for us today.

"It would be premature to try to form definite opinions on the questions of mathematical history that are raised here. The argument that similar ideas and concepts imply cultural contact is not always convincing to mathematicians. It is easy for them to believe, for instance, that a concern for prime numbers could develop or Pascal's triangle could be discovered independently in several places, since good mathematical ideas are a reflection of the nature of things.

"Even more interesting than what is shown of the ancient mathematical technique are the views of the relationship between mathematics and the rest of human knowledge. There appears to have been an early understanding of the way that abstract concepts can unify thought about diverse aspects of reality, but perhaps even more important is the insight into the dialectical process by which abstract systems can raise levels of thinking. One finds the following pattern repeated over and over. At first there is an attempt to complete a system by carrying an established process one step further. In music, for example, the motivation might stem from a desire to be able to construct certain intervals beginning from any point on a scale, but mathematically what is involved is an effort to satisfy certain axioms such as those of closure and inverses. The new step generally fails to solve the problem and often raises new and disturbing questions. From the original standpoint there is no way to avoid chaos, and the only way out is to adopt a more sophisticated point of view. Initially this might be painful, as with the discovery of irrational numbers, but in the end there is such an enrichment that one would never want to return to the lost state of innocence. Mathematics is made more interesting because there are irrational numbers, and music is made more exciting because certain intervals are incompatible. Even if we are no longer interested in the ancients' computation of the number of steps in the ladder to heaven or of the number of days since the creation we can still admire their use of one of the basic processes of intellectual creativity."[7]

CODETTA

If a mathematician can find no "lost wisdom" in these pages it is, I suggest, because whatever wisdom was acquired originally through music and mathematics has never really been lost to the larger family of man, although one civilization after another has perished from the earth. What is most easily transmitted between cultures is mathematics, what is most universally shared (although in different styles) is music. But neither music nor mathematics can lead to wisdom except via the mediating influence of tradition. The family of cultures we have met in the course of this study possessed the mediating traditions by which musical and mathematical logic operated to structure a wisdom conceived as the expression in closed form of all that is. This aim led along the dynamic path of ever more complex but complementary frameworks where number embodied in sound was the medium through which the universe manifest was a universe-as-sung. Various tunings are complementary, that is, context dependent, the context being set arithmetically by the least common denominator and physically by the chosen lengths of pipes and strings. In this mode of expression no universal context exists, hence whatever exists is in the array of particular contexts. The array of particular contexts, however, is not without its own order: we have seen how the notes of one tuning can approach those of another tuning until the distinction is inaudible, although the number ratios remain differentiated.

Patrick Heelan has claimed that there is in quantum mechanics an internal logic expressing the articulation of multiple context-dependent frameworks, with different contexts embodied in different kinds of measuring apparatus.[8] The structure of multiple relationships between frameworks is that of a non-distributive lattice. Thus, the two elements we have noticed—a plurality of mathematical structures and the embodiment of each in a material medium—are common to both quantum mechanics and the musical-mathematical cultures we have been studying.

I propose that both will be found to obey a form of quantum logic in the sense that Heelan gives to that term.

The question of embodiment is a central concern in the work of Antonio de Nicolás. My work here was intended as a musical illustration of what he means by "embodied vision." It is a disciplined awareness that every partial vision a culture provides must be lovingly sacrificed to preserve man's right to innovation and continuity and his freedom to act in the present unconstrained by idolizing any single perspective. For de Nicolás the basic activity of man as man is radically philosophical, every perception, every sensation, every judgment being part of the process by which he both embodies his culture and creates himself.[9] "I doubt, however," de Nicolás writes, "that anyone will follow the way of philosophy unless he loves his own culture enough not to settle for imitations of life."[10]

There is the philosopher's challenge to the musician, one he actually learned from music. It is love of an authentic experience with tone which has been the "invariant" responsibility of musicians to teach all cultures through all the vicissitudes of the ages.

FOOTNOTES

1. *The Gilgamesh Epic and Old Testament Parallels*, Alexander Heidel, trans. (Chicago: The University of Chicago Press, 1946; first Phoenix Edition, 1963), p. 79.
2. J. Norman Lockyer, who believed the Egyptians first developed an accurate measure of the solar year, discusses at length the ease with which an initial estimate of 360 days would have been proved wrong. See *The Dawn of Astronomy* (Cambridge, The M.I.T. Press, 1964; reprint of the first edition by Cassell and Company, 1894), Chapter 7.
3. Siegmund Levarie and Ernst Levy, *A Dictionary of Musical Morphology*, (now in preparation by The Institute of Mediaeval Music).
4. Aristotle's very extensive comments on Pythagorean mythology and mathematics, spread through many of his books, have been profoundly misunderstood and are in urgent need of a new study. From my point of view he appears to be an infallible guide to the ancient mathematics I have expounded here. Similarly, the *Harmonics* of Aristoxenus, Aristotle's pupil, is in urgent need at least of a new and extensive commentary, for he has been read out of context so very seriously that many interesting concerns have been misunderstood. Aristotle wrote a lost book on Pythagoreanism and Aristoxenus was trained as a Pythagorean before studying with Aristotle. They vigorously criticized Pythagoreanism from within, from having first learned what it could teach, and from feeling within themselves the tensions which inevitably arose during the dramatic increase in the Greek power of abstract reasoning. Modern classical scholarship has done powerful injustices not only to these two men but even more so to Plato and, less importantly perhaps, to Plutarch by its own ignorance of and indifference to the role of mathematical harmonics.

FOOTNOTES

5. *Four-Dimensional Man*, p. 169.
6. *Ibid.*, p. 174.
7. Richard Sacksteder is Professor of Mathematics in the Ph.D. program at the Graduate Center of the City University of New York.
8. Patrick Heelan, "Complementarity, Context-Dependence, and Quantum Logic," *Foundations of Physics* (1970) pp. 95–100; "Logic of Framework Transpositions," *International Philosophical Quarterly*, 11 (1971), pp. 314–334.
9. Antonio T. de Nicolás, *Avatāra: The Humanization of Philosophy through the Bhagavad Gītā* (New York: Nicolás Hays, Ltd., 1976). In the grand scale in which de Nicolás works, music is once again employed as the fundamental tool of philosophy, occupying not the highest place but the lowest, the most primitive in the sense of prime, a role it has not played in the works of major philosophers since Plato.
10. Antonio T. de Nicolás, "The Humanization of Philosophy," *Main Currents in Modern Thought*, Vol. 30, No. 5, May-June, 1974, pp. 167–173, p. 173.

APPENDIX I

Conversion Tables

The intervals of central concern are displayed here in three ways: (1) as the ratios of integers, (2) as logarithmic cents, and (3) as degrees in a one-octave tone-mandala.

To convert ratios to cents, subtract the log of the smaller number from the log of the larger, then multiply by 1200/log 2 ($\approx$3986).

To convert cents to degrees, multiply by 360/1200 = .3.

All conversions are *approximations* except that of the octave, ratio 1:2 = 1200 cents = 360 degrees.

SUPERPARTICULAR RATIOS

Ratios	Intervals	Cents	Degrees
1:2	octave	1200	360.
2:3	perfect 5th	702	210.6
3:4	perfect 4th	498	149.4
4:5	major 3rd	386	115.8
5:6	minor 3rd	316	94.8
6:7	septimal 3rd	267	80.1
7:8	septimal 2nd	231	69.3
8:9	major tone	204	61.2
9:10	minor tone	182	54.6
15:16	just diatonic semitone	112	33.6
17:18	approximation to equal-tempered semitone	99	29.7
19:20	approximation to Pythagorean diatonic semitone of 243:256	89	26.7

SUPERPARTICULAR RATIOS (*Continued*)

Ratios	Intervals	Cents	Degrees
24:25	just chromatic semitone	70	21.
35:36	approximation to equal-tempered quarter-tone	49	14.7
73:74	approximation to Pythagorean comma of 524288:531441	24	7.2
80:81	syntonic comma	22	6.6

OTHER RATIOS

Ratios	Intervals	Cents	Degrees
64:81	Pythagorean "ditone" third	408	122.4
243:256	Pythagorean *leimma* (semitone)	90	27.
125:128	diesis	41	12.3
2025:2048	diaschisma	20	6.
32768:32805	schisma	2	.6

APPENDIX II

Multiplication Tables for Numbers 3^p5^q

The following multiplication tables for products of the male prime numbers 3 and 5 are limited by the "Revelation Index" of $12{,}000^3 = 1{,}728{,}000{,}000{,}000$. The number $3^0 = 1$ is graphed in the lower-left-hand corner of all yantras except the Revelation yantras, in which left and right are reversed. In the yantras, powers of 3 can be counted as places along the horizontal axis, and powers of 5 as places along the vertical axis; directions are reversed here to simplify tabulation. Multiplication by 2^n is merely for the convenience of projecting these tone-numbers into some desired "octave-double" and does not change their loci as "cuts" in a tone-mandala. The tonal meanings of a number are entirely dependent on context. In all cases I have assigned the tone-value of "D" to the terminal number of the set.

For correlations with equal-temperament, remember that every multiplication by 3 exceeds some equal-tempered fifth by about 2 cents, while every multiplication by 5 falls short of a major third by about 14 cents, assuming octave-equivalence.

Item	Row 1 3^p	Row 2 $3^p \times 5$	Row 3 $3^p \times 5^2$	Row 4 $3^p \times 5^3$	Item
1	$3^0 =$ 1	5	25	125	1
2	$3^1 =$ 3	15	75	375	2
3	$3^2 =$ 9	45	225	1,125	3
4	$3^3 =$ 27	135	675	3,375	4
5	$3^4 =$ 81	405	2,025	10,125	5
6	$3^5 =$ 243	1,215	6,075	30,375	6
7	$3^6 =$ 729	3,645	18,225	91,125	7
8	$3^7 =$ 2,187	10,935	54,675	273,375	8
9	$3^8 =$ 6,561	32,805	164,025	820,125	9
10	$3^9 =$ 19,683	98,415	492,075	2,460,375	10
11	$3^{10} =$ 59,049	295,245	1,476,225	7,381,125	11
12	$3^{11} =$ 177,147	885,735	4,428,675	22,143,375	12
13	$3^{12} =$ 531,441	2,657,205	13,286,025	66,430,125	13
14	$3^{13} =$ 1,594,323	7,971,615	39,858,075	199,290,375	14
15	$3^{14} =$ 4,782,969	23,914,845	119,574,225	597,871,125	15
16	$3^{15} =$ 14,348,907	71,744,535	358,722,675	1,739,613,375	16
17	$3^{16} =$ 43,046,721	215,233,605	1,076,168,025	5,380,840,125	17
18	$3^{17} =$ 129,140,163	645,700,815	3,228,504,075	16,142,520,375	18
19	$3^{18} =$ 387,420,489	1,937,102,445	9,685,512,225	48,427,561,125	19
20	$3^{19} =$ 1,162,261,467	5,811,307,335	29,056,536,675	145,282,683,375	20
21	$3^{20} =$ 3,486,784,401	17,433,922,005	87,169,610,025	435,848,050,125	21
22	$3^{21} =$ 10,460,353,203	52,301,766,015	261,508,830,075	1,307,544,150,375	22
23	$3^{22} =$ 31,381,059,609	156,905,298,045	784,526,490,225		23
24	$3^{23} =$ 94,143,178,827	470,715,894,135			24
25	$3^{24} =$ 282,429,536,481	1,412,147,682,405			25
26	$3^{25} =$ 847,288,609,443				26

Item	Row 5 $3^p \times 5^4$	Row 6 $3^p \times 5^5$	Row 7 $3^p \times 5^6$	Row 8 $3^p \times 5^7$	Item
1	$3^0 =$ 625	3,125	15,625	78,125	1
2	$3^1 =$ 1,875	9,375	46,875	234,375	2
3	$3^2 =$ 5,625	28,125	140,625	703,125	3
4	$3^3 =$ 16,875	84,375	421,875	2,109,375	4
5	$3^4 =$ 50,625	253,125	1,265,625	6,328,125	5
6	$3^5 =$ 151,875	759,375	3,796,875	18,984,375	6
7	$3^6 =$ 455,625	2,278,125	11,390,625	56,953,125	7
8	$3^7 =$ 1,366,875	6,834,375	34,171,875	170,859,375	8
9	$3^8 =$ 4,100,625	20,503,125	102,515,625	512,578,125	9
10	$3^9 =$ 12,301,875	61,509,375	307,546,875	1,537,734,375	10
11	$3^{10} =$ 36,905,625	184,528,125	922,640,625	4,613,203,125	11
12	$3^{11} =$ 110,716,875	553,584,375	2,767,921,875	13,839,609,375	12
13	$3^{12} =$ 332,150,625	1,660,753,125	8,303,765,625	41,518,828,125	13

14	3^{13} = 996,451,875	4,982,259,375	24,991,296,875	124,556,484,375	14
15	3^{14} = 2,989,355,625	14,946,778,125	74,733,890,625	373,669,453,125	15
16	3^{15} = 8,968,066,875	44,840,334,375	224,201,671,875	1,121,008,359,375	16
17	3^{16} = 26,904,200,625	134,521,003,125	672,605,015,625		17
18	3^{17} = 80,712,601,875	403,563,009,375			18
19	3^{18} = 242,137,805,625	1,210,689,028,125			19
20	3^{19} = 726,413,416,875				20

Item	Row 9 $3^p \times 5^8$	Row 10 $3^p \times 5^9$	Row 11 $3^p \times 5^{10}$	Row 12 $3^p \times 5^{11}$	Item
1	3^0 = 390,625	1,953,125	9,765,625	48,828,125	1
2	3^1 = 1,171,875	5,859,375	29,296,875	146,484,375	2
3	3^2 = 3,515,625	17,578,125	87,890,625	439,453,125	3
4	3^3 = 10,546,875	52,734,375	263,671,875	1,318,359,375	4
5	3^4 = 31,640,625	158,203,125	791,015,625	3,955,078,125	5
6	3^5 = 94,921,875	474,609,375	2,373,046,875	11,865,234,375	6
7	3^6 = 284,765,625	1,423,828,125	7,119,140,625	35,595,703,125	7
8	3^7 = 854,296,875	4,271,484,375	21,357,421,875	106,787,109,375	8
9	3^8 = 2,562,890,625	12,814,453,125	64,072,265,625	320,361,328,125	9
10	3^9 = 7,688,671,875	38,443,359,375	192,216,796,875	961,083,984,375	10
11	3^{10} = 23,066,015,625	115,330,078,125	576,650,390,625		11
12	3^{11} = 69,198,046,872	345,990,234,375	1,729,951,117,875		12
13	3^{12} = 207,594,140,625	1,037,970,703,125			13
14	3^{13} = 622,782,421,875				14

Item	Row 13 $3^p \times 5^{12}$	Row 14 $3^p \times 5^{13}$	Row 15 $3^p \times 5^{14}$	Row 16 $3^p \times 5^{15}$	Item
1	3^0 = 244,140,625	1,220,703,125	6,103,515,625	30,517,578,125	1
2	3^1 = 732,421,875	3,662,109,375	18,310,546,875	91,552,734,375	2
3	3^2 = 2,197,265,625	10,986,328,125	54,931,640,625	274,658,203,125	3
4	3^3 = 6,591,796,875	32,958,984,375	164,794,921,875	823,974,609,375	4
5	3^4 = 19,775,390,625	98,876,953,125	494,384,765,625		5
6	3^5 = 59,326,171,875	296,630,859,375	1,483,154,296,875		6
7	3^6 = 177,978,515,625	889,892,578,125			7
8	3^7 = 533,935,546,875				8
9	3^8 = 1,601,806,640,625				9

Item	Row 17 $3^p \times 5^{16}$	Row 18 5^{17}
1	3^0 = 152,587,890,625	762,939,453,125
2	3^1 = 457,763,671,875	
3	3^2 = 1,373,291,015,625	

APPENDIX III

Simplified Acoustical Theory for Fretted Instruments

The popularity of fretted instruments like the ukelele, guitar, banjo, and mandolin has created a multitude of musical amateurs with considerable expertise in their ears and fingers. Players of such instruments, regardless of their theoretical training in music, already "embody" the musical systems discussed here. The following table translates formal musical and mathematical language into the simpler language of frets—and with negligible acoustical error. Only in the sustained harmonies of piano and organ could the discrepancies be made clearly audible, and only on a monochord string three to five feet in length would they become clearly visible. Two sets of assumptions make this simplification possible:

1) A change of string length by one fret is accompanied by a change in pitch of one semitone, meaning by 100 cents in the language of equal-temperament. Shortening a string by one fret is equivalent to division by the twelfth root of 2 = 1.059463+; lengthening it by one fret is equivalent to multiplication by the same ratio. Changes in vibration rates are the reciprocals of changes in length. Vincenzo Galileo's approximation by the ratio 17:18 contains a negligible error, but the instrument maker must introduce slight modifications, depending on the height of bridge and/or frets to compensate for any stretching when the string is depressed to the fingerboard.

2) We shall happily agree with Aristoxenus that pitch discrepancies become inaudible at about one-twelfth of a wholetone, meaning 200/12 = 16+ cents, for all practical purposes of music making. Notice how few of the pitches reached via the "pure" intervals defined by integer ratios exceed this amount of deviation from the idealized location of equal-temperament frets. In the following table I have labelled the tones in

Correlation of Equal-Temperament with "Just" and "Pythagorean Tunings"

Frets	Formula	Musical Interval	Cents	Derivation from "Pure" Integer Ratios	Tones (D-D′)	Deviation from E.T. Frets
1	$\sqrt[12]{2}$	semitone or minor second	100	243:256 15:16	E♭ e♭	−11 +12
2	$\sqrt[6]{2}$	wholetone or major second	200	9:10 8:9	e E	−18 +4
3	$\sqrt[4]{2}$	minor third	300	27:32 5:6	F f	−6 +16
4	$\sqrt[3]{2}$	major third	400	4:5 64:81	f♯ F♯	−14 +8
5	$\sqrt[5/12]{2}$	perfect fourth	500	3:4	G	−2
6	$\sqrt{2}$	tritone or augmented fourth	600	32:45 512:729	g♯ G♯	−10 +12
7	$\sqrt[7/12]{2}$	perfect fifth	700	2:3	A	+2
8	$\sqrt[2/3]{2}$	minor sixth	800	81:128 5:8	B♭ b♭	−8 +14
9	$\sqrt[3/4]{2}$	major sixth	900	3:5 16:27	b B	−16 +6
10	$\sqrt[5/6]{2}$	minor seventh	1000	9:16 5:9	C c	−4 +18
11	$\sqrt[11/12]{2}$	major seventh	1100	8:15 128:243	c♯ C♯	−12 +11
12	2	perfect octave	1200	1:2	D′	0

("Pythagorean tuning," shown in capital letters and numbers 2^p3^q, is a "sub-set" of "Just tuning".)

rising order in the octave on D, but the same interval pattern applies to any set of twelve consecutive frets and to both rising and falling pitch sequences.

The virtue of the "irrationals" in the formulas is that they mediate contradictory integer "norms," and they ensure a restriction to a cyclic group of only twelve tones. While the maximum range of variability for a given tone does lie within the threshold of audibility for sensitive ears, deviations from equal-temperament loci are generally too small to be noticed, hence performing the intervals and scales of this study on a fretted instrument will not mislead the ear in any important way—provided, that is, that the qualifications introduced here are kept in mind. In number theory, however, there are no "negligible" discrepancies whatever; tuning "theory" thus involves far greater subtleties than the ear can notice while casually listening to a scale.

INDEX